IMAGES of America
TISHOMINGO COUNTY

On the Cover: Logging was a serious business enterprise in north Mississippi. Timber provided material for building homes, furniture, farm implements, and tools. It was also a source of heat. At one time in Mississippi's early history, the state ranked third in lumber-producing states in the United States. Although logging continues to be a viable industry, there are fewer small sawmills today. (Courtesy of Tishomingo County Historical & Genealogical Society.)

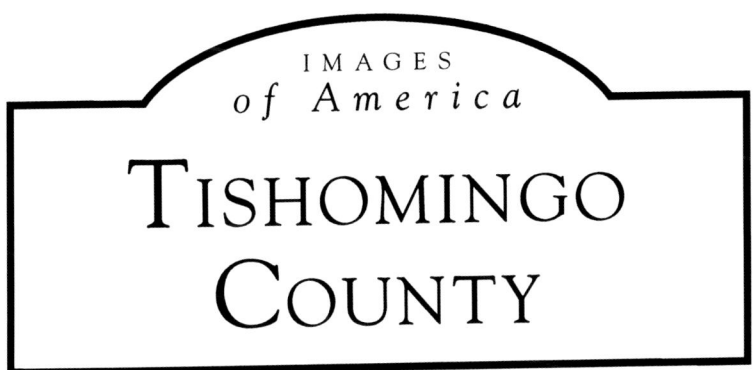

Cindy W. Nelson, RaNae S. Vaughn,
and Tishomingo County Historical & Genealogical Society

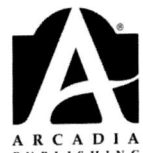

ARCADIA
PUBLISHING

Copyright © 2013 by Cindy W. Nelson, RaNae S. Vaughn, and Tishomingo County Historical
    & Genealogical Society
ISBN 978-0-7385-9816-1

Published by Arcadia Publishing
Charleston, South Carolina

Printed in the United States of America

Library of Congress Control Number: 2012948677

For all general information, please contact Arcadia Publishing:
Telephone 843-853-2070
Fax 843-853-0044
E-mail sales@arcadiapublishing.com
For customer service and orders:
Toll-Free 1-888-313-2665

Visit us on the Internet at www.arcadiapublishing.com

*This book is dedicated to the exceptional volunteers and
committed individuals who continue to strive to preserve the
unique and incomparable history of northeast Mississippi.*

CONTENTS

Acknowledgments		6
Introduction		7
1.	Business and Industry	9
2.	Churches and Cemeteries	33
3.	Cities, Towns, and Communities	43
4.	Clubs and Events	55
5.	County Government	61
6.	Historic Homes and Buildings	65
7.	Military	69
8.	Schools	99

Acknowledgments

Founded in 1996 by Cindy Whirley Nelson, the Tishomingo County Historical & Genealogical Society (TCHGS) has a strong and unwavering commitment to the preservation of local history. Tishomingo Countians encourage and instill habits of character that are prized within each community. TCHGS is pleased to be a part of the exploration of the rich history of Tishomingo County, Mississippi, by sharing a pictorial view of its people and history.

Eight years after the society was organized, an official archives and history museum became a reality when the locally owned First American National Bank built a new bank and relinquished its branch bank building to the Tishomingo County Development Foundation and Tourism Office, which had been tenants of the Old Tishomingo County Courthouse.

TCHGS was established with a mission of promoting the collection and preservation of local history. To assist in this endeavor, a genealogical research library and historical museum was established to collect, preserve, index, and provide access to the archival resources of Tishomingo County. The archives and history museum is dedicated to the collection, preservation, exhibition, and interpretation of articles that relate to the lives and accomplishments of Tishomingo County. Special emphasis is on the period from 1870 to 1971, when the historic courthouse was in use. RaNae Smith Vaughn is the volunteer librarian.

We would like to thank the staff and volunteers for their assistance in researching the photographs used in this book. Eunell Handy, Janice Switcher, and Helah Wilson are commended on their many hours spent locating, retrieving, and scanning the photographs compiled herein. Most of all, thanks to all the people who have donated materials and collections to the Tishomingo County Historical & Genealogical Society over the years. We hope that our public will continue to entrust their valuable Tishomingo County history to TCHGS for future publications. Unless otherwise noted, all images are courtesy of the Tishomingo County Historical & Genealogical Society. Every image included in this volume may be found at the Tishomingo County Archives & History Museum. Welcome to your pictorial exploration of Tishomingo County!

INTRODUCTION

Tishomingo County, which forms the extreme northeast corner of Mississippi, was established on February 9, 1836, and was one of 12 counties formed that year from the Chickasaw Indian cession of 1832. It was named for a king of that tribe, Chief Tishomingo. Tishomingo, meaning "warrior chief," was indeed the big chief among the Chickasaws. He was the last of the full-blooded warriors. Tradition has it that Tishomingo once lived near what is now the town of Tishomingo. On February 14, 1836, Peter G. Rives, A.M. Cowan, James M. Matthews, and James Davis were appointed by legislative act to organize the county. It was originally large, containing an area of about 30 townships, or 1,080 square miles. Due to its size, it was often called the "Free State of Tishomingo." Jacinto became the county seat of government for Tishomingo County.

Tishomingo County's first settlers lived in log houses and made their own implements for farming. Tools were mostly made of wood, although plows were made at the blacksmith shop and were similar to half shovels. Spinning wheels and looms were homemade and vital in the development of the county. All clothing was made by the women. When a surplus was made, it was exchanged at the general store for other needs. Shoes and boots were homemade out of leather the farmers tanned themselves. During the winter months, log-rollings and house-raisings were important social events. The men and boys cleared the land and built the houses while the women and girls put together quilts. Other social events included weddings, speeches, camp meetings, all-day singings, and religious-related activities. Spelling bees were enjoyed by old and young alike. Transportation was by stagecoach, buggy, wagon, and horseback. Mail was delivered by carriers on horseback or stagecoach. The major stage line by way of Jacinto was the route from Nashville to Memphis, which also had a telegraph line as a major means of communication to outside communities. Education took place in private schools in church buildings. School terms lasted only three to four months. Due to poverty, few books were available for study. However, Tishomingo County did manage to develop a system of public education before the Civil War.

Bear, deer, panthers, wildcats, turkeys, squirrels, coons, foxes, and wolves were abundant in the "Free State of Tishomingo" in the years of 1836 to 1839. Indians and whites roamed to and fro throughout the area, enjoying hunting with much success. Early settlers had trouble with bears attacking their calves and sheep. Often, hunters would have to hack their way through canebrakes as such places were favorite places for bears to make their beds or to try to evade hunters and dogs. Going through such canes, it was necessary for hunters to unload their guns for safety. Short double-barreled shotguns were thought to be the best weapons for bear hunts. These were loaded with buck and ball. Rifles were less used because bears were usually shot at close range in a tree or on the ground. As more settlers came into the area and more cane brakes were cleared, bears were seldom seen.

Among the prominent names noticed in the beginning history of Tishomingo County were Reuben Boone, Stephen Gibbs, Terrell and Jeremiah Phillips, H.B. Mitchell, Reuben Rorie, William Walker, John Duncan, Elias Rinehart, B.F. Liddon, John Jobe, Allen H. Kemp, Taylor Jobe, Isaac

Essary, William Rowsey, Peter Searcy, E.W. Carmack, and many men surnamed Morrison. The first marriage license was issued on April 2, 1837, to John P. Azbell and Jane Phillips. Other licenses issued in 1837 were for William Hancock and Delilia Roden, Asabel Atherton and Bearzilla Cattel, William Fitzpatrick and Sarah Wilson, and Thomas Douglass and Mariom McIntore. The first four newspapers established in the county were the *Jacinto Reporter* in 1849, the *Eastport Gazette* in 1850, the *Eastport North Mississippi Union* in 1848, and the *Eastport Republican* in 1851. The first sawmill of record was established on Seven Mile Creek in May 1838 by Hickman Hensley. Sawmills manufactured lumber, and there were also various grist mills where farmers brought their grain to be ground into meal or flour, minus a percentage called the "miller's toll."

In 1870, Old Tishomingo County was divided to form present-day Tishomingo, Prentiss, and Alcorn Counties. At the time the county was divided, its population was 27,129. After the division, Tishomingo County had the smallest population of the three new counties, with 7,440 residents. This division reduced the area to 428 square miles. E.W. Carmack was elected to transcribe the records of the old county for the new counties of Prentiss and Tishomingo, and the original records went to Alcorn County. Carmack accepted the old courthouse at Jacinto as payment for his transcription, and in 1871, he established a school in the former courthouse, which continued until his death in 1882. Most of the old county records have been microfilmed and are retained in the Mississippi State Archives.

Burnsville, Eastport, and Iuka were the largest towns in the new county. Burnsville, situated in the northwest, was established about 1832. It was located on the Iuka-to-Corinth stage route and, in 1857 or 1858, became a major stop on the Memphis & Charleston Railroad. Iuka, located in the northeast section of the county, began about 1844 as a settlement with the sale of a large block of land by Chief Iuka to David Hubbard and his son. Iuka was incorporated in 1857, which was the year for the Memphis & Charleston Railroad. It was a main terminal for the Iuka-Jacinto Road and the Iuka-Corinth Stage Line. After the Civil War years (1861–1865), many of the prominent citizens of Eastport moved to Iuka; Eastport had lost its status as a business hub. By the 1870s, Iuka was a thriving and growing community with its well-known mineral springs.

One
BUSINESS AND INDUSTRY

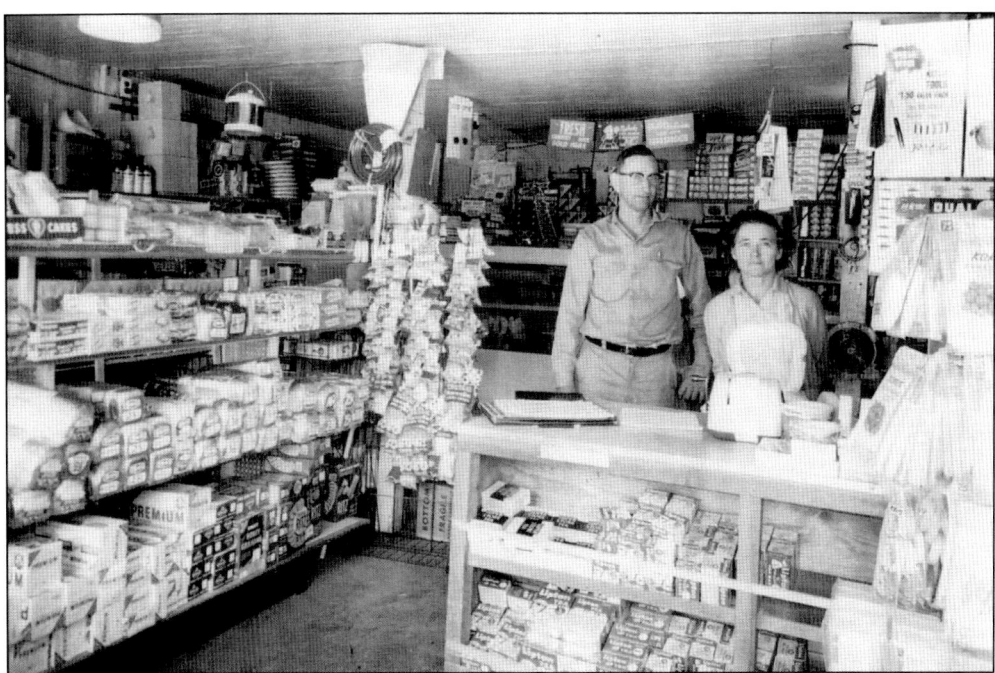

C.J. "Cap" Arnold and his wife, Mae, purchased this business, formerly known as Ross Tucker Grocery, in the 1950s. In the 1959 grand opening, Arnold gave away five gallons of gas with each cash purchase of $7.50 or more of groceries. The store carried a full line of staple groceries and meats and also offered complete auto service. Pictured here is the couple at their business in 1963.

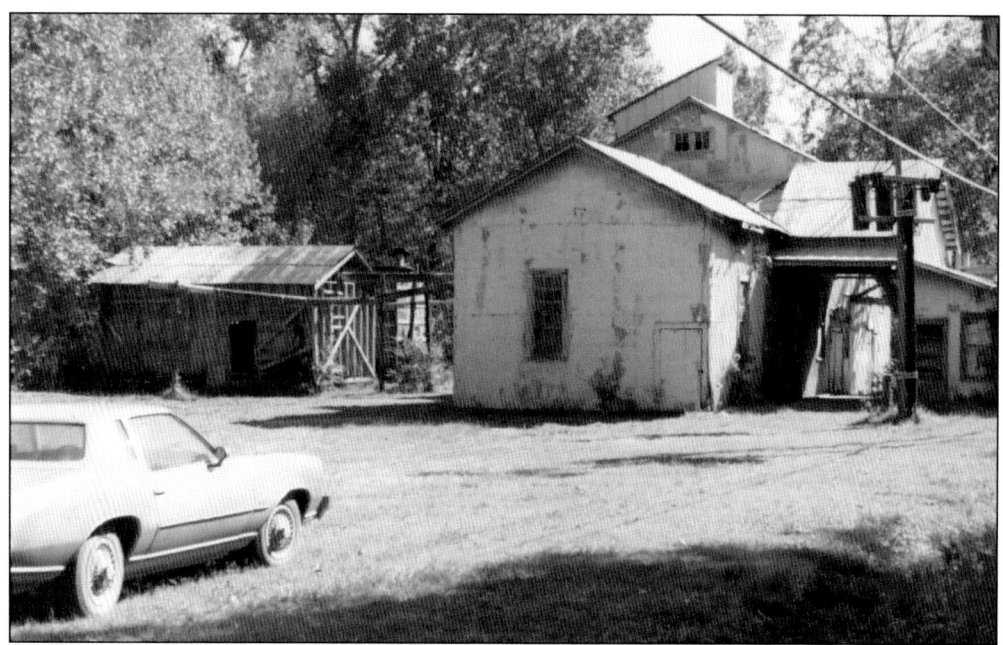

Iuka Gin Company, built in 1926, was located at 609 Main Street in Iuka. Owned and operated by Oscar and Clay Pruitt, it was the first electric gin in Tishomingo County. Two of Clay's four sons, Dayton and Ward "Pinky" Pruitt, assumed their father's role after his death in 1931. Oscar's oldest son, George Hampton Pruitt, worked at the gin until his death in 1929 and his youngest son, Perry Joe Pruitt, worked there until the mid-1950s. During the height of the gin's busiest years, farmers with wagonloads of cotton would form a line that ran from the gin and around Mineral Springs Park. It was common for farmers to have to wait two or three days for their cotton to be ginned, even though the gin crew worked around the clock.

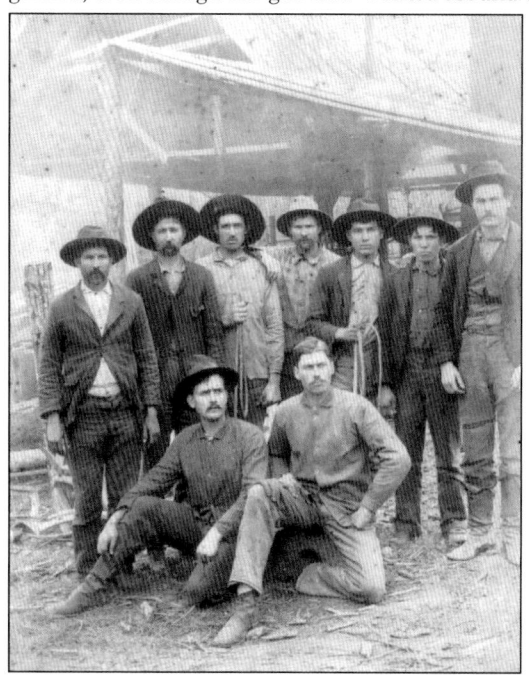

The Golden Sawmill operated in the 1920s and had a long-lasting impact on north Mississippi. The mill decimated vast stands of virgin timber, but it attracted laborers and brought an economic surge to an economically depressed area. The Golden Sawmill shut down in 1933 and completely closed in 1934. These sawmill workers are unidentified.

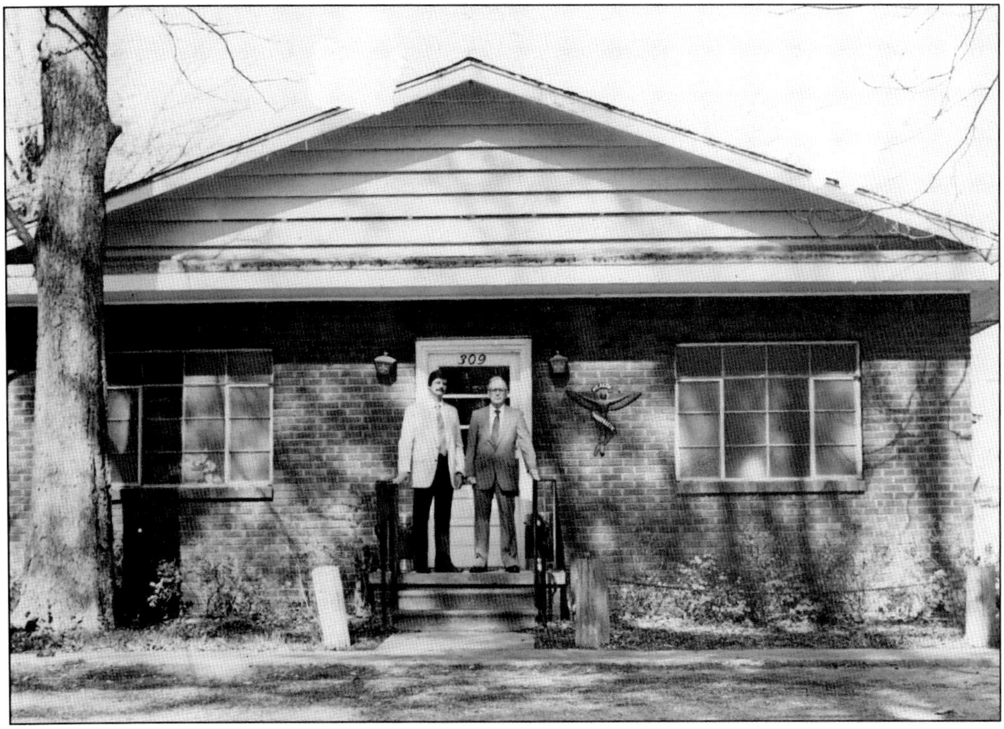

The Cosby Clinic and Hospital opened in May 1950 as Tishomingo County's first hospital. Operated by Dr. Harry Cosby Jr., the hospital boasted six beds and rapidly grew to nine beds. Physicians associated with Dr. Cosby included Dr. John Hensleigh, Dr. Louie Coker, Dr. Gene Birdsong, and Dr. Charles Atkins. Drs. Thomas Rolleigh (left) and Harry Cosby (right) are pictured here. The building is now Dr. Rolleigh's chiropractic clinic.

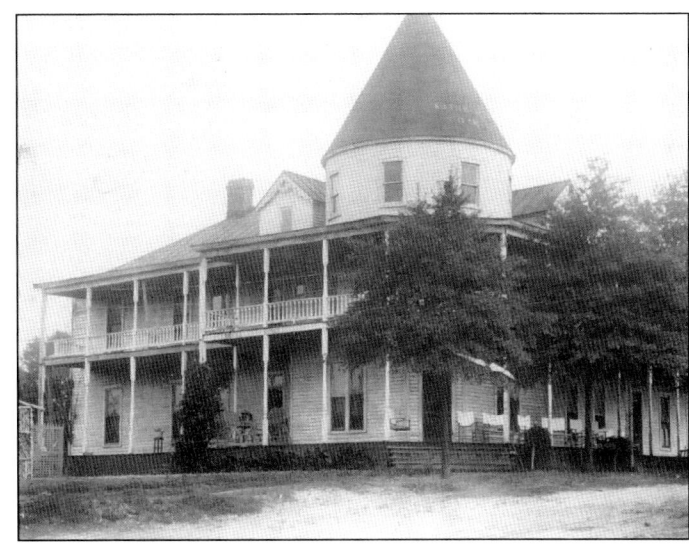

The Leatherwood Hotel was one of the leading hotels in northeast Mississippi. Iuka, known as a resort town, entertained visitors who came to partake of the mineral water from the springs located in the Mineral Springs Park. Rates were $2 per day and $8 or $10 per week. W.B. Leatherwood was the proprietor. The building was torn down around 1956.

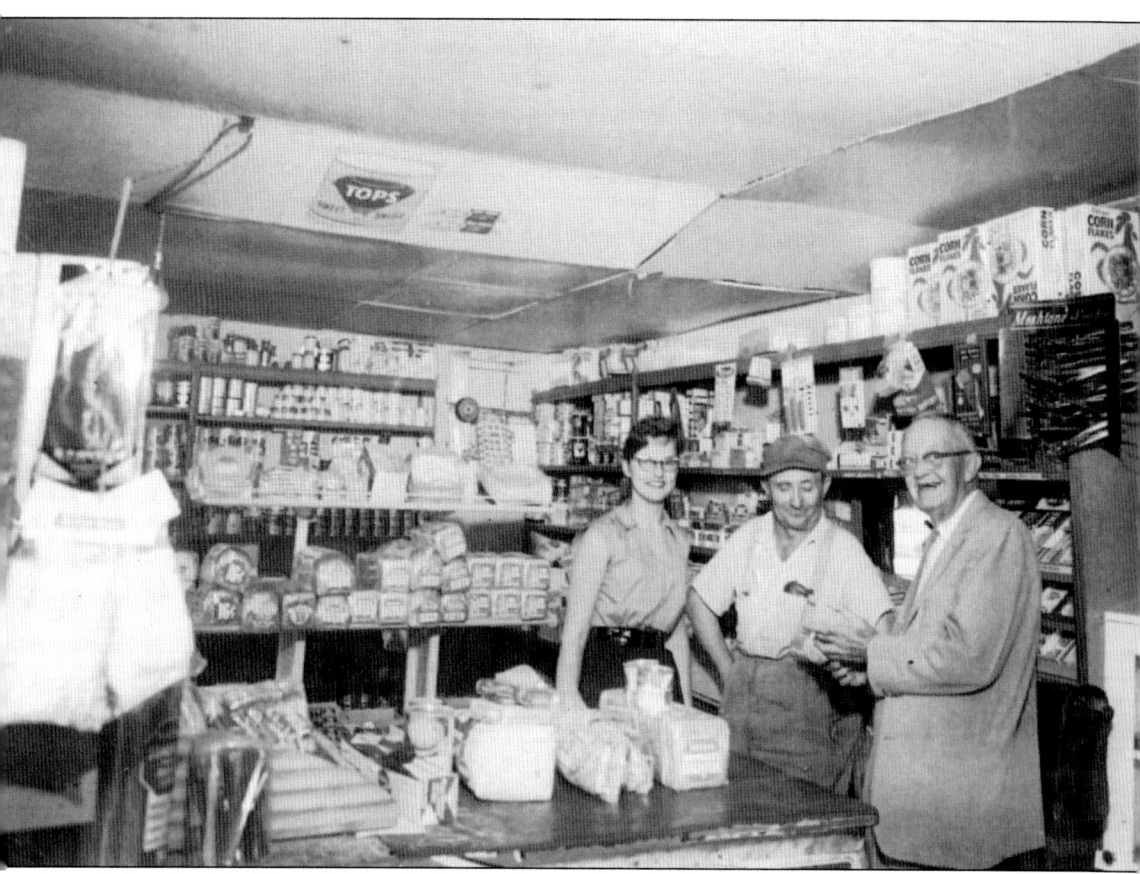

Ed Hudson and his wife, Lavonia, owned the Hudson Grocery Store and Garage in Iuka. Hudson is pictured in the business with their daughter Earline. Purvis and Ruth Cappleman purchased the building in 1975 and opened Cappleman's Antiques. Their son-in-law Lee Everitt and daughter Kathy joined the business in 1979 and purchased the store in 1991. The couple continues to operate the business today. (Courtesy of Kathy Everitt.)

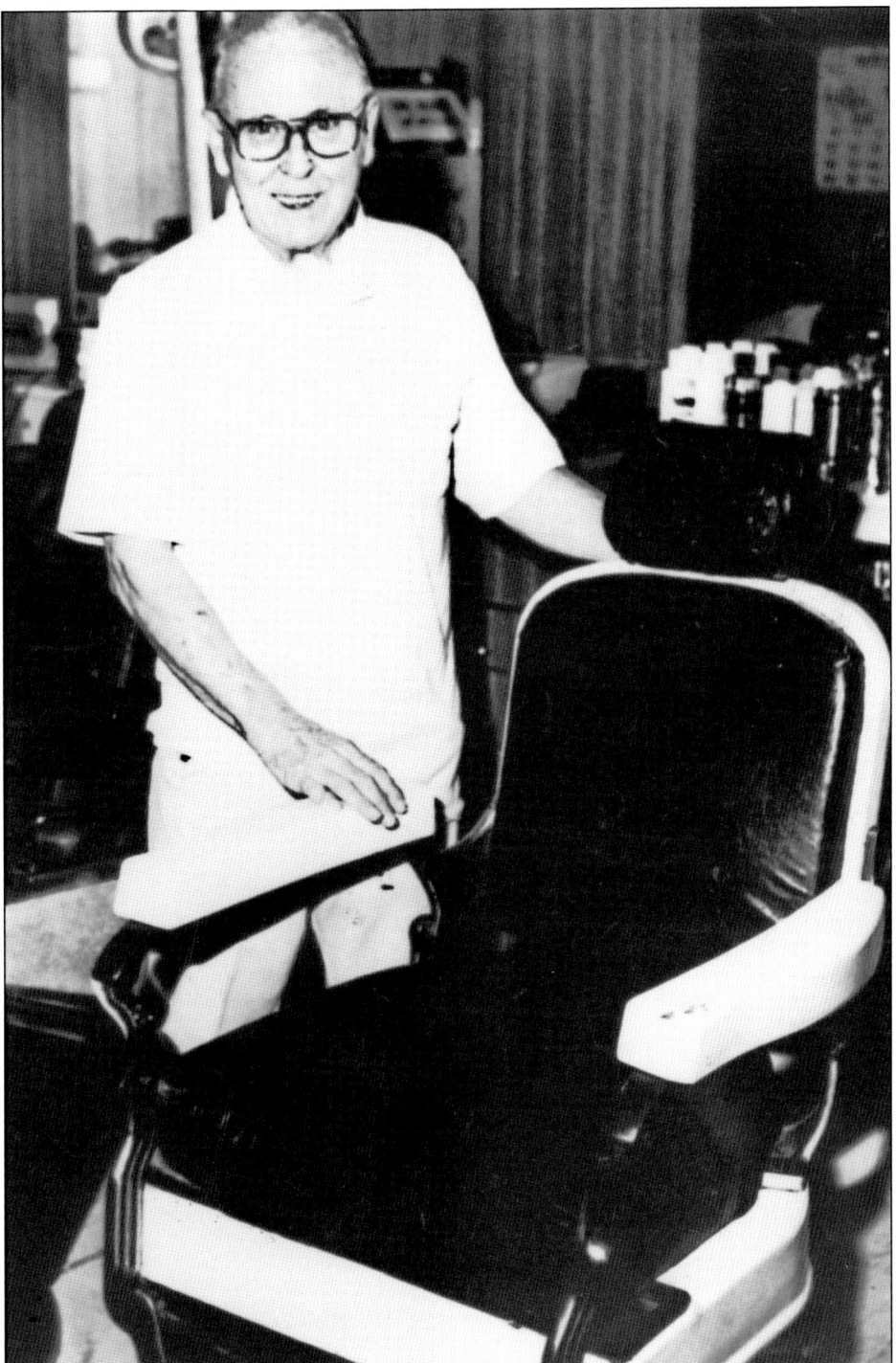

Charles A. Daugherty was a barber in Iuka for 50 years. Daugherty's Barber Shop was a town fixture to acquire a shave, haircut, or "two bits" worth of political wisdom. A hot shower was available on Saturdays. Charlie wore white clothing and a smile to oversee the four-chair operation that his father, D.C., began in 1912. Charlie cut his first hair in 1928 and bought the business in 1967.

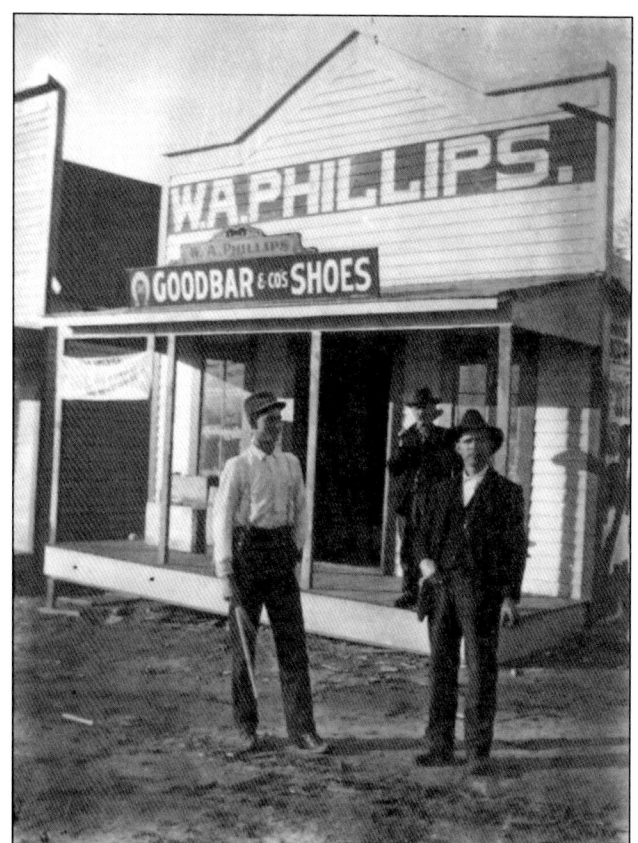

Three men pose for a photograph in front of the W.A. Phillips Store in Dennis. Daily Burleson, wearing a black suit, is the gentleman on the right; the identities of the other gentlemen are unknown. Phillips enjoyed success as a farmer in the Dennis community. (Courtesy of Sharon Embrey.)

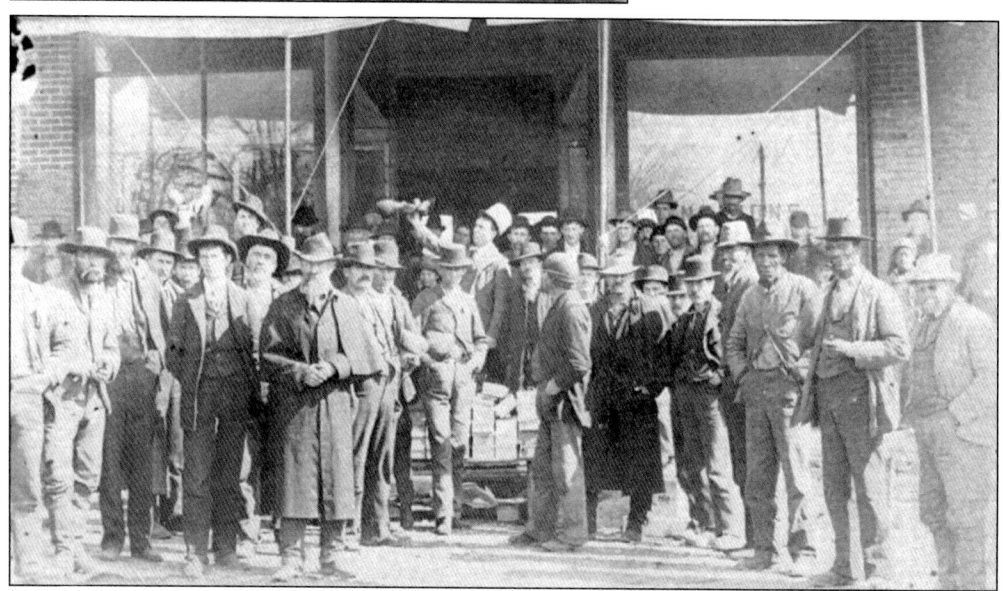

The W.S. Brown Store in Iuka was a general merchandise business. Brown ran his shop with a fair deal for every customer, large or small. He kept abreast of the times, and his policy from the very outset was to give each and every customer extra value and service—just a little more than what the customer paid for or expected to receive.

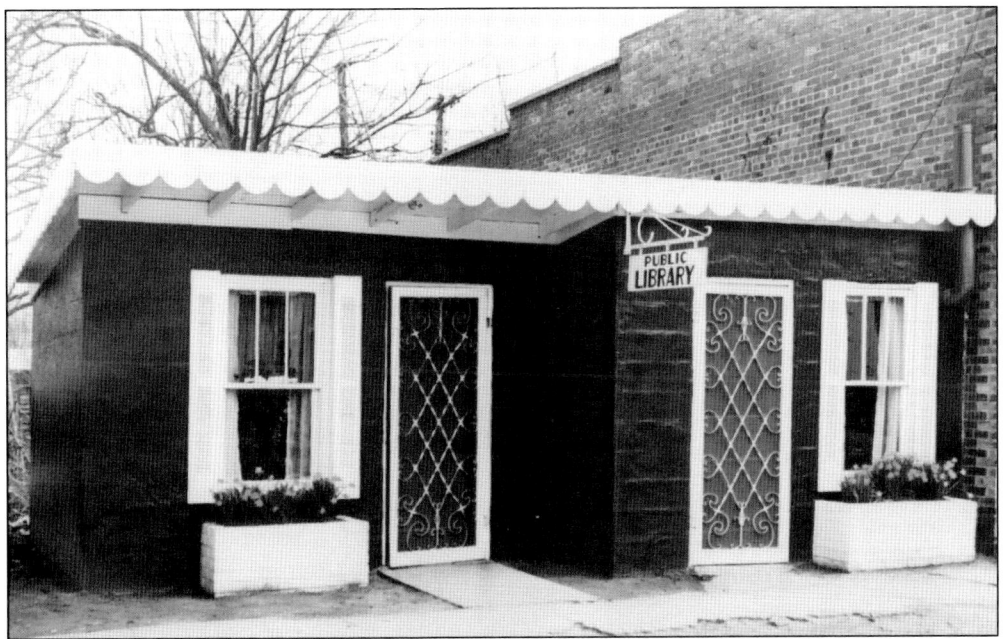

The Iuka Public Library was the first nonsegregated library in Mississippi. It opened on Eastport Street in Iuka on February 11, 1952. Iuka's first librarian was Hallie Jackson Little, wife of Henry Little. She served as librarian until 1964. When her house at 204 North Main Street in Iuka was destroyed by fire, she donated the property to build the public library facility that is now in existence.

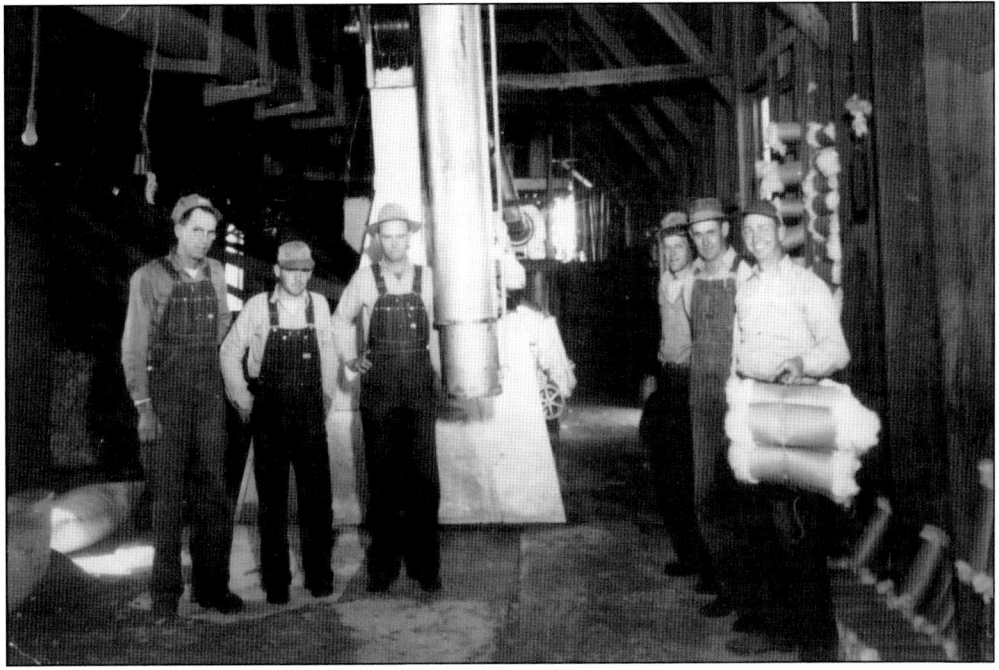

These 1960 workers at the Burnsville Gin, pictured from left to right, are Lex Sellers, J.C. Bain, Kermit Orick, Thurston Bain, Homer Sitton, and Farris Bain. The Burnsville Gin was operated by Homer Sitton and T.B. Woodruff. One of the largest cotton farmers during this time was Allen Hale. The gin was located behind the Burnsville Methodist Church in Burnsville.

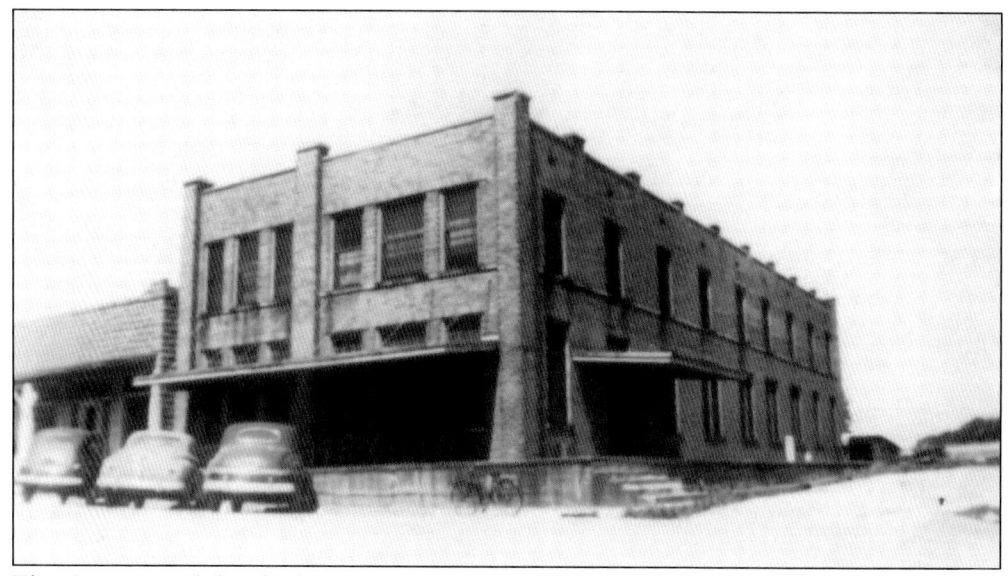

This Georgian-style hotel is located in downtown Belmont at 121 Main Street. Built in 1924, it has been called the "oldest hotel in Mississippi." The Belmont Hotel is a gem. Although it has been restored, the decor of an earlier, more gracious time has been retained. It boasts wide hallways, high ceilings, and a relaxing atmosphere.

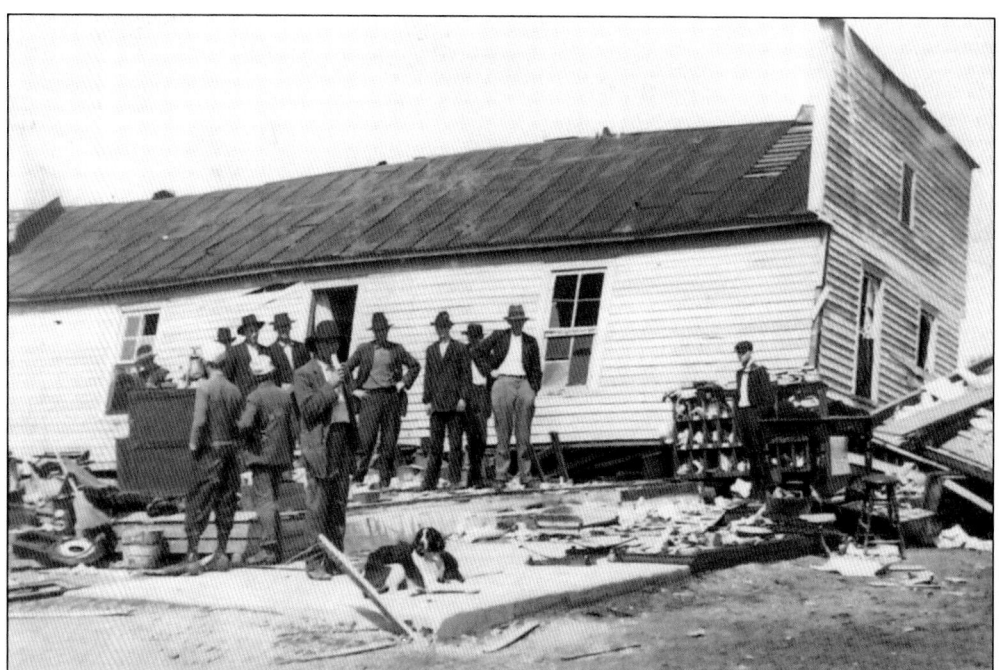

In March 1913, a tornado devastated the town of Tishomingo. The Tishomingo School was picked up from its foundation and severely damaged; however no children were seriously hurt. The tornado destroyed most of the store buildings in town, and the remainder of the town was heavily damaged. This photograph of the school was taken from southeast of the post office. (Courtesy of Anne Taylor.)

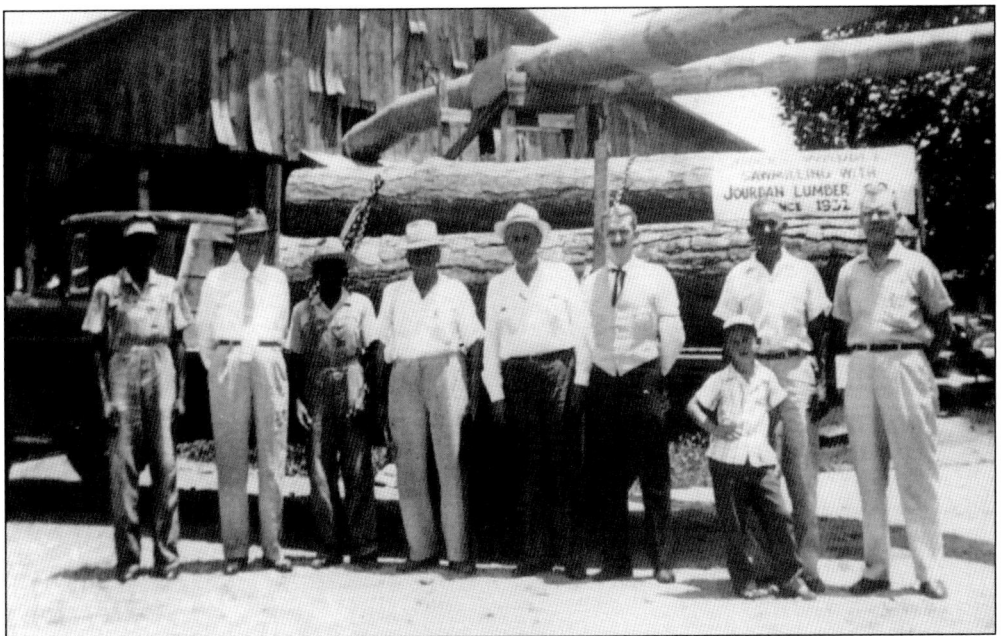

The J.C. Jourdan Lumber Company, founded in 1898, manufactured and shipped lumber, pallets, and crating material. The company served Mississippi, Alabama, Arkansas, Louisiana, and Tennessee for 113 years. Jourdan either sold a wagonload of lumber or traded it to obtain a planer. He then earned enough to buy land near the railroad depot in Iuka to run his business. This photograph was taken in 1932.

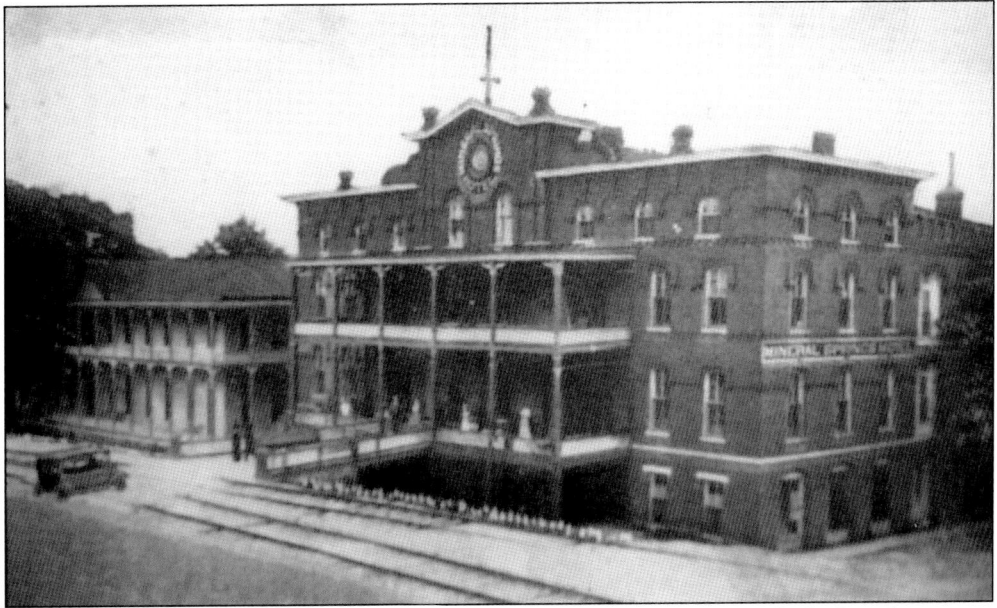

The Iuka Mineral Springs Hotel was a flourishing resort hotel. Tourists flocked to the area to partake of the famous mineral waters. At the 1904 World's Fair in St. Louis, the mineral springs were awarded first prize and a medal for the purest and best mineral water. The hotel hosted lavish parties with dancing and orchestras. W.C. Handy, known as the "Father of the Blues," performed in Iuka several times.

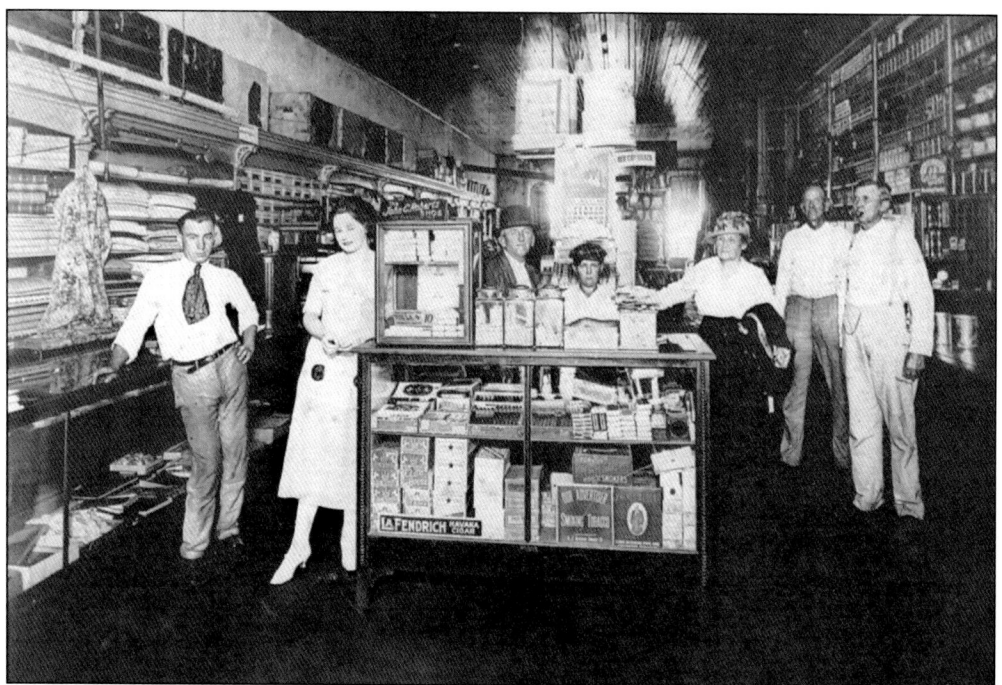

G.T. Carmichael and Son was one of the oldest mercantile firms in Tishomingo County. The Carmichaels were dealers in pure foods, groceries, fancy table delicacies, fruits, vegetables, produce, flour, and feed. Also available was staple hardware, household necessities, tools, farm and home supplies, and stoves and ranges. Various brands carried included the celebrated Hot Point Electric Line, Bendix Radios, and Allen's Princess Ranges.

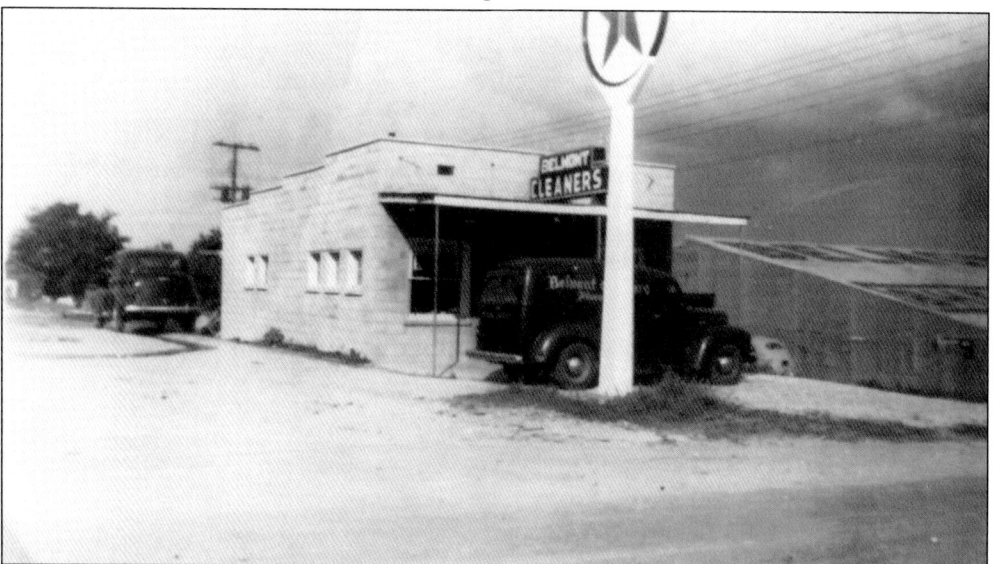

Belmont Cleaners, located in Belmont, was founded by Raymond E. Patrick and Freed Lindsey in July 1945 in a building on Main Street. One year later, the business moved to its current location. This is quite possibly the oldest business under the same ownership in the town of Belmont. In 2004, the business was sold to Bobby Credille, who died in a drowning incident two months after the transaction.

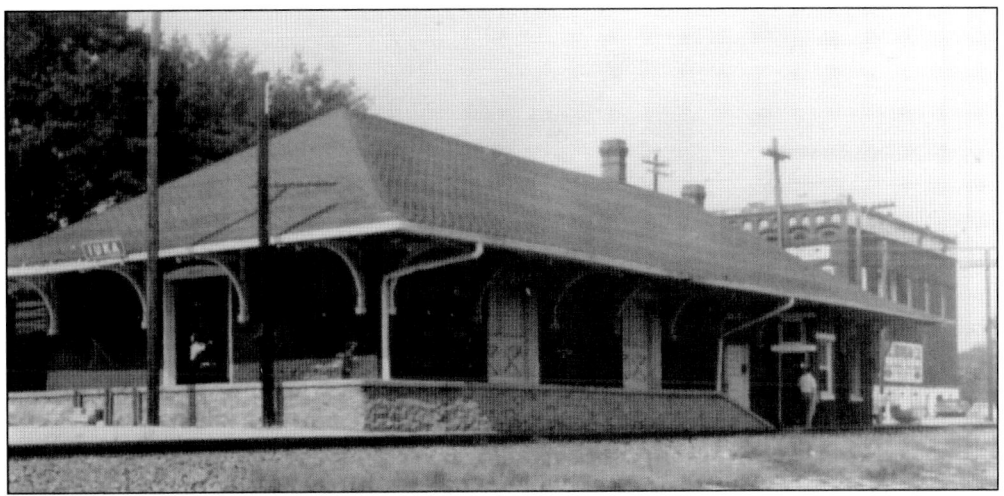

Three railroad agents—John M. Stone, Edwin Merrill, and Brother Berry Martin—worked during the 81 years of the railroad's existence in Iuka. The first depot was used until 1907. Iuka received and distributed all freight and mail for Tishomingo County, Hardin County in Tennessee, and Colbert and Franklin Counties in Alabama. During the Civil War, Gen. Ulysses S. Grant, Brig. Gen. Louis Hébert, Maj. Gen. Edward Ord, and other military personnel used this telegraph line.

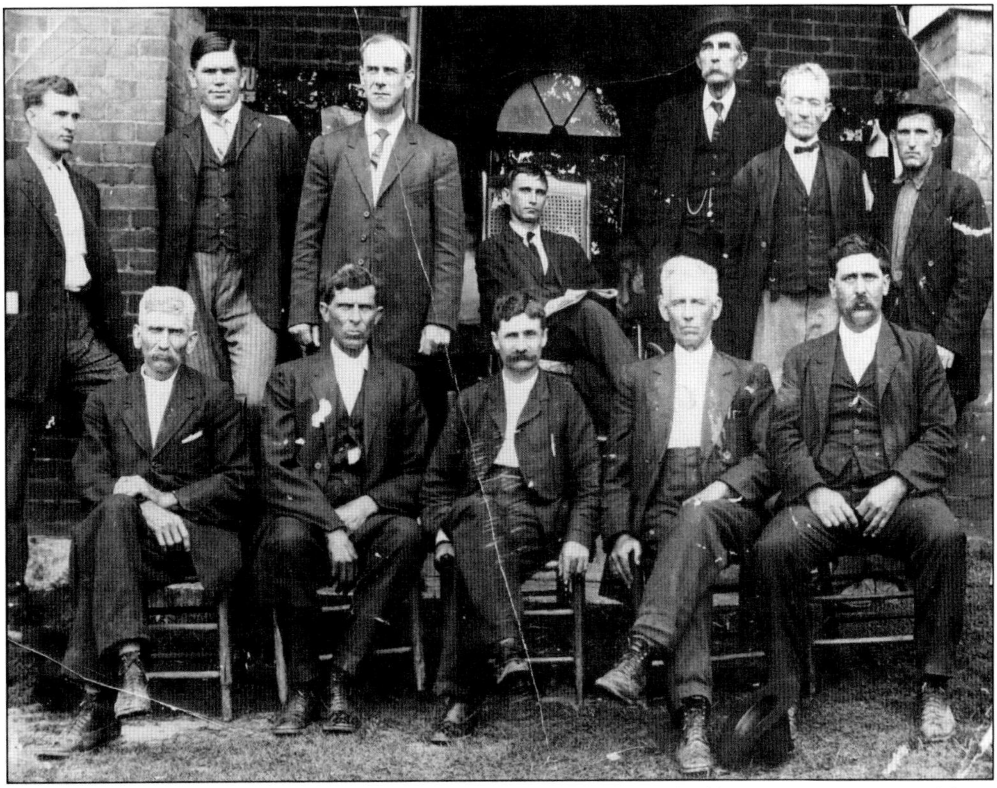

This photograph depicts a group of Tishomingo County distinguished businessmen. Pictured from left to right, are (seated) David Laranzo Anderson, unidentified, G. N. Gober, Russ Owens, and Will Harris; (standing) Walter Goodman, unidentified, N.L. Phillips, Ben C. Pace (sitting in a chair in the middle), Jess Adams, Thomas J. Storment, and C L. Pace Jr.

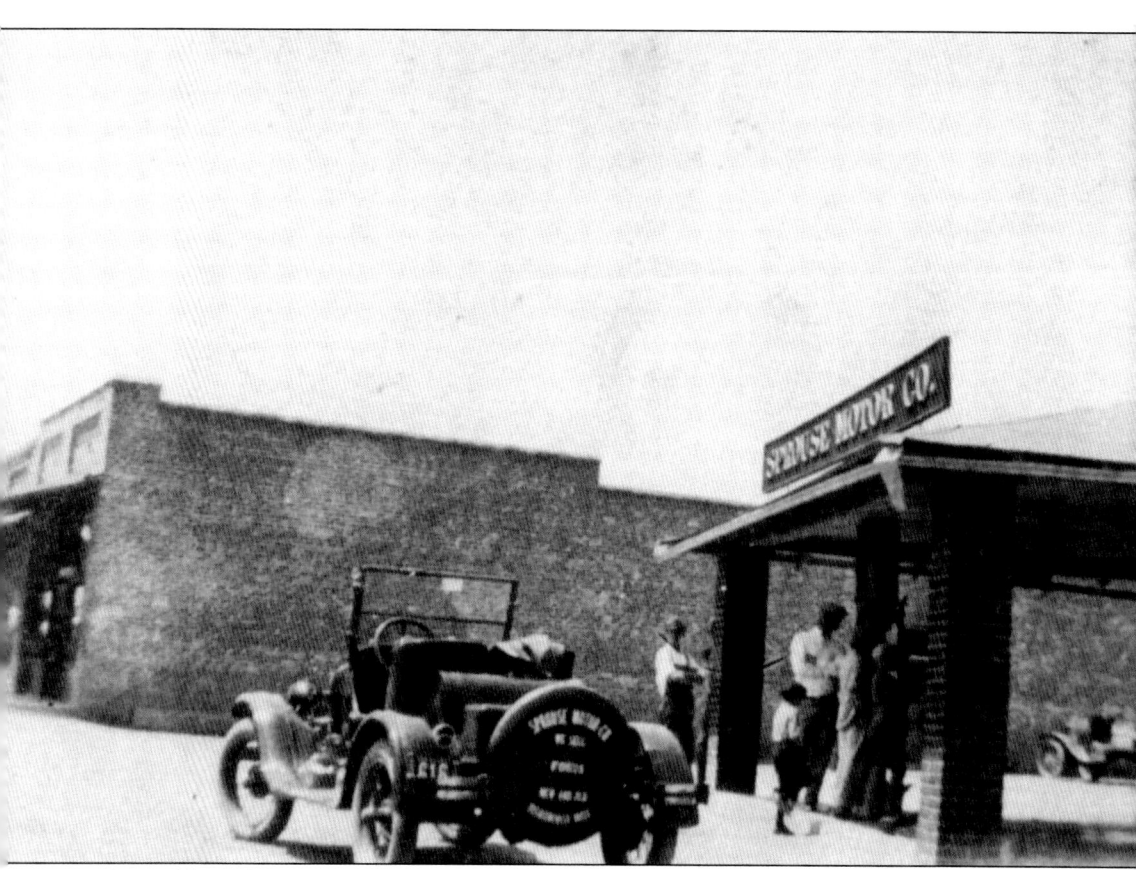

Owned by Milton Sprouse Sr., the Sprouse Motor Company in Tishomingo sold Ford vehicles. Pictured is the company's new building in the 1920s. Sprouse was especially fond of driving a touring car that started with a crank. After the Sprouse family moved to Iuka, Sprouse opened a service station on the corner of Highway 25 and Highway 72 across the street from Deaton's Service Station.

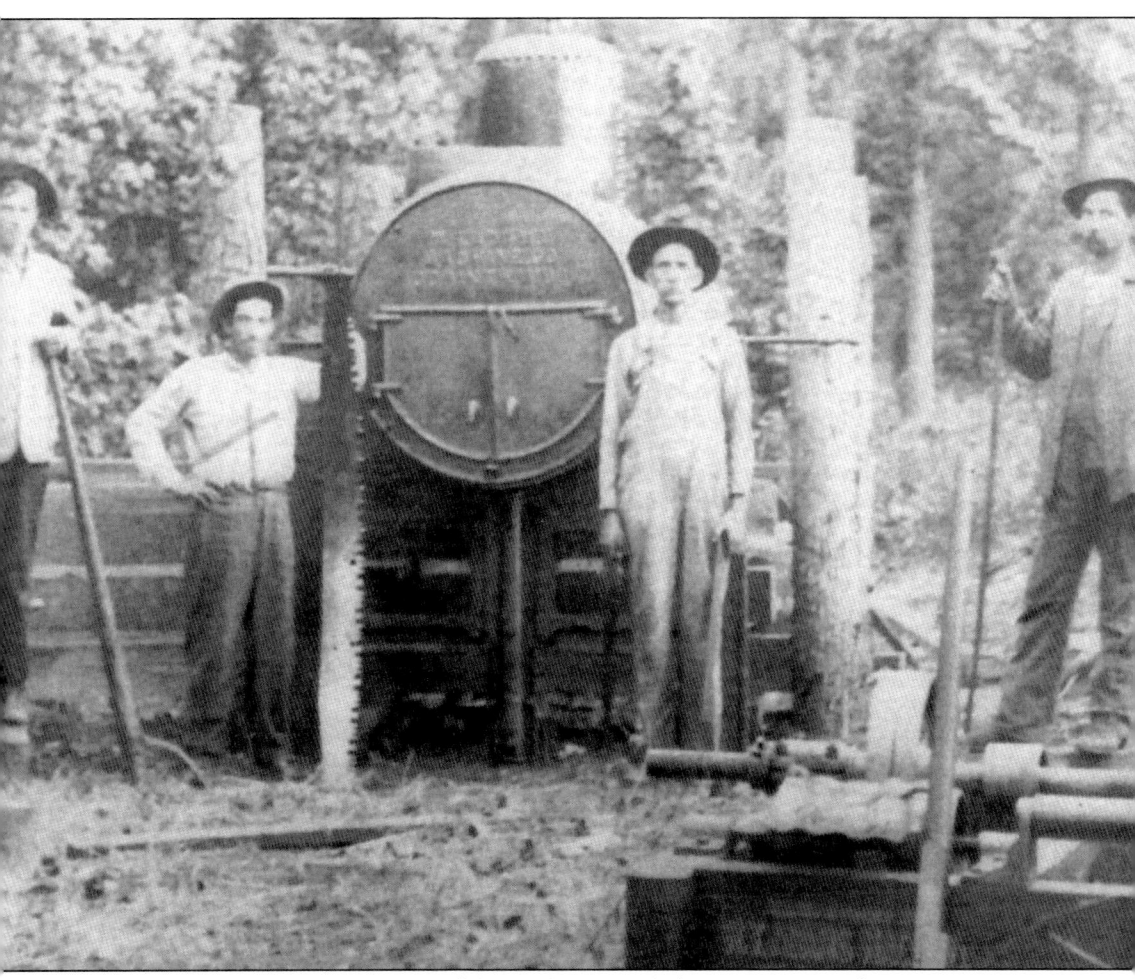

This 1912 photograph depicts a sawmill located in Crippled Deer Bottom. The steam engine's whistle blew for lunch and was heard from miles away. Leland Henry Turner, a 22-year-old deaf man, ran the engine by sensing when the engine needed smoking. This sawmill cut the timber for the pews in the original Rutledge-Salem Methodist Church; they were moved into the new church when it was rebuilt. (Courtesy of Joseph Gist.)

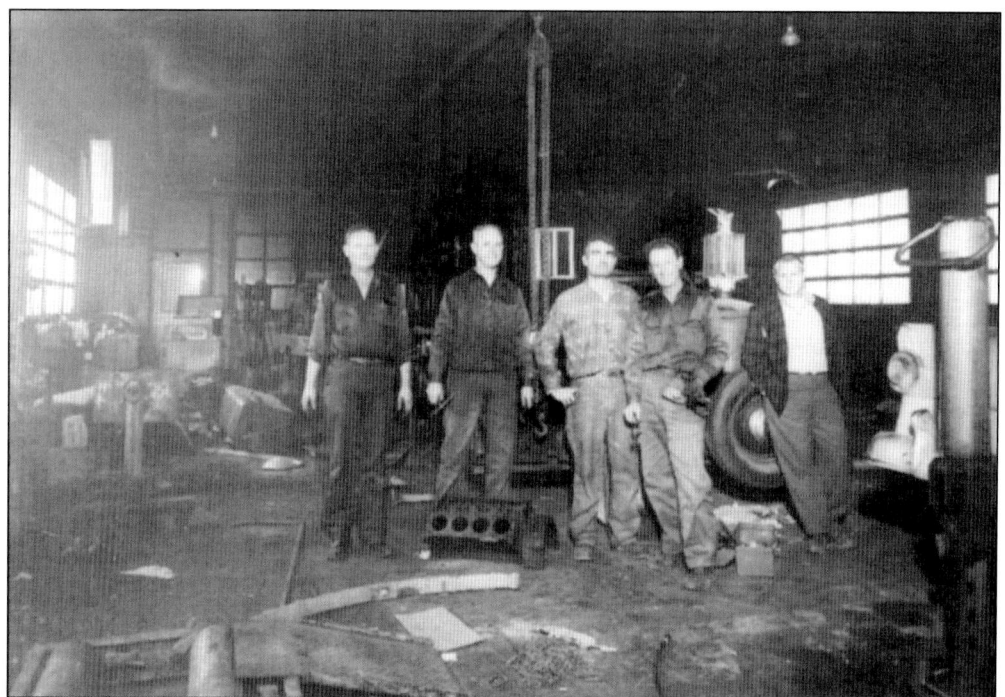

As a boy, Hoyt Phillips worked at his father's garage and then went to Dallas, Texas, to work as a mechanic. After his brother's tragic and paralyzing accident, he returned to Tishomingo. Hoyt opened a garage in Tishomingo, where he stayed for about 27 years. The garage was closed during World War II, but after his discharge from military service, he returned home to reopen his business.

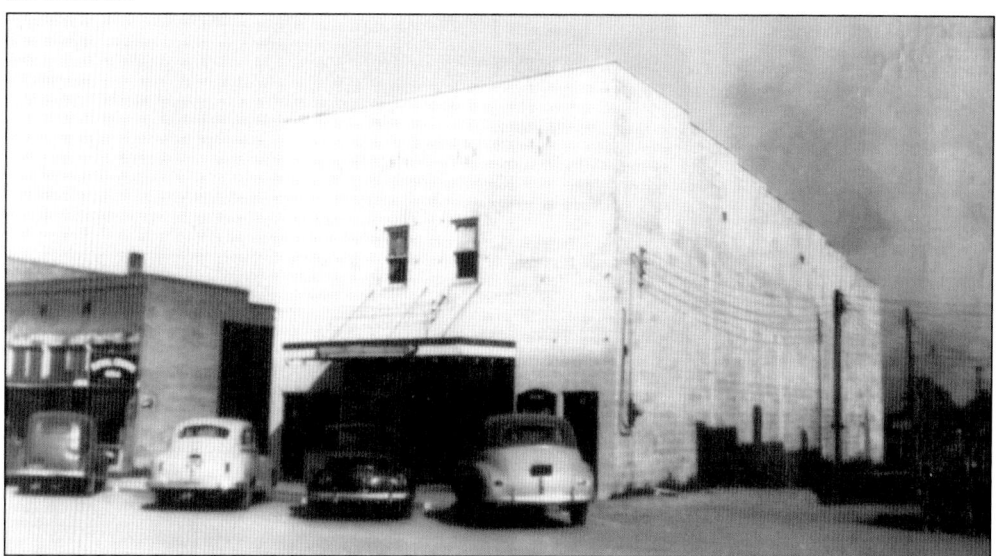

In 1945, the Belmont Bal Theatre, owned by J.E. Clement, opened. The first picture shown was *Passage to Marseilles*. Each Saturday was a busy movie day with a daytime show—usually a Western "shoot 'em up"—an early night show, and a night "Owl Show." The Saturday night movies increased evening business activity and gatherings of people, which was beneficial for the town of Belmont.

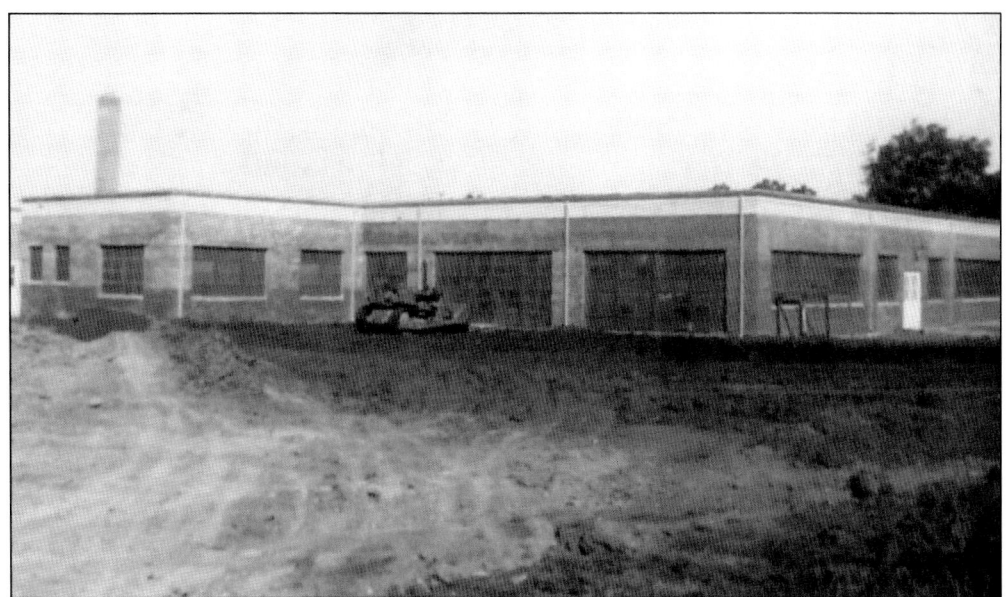

During Belmont's April 1948 town meeting, the board agreed to buy 1.77 acres from Hattie V. Smith at a cost of $7,000 for a factory site between Front and Second Streets. In 1953, Blue Bell, Inc., opened a manufacturing business at this site. Blue Bell was the original Wrangler jeans company before several name changes. Murray C. Adams was the plant manager. (Courtesy of the *Belmont Journal*.)

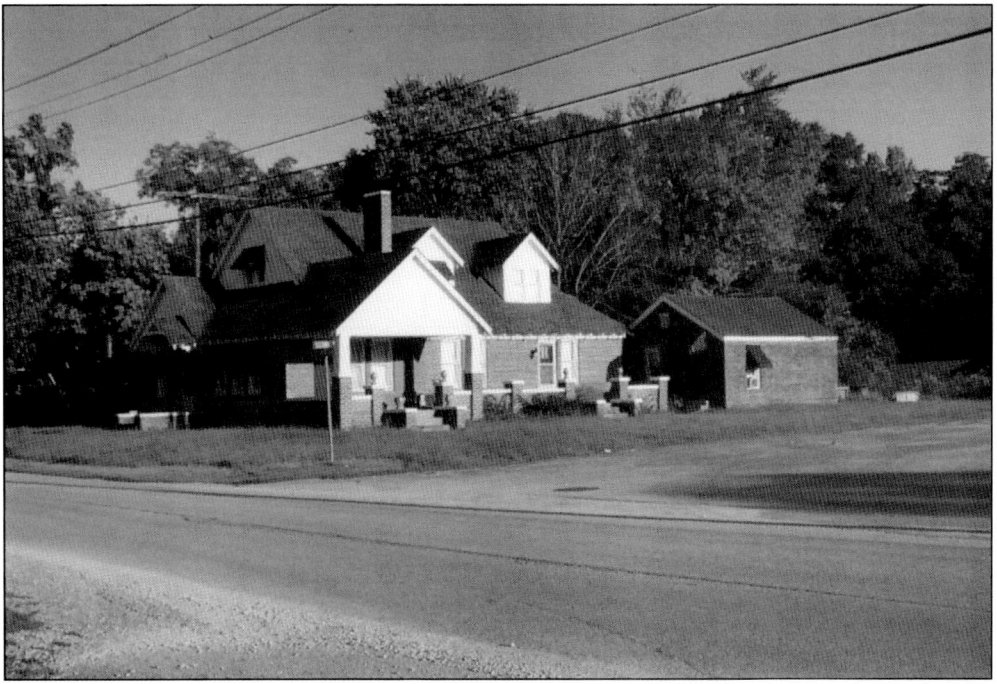

Dr. Arlander Houston Montgomery was Tishomingo County's oldest doctor when he died at the age of 89 on October 10, 1963. This photograph portrays his medical practice in his home office, which was located on Front Street in Burnsville. Dr. Montgomery practiced medicine in Tishomingo County for almost 50 years. During this time, he delivered more than 5,000 babies.

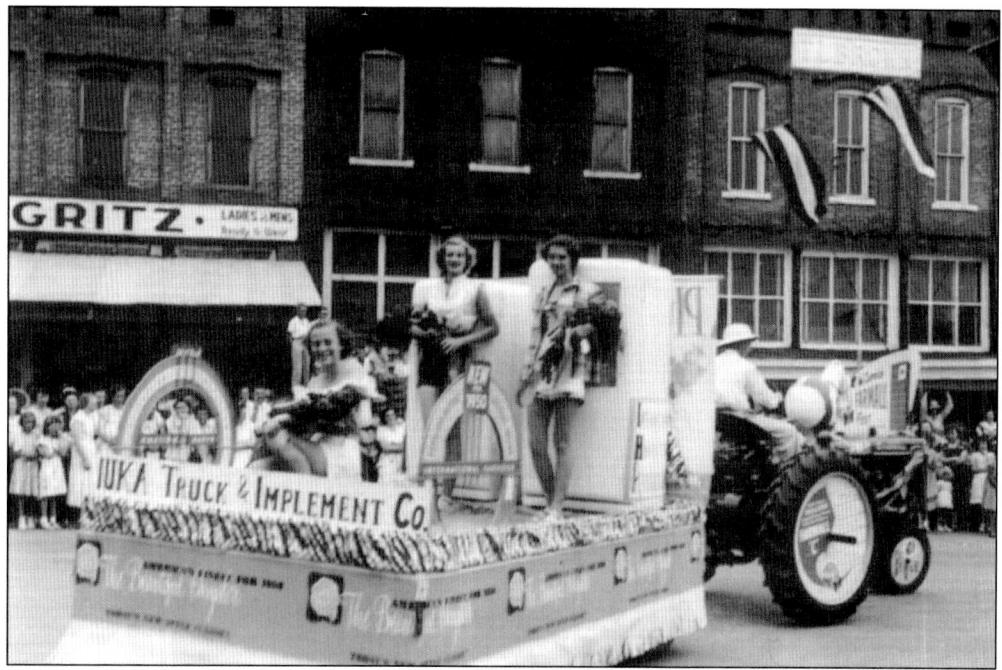

The Iuka Truck & Implement Company was one of the sponsors in a 1950 downtown Iuka parade. The company's float is shown traveling by the Gritz Ladies' & Men's Ready to Wear Clothing Store and the T.L. Brown Store. The proprietors of the Iuka Truck & Implement Company were L.A. Whitten and R.L. Grisham.

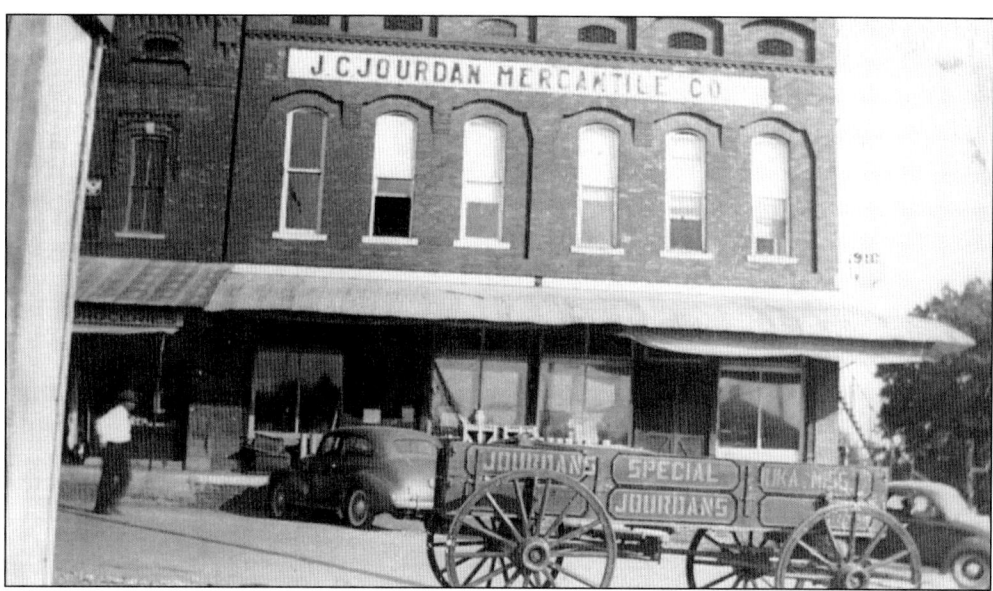

The J.C. Jourdan Mercantile Company was founded by local businessman J.C. Jourdan Sr. The thriving business, located on the south end of the Fulton Street block, offered the famous Florence wagons as a specialty product. In the 1950s, the company name was changed to Jourdan Lumber Company and was managed by the next generation of the family: David O. Jourdan Jr. and Robert L. Brown Jr.

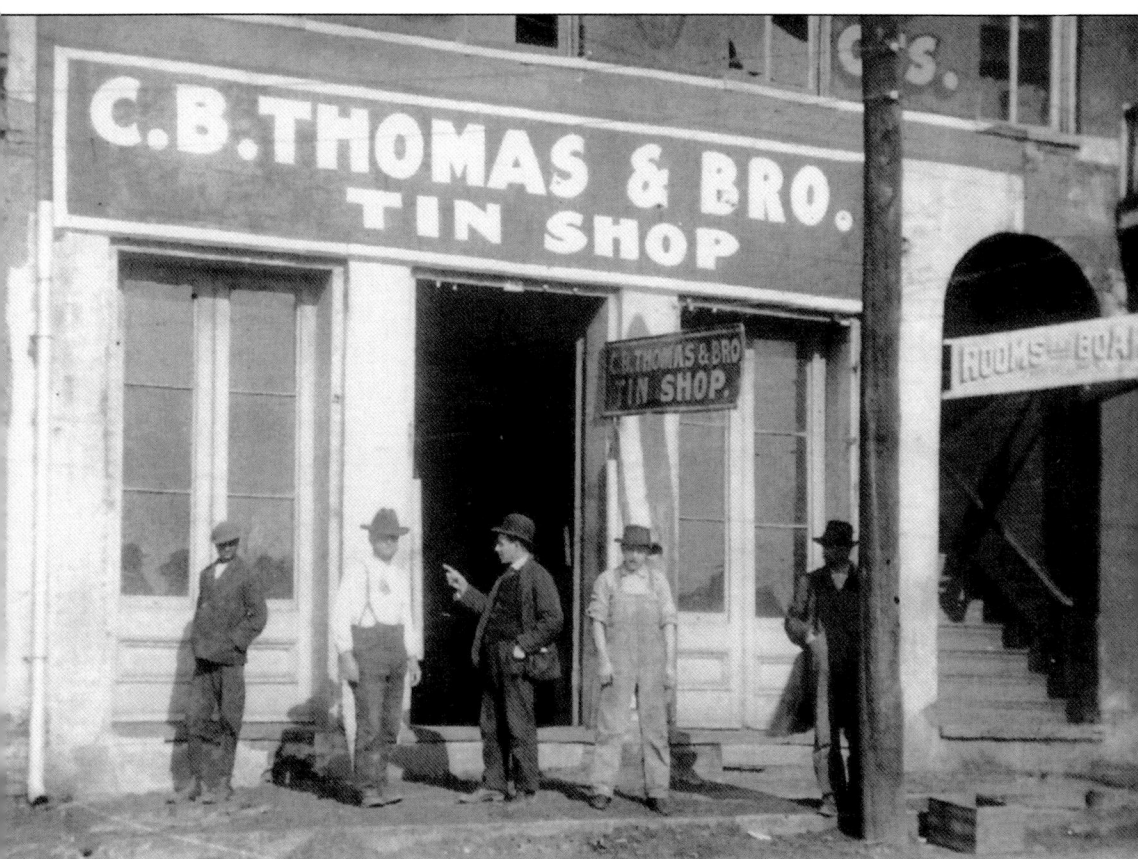

C.B. Thomas & Bro. Tin Shop was located in Iuka. The date of the business is not known; however, a C.B. Thomas married Mary C. Hallmark in November 1868 in Alcorn County. Tin shops often accompanied hardware stores and made pans, cups, and pots and even specialized in roofing and spouting.

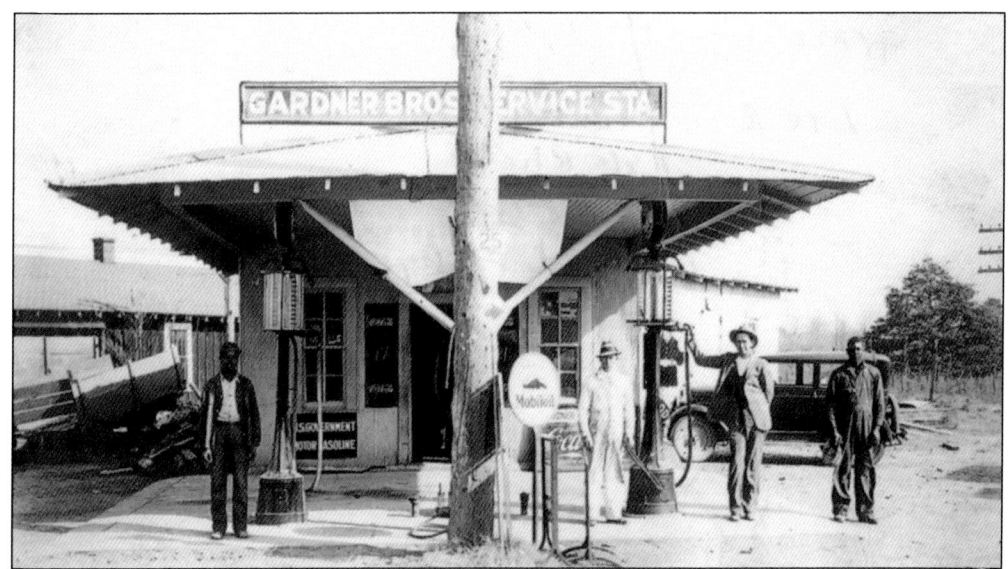

The Gardner Bros. Service Station was located at the corner of Main Street and Trace Street in Tishomingo, Mississippi, in the 1920s. Pictured from left to right are an unidentified man, Kyle Rhodes, O.E. Garner, and Mack Finley. This business was a full-service station that offered gasoline, fixed flats, and offered various other automotive services, including oil changes and minor automotive repairs.

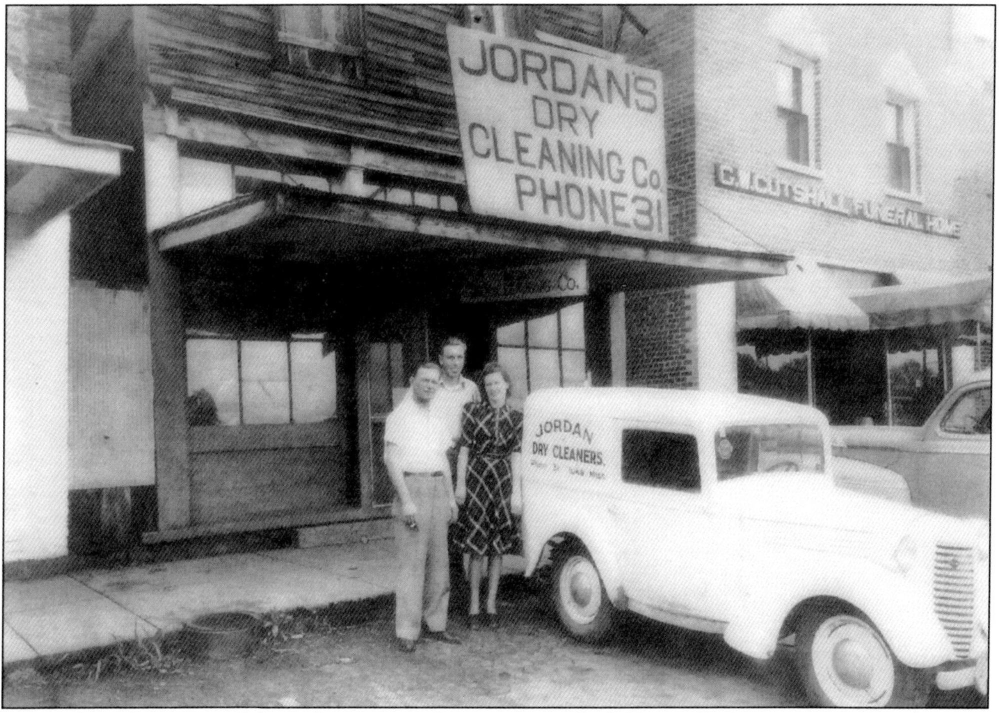

Located in downtown Iuka, adjacent to the G.W. Cutshall Funeral Home, was a dry cleaning service operated by the Jordan family. Notice the telephone number "31" written on the side of the company's delivery vehicle. Dry cleaning was picked up and delivered upon request. The date this family-owned company was in business is unknown.

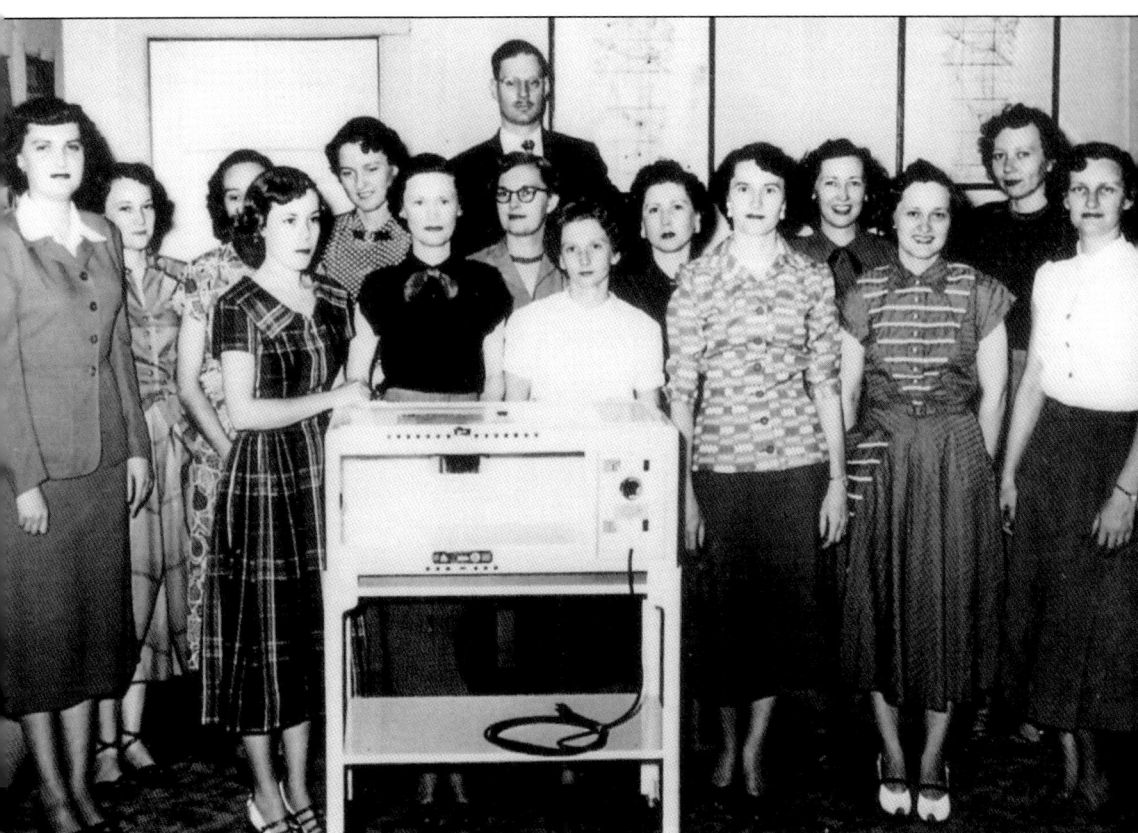

Personnel at the Tishomingo County Health Department are displaying a new piece of machinery. Pictured from left to right are (first row) Betty Dexter, Laura Waddy, Montez Edmondson, Marion McDonald, Lucille Page, Eloise Ramsey Foote, Lynn Reid, and Edith Byram; (second row) June Pruitt, Syble Edmondson, Margaret Whitten, Carolyn Crawford, a health department doctor, France McCune, and Lucille Pruitt.

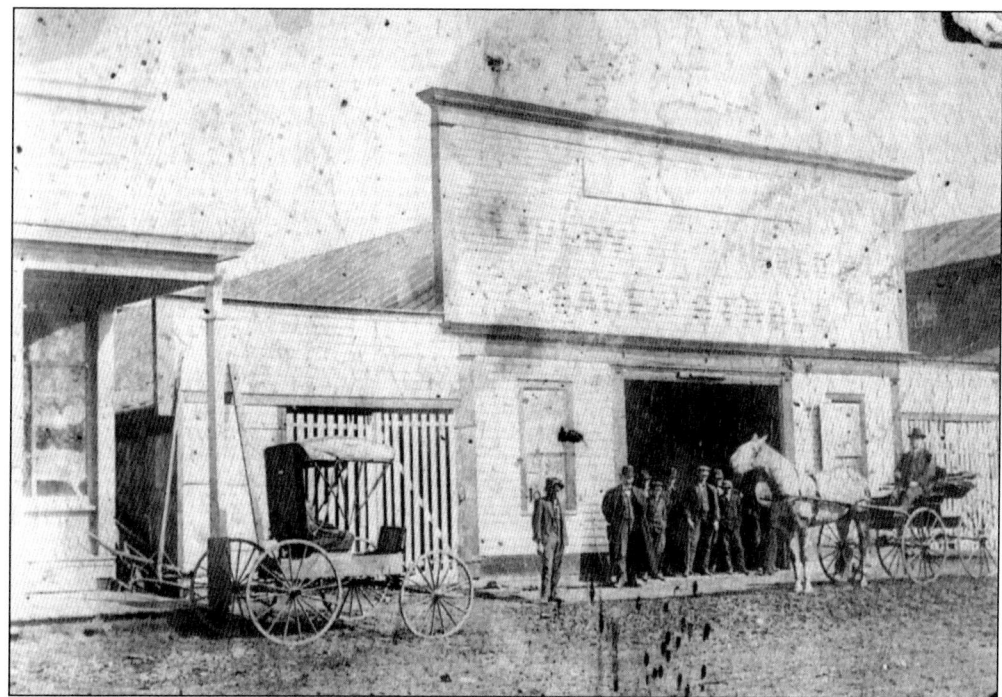

This livery stable ran by Claude Kendrick "C.K." Linton was located in downtown Iuka. The stable hired out horses, teams, and wagons but also boarded privately owned horses. The livery stable was also a source for hay and grain. During the early 1900s, many livery stables were attached to hotels or boardinghouses. With the advent of the automobile after 1910, livery stables quietly disappeared.

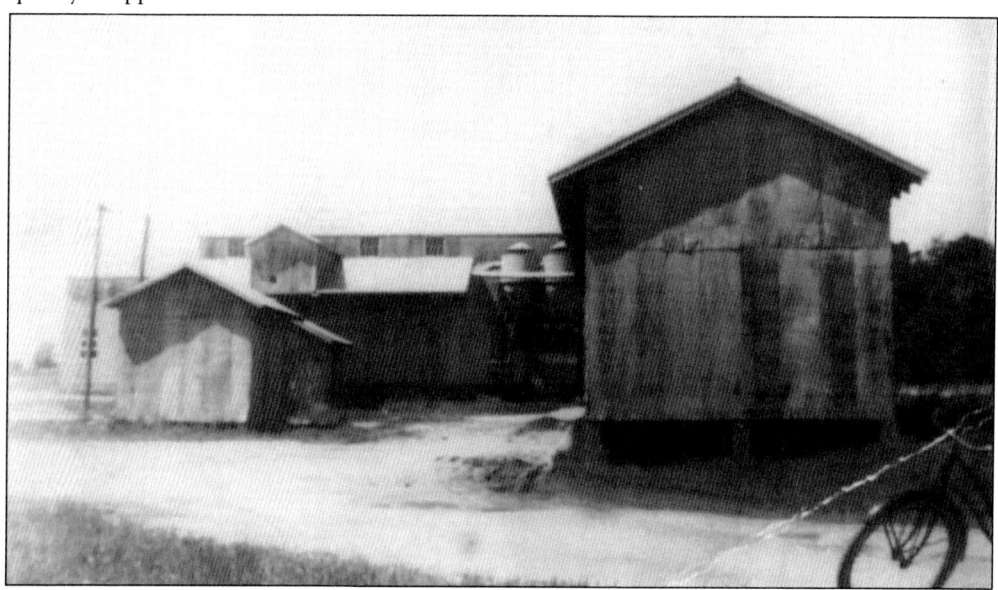

Shown here is the Belmont Cotton Gin. According to industrial data in April 1934, Belmont had two cotton gins. D.D. Patterson was owner of one four-stand gin, used as a standby unit. The gin employed five men. The capacity was three bales an hour. Combined output of both gins in 1933 and 1934 was 2,075 bales. (Courtesy of the *Belmont Journal*.)

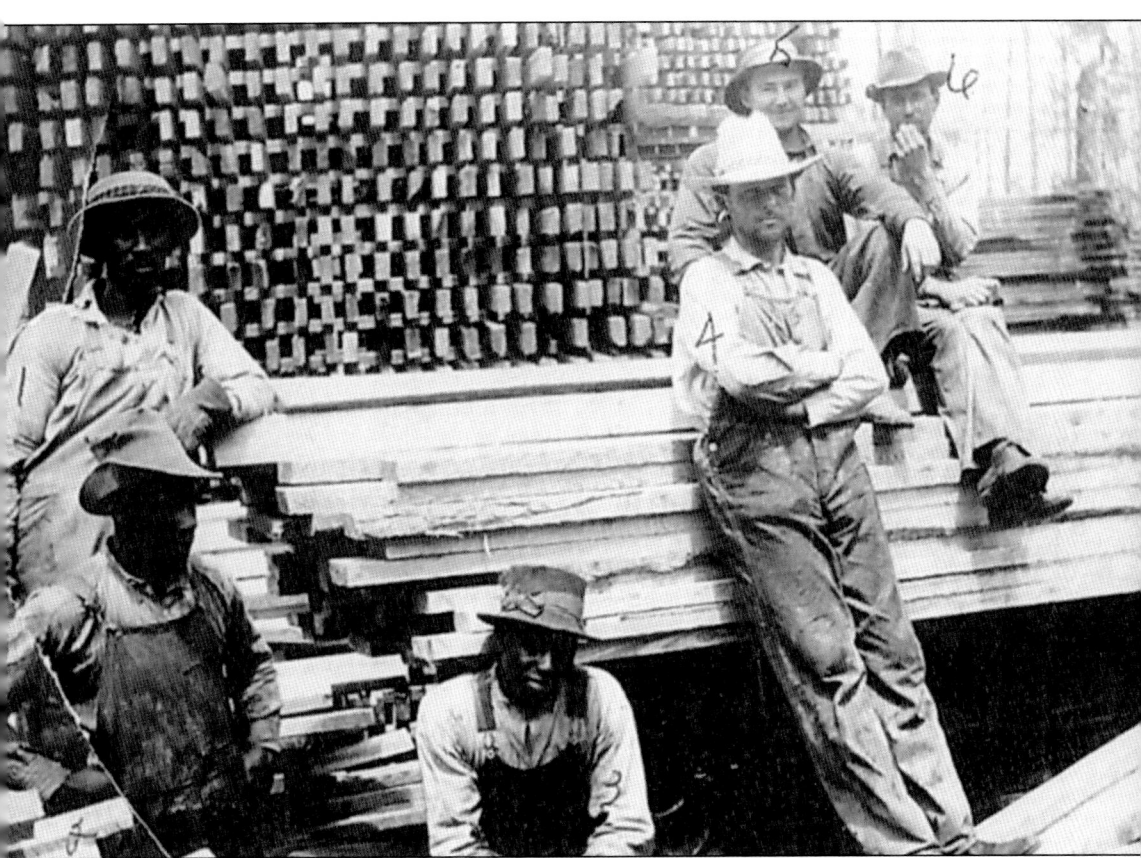

Pictured here are employees of Dan B. Delp Lumber Company in Tishomingo, Mississippi. Leaning against the lumber on the far left is an unidentified man. Others, from left to right, are Alden Hodges, Jim Southward (sitting in center), Steve McDougal (standing), and Ward Wimbish (left of two on right). (Courtesy of Anne Taylor.)

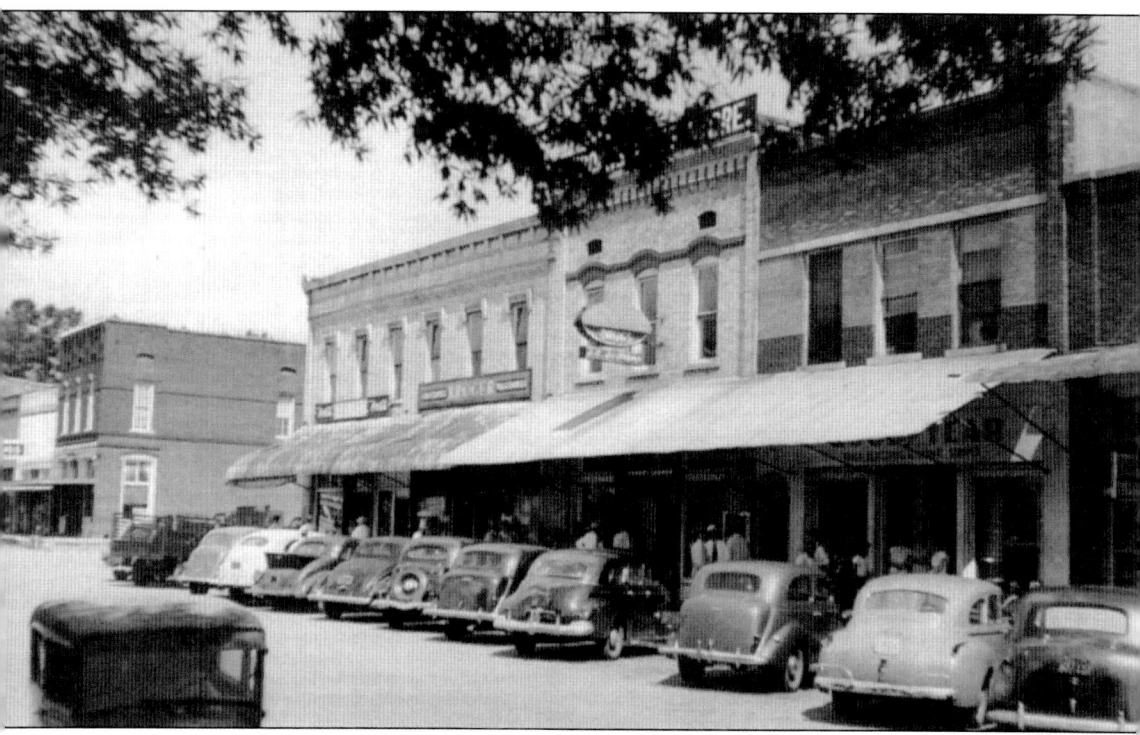
People in Iuka remember July 6, 1950, as the day the Kroger Company awarded the grand prize of $10,000 to the Twentieth Century Club for winning a nationwide contest in community improvement. Iuka celebrated with a huge parade and cookout. Pictured is the Kroger's in Iuka.

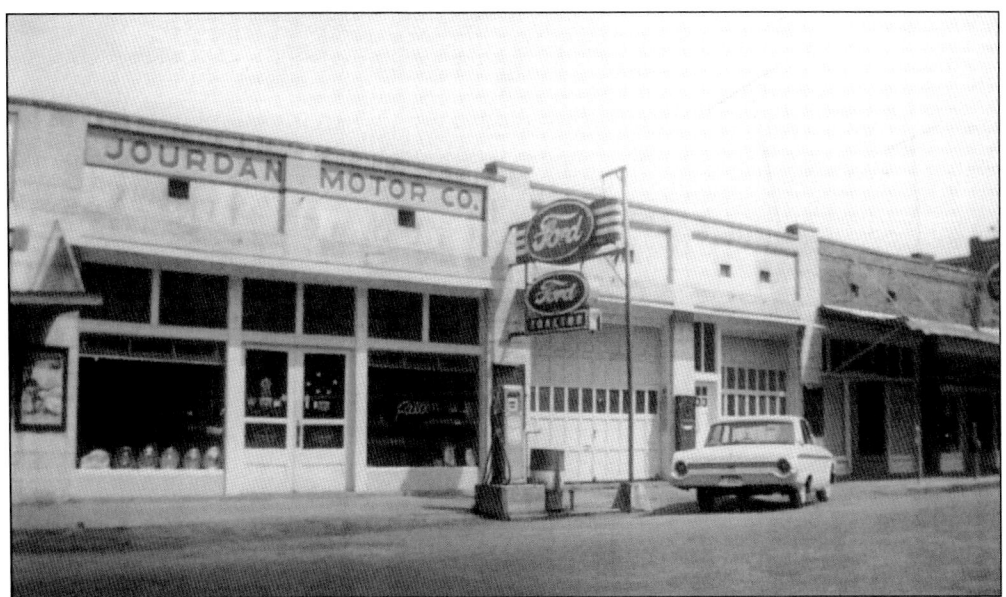

Jourdan Motor Company was founded by local Iuka business leader J.C. Jourdan Sr. After Jourdan's oldest son, Talmage M., finished his formal schooling, he returned home to Iuka and worked closely with his father. The Jourdan Motor Company was located at the northeastern end of the Fulton Street block. It was managed by Talmage for many years until he relinquished active control due to failing health.

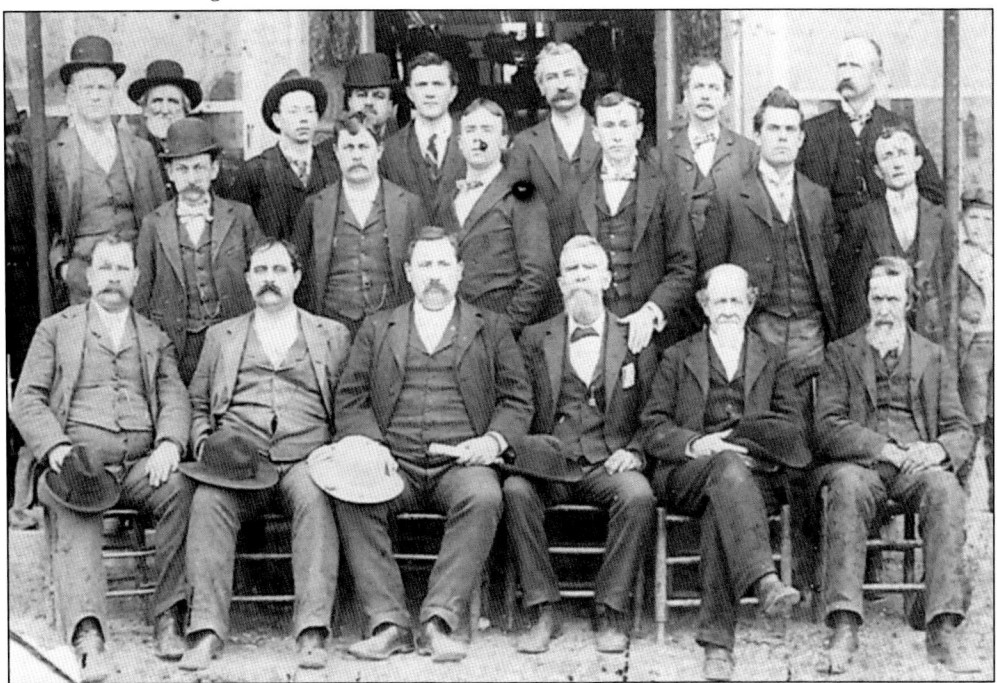

Pictured here are Iuka merchants in 1901. Although they have not been identified, it is important to share what is known of their history. The early 1900s must have been an exciting time for them, as Iuka's electric lights were turned on in 1901, and the Iuka mineral springs water won first prize at the 1904 World's Fair in St. Louis.

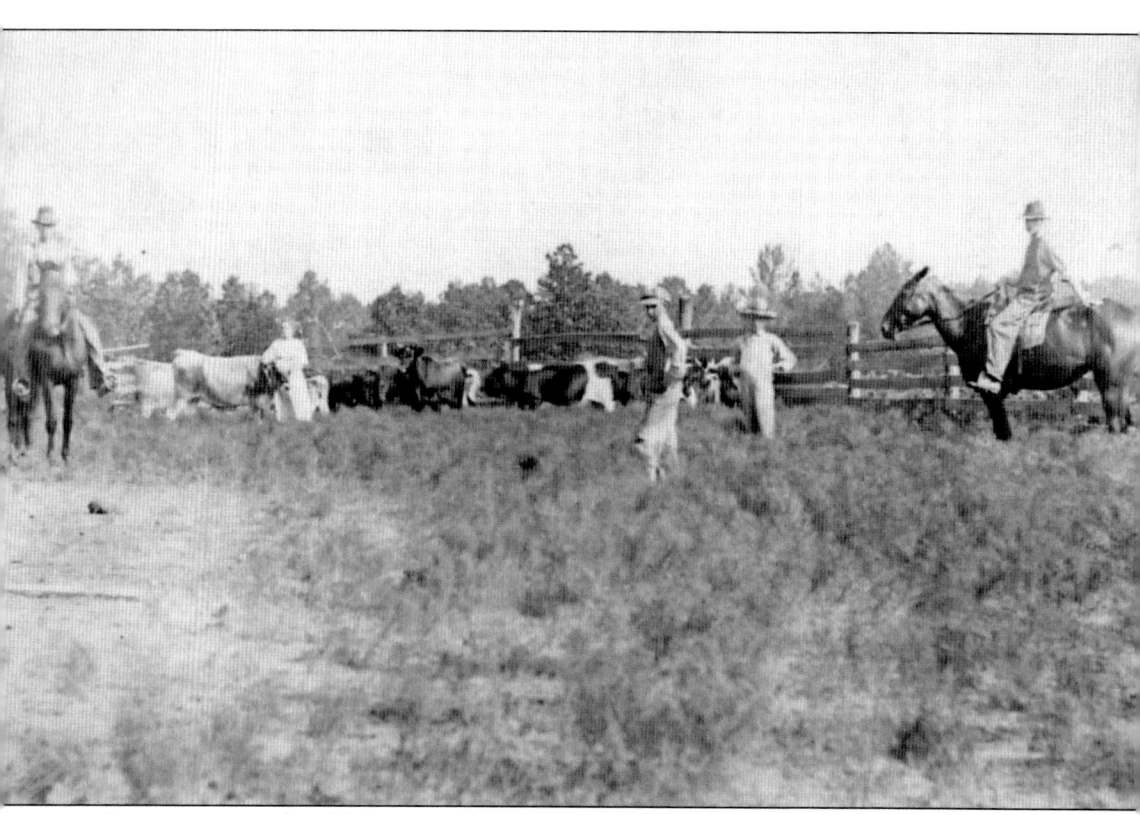

An important trade in Tishomingo County was and continues to be cattle farming—not only for personal family provision, but also because other families depend on the farmer for food. Cattle were raised on land which had few other uses, such as areas of land that were unsuitable for any other crop except grass. Cattle farming operations continue to be popular today.

Two

CHURCHES AND CEMETERIES

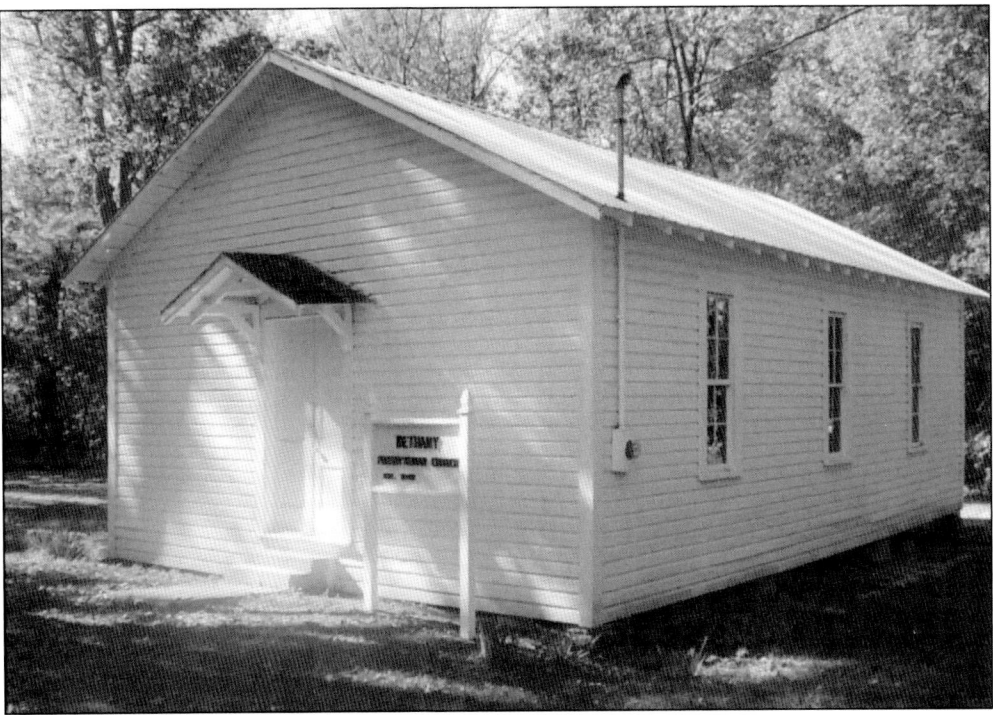

The Bethany Presbyterian Church of Tishomingo held its first service in December 1840. Seven acres were deeded to the church in September 1853 by James McDougal. A school, Euclid Academy, was also established at Bethany by E.W. Carmack. This school first met in the church and accommodated 50 students. Most students boarded with either nearby residents or Cornelius Carmack. Board was $30 for a five-month session.

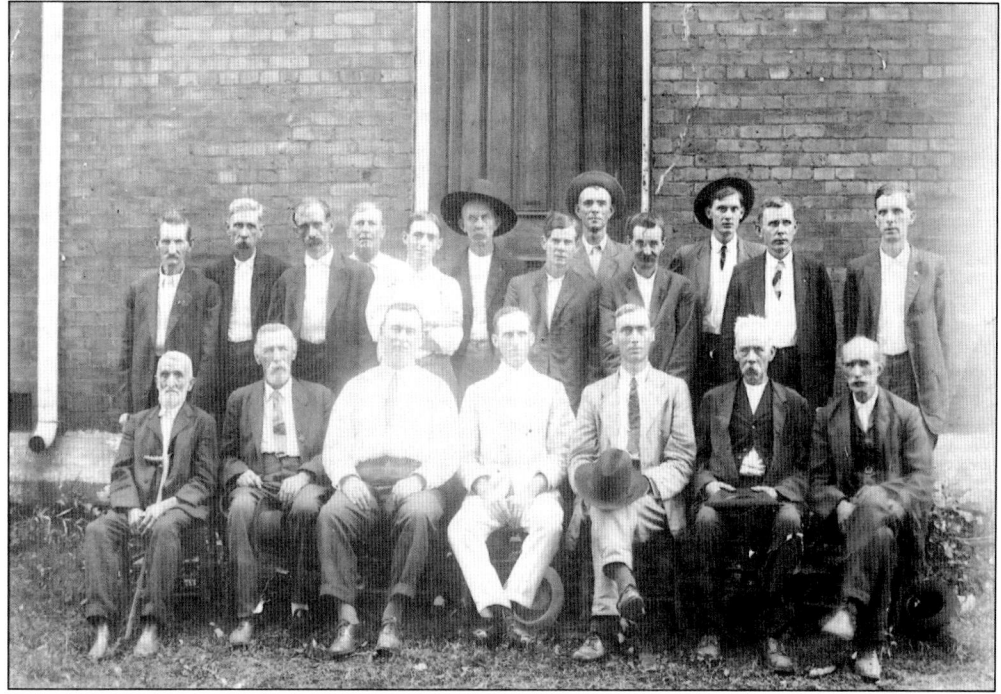

First known as a Church of Baptist Faith, the Iuka Baptist Church was organized in 1859, two years after the town was established. Reverend Hughes served as the first pastor of the church. Men of the Iuka Baptist Church gathered on Monday night, December 27, 1920, for a photograph; J.J. Moore is located in the lower left-hand corner. The others are unidentified.

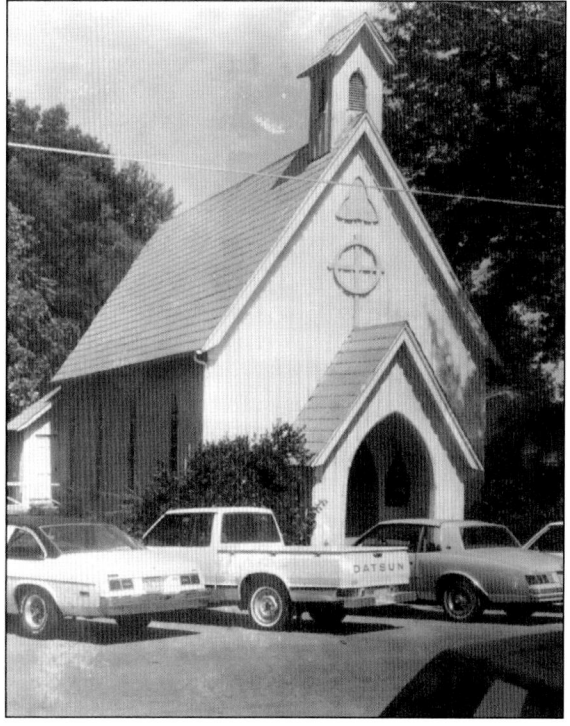

This beautiful, historic, Carpenter Gothic–style church located on Eastport Street in Iuka is one of the oldest places of worship in Tishomingo County. Built in 1873, the Episcopal Church of Our Savior was designed by architect James B. Cook. A small congregation formed in 1866, and the building was formally consecrated on September 28, 1873, by the first bishop of Mississippi, William Mercer Green. It was listed in the National Register of Historic Places in 1991.

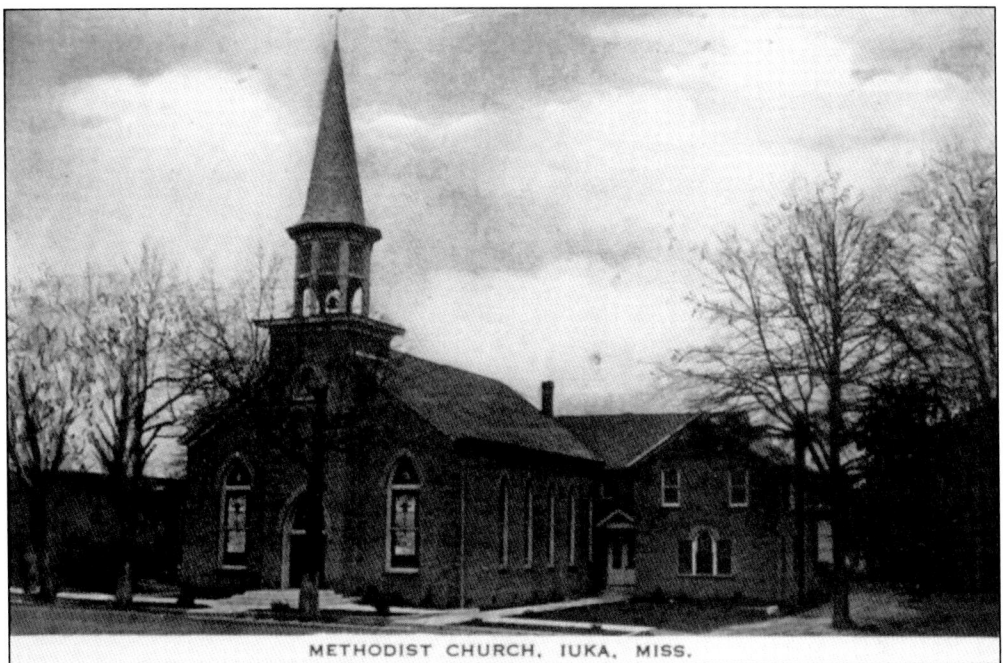

METHODIST CHURCH, IUKA, MISS.

In 1859, Methodists erected a church in Iuka on Eastport Street. This edifice was a frame structure with two large front windows and a broad porch supported by Corinthian columns. A gallery was built for slaves to hear the gospel as well. During the Civil War, the Iuka Methodist Church served as a hospital, and wounded and dying Union and Confederate soldiers were carried through its sacred portals.

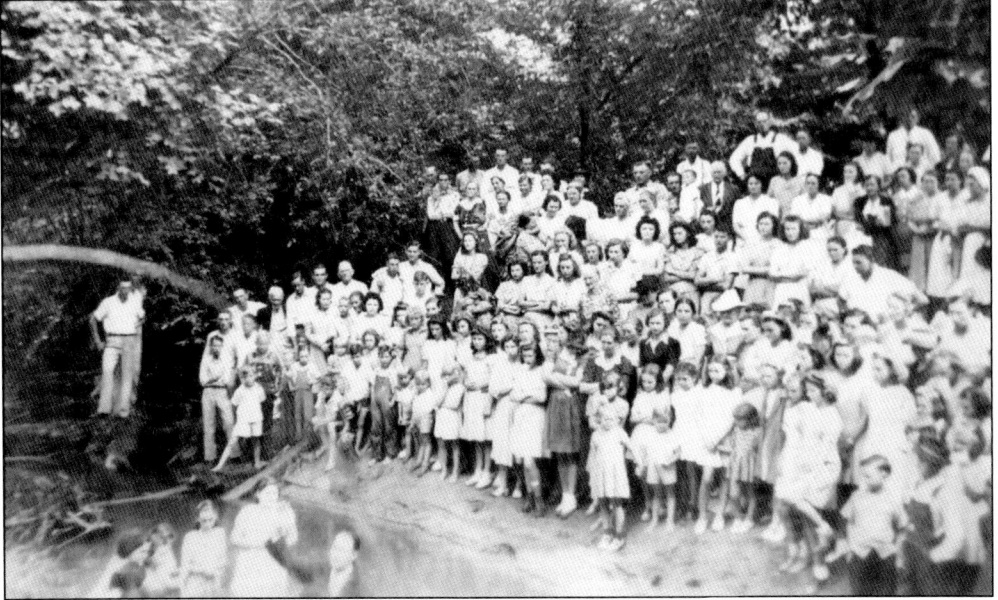

Records show that the Mount Gilead Baptist Church was organized in 1844. Mount Gilead also had a school before Tishomingo County was divided in 1870. According to 1856–1858 records, the school was held in the church facility. This photograph of Mount Gilead Missionary Baptist Church, taken in the 1940s, was the scene of a baptismal service following a revival.

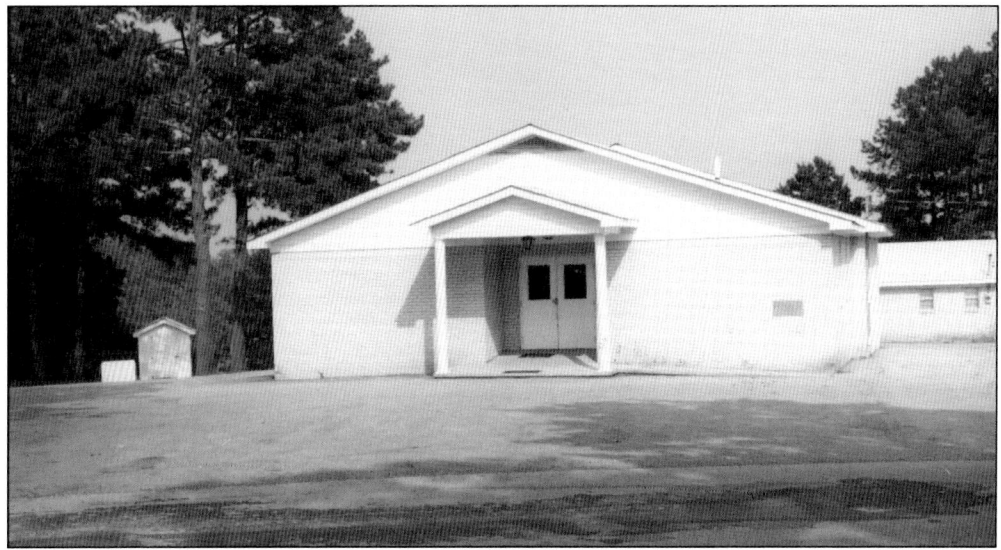

Harmony Hill Baptist Church was organized in August 1962 in the Burnsville community. Clyde Sullivan was the first pastor. Church members met in the Old Burnsville Elementary School while building a sanctuary. The first service was held on October 7, 1962, and the first homecoming service was held on October 13, 1963. The Harmony Hill Baptist Church celebrated its 50th anniversary in 2012.

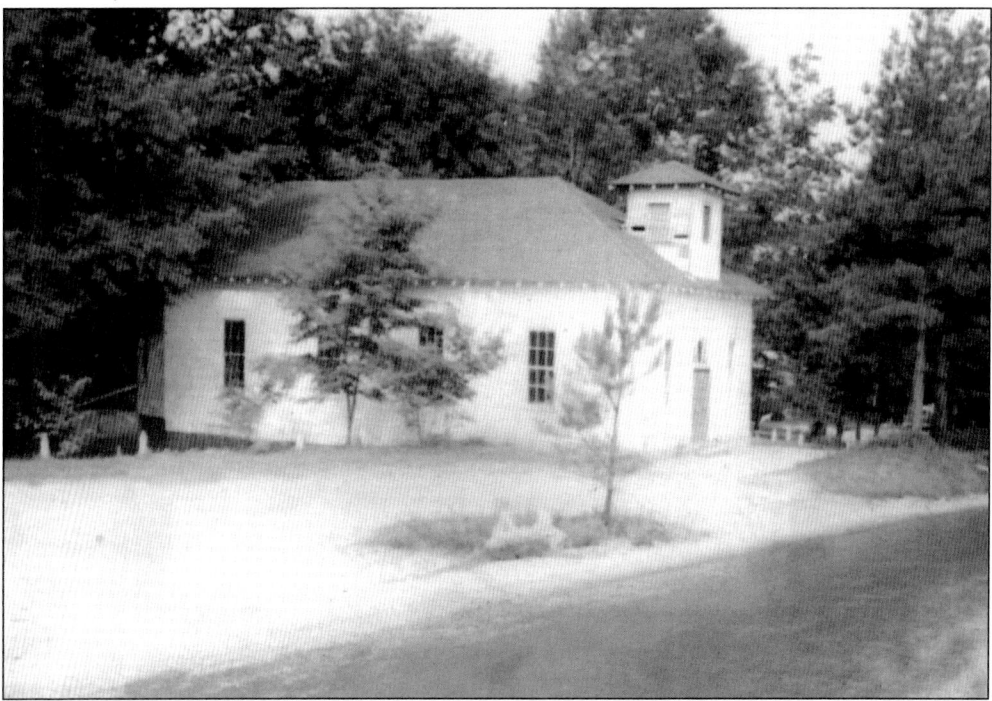

The First Missionary Baptist Church in Iuka was established in 1867. Records show that the present location was purchased from Paul Bonds in 1905. Early known members of the church from the 1800s and early 1900s include Bob Brown, Tim Creighton, Edd Walker, George Armstrong, Jay Winbush, Lewis Moody, Charlie Clement, Edith Grizzard, Laura Brown, Emily Creighton, Cherry Gholston, Margarette White, Belle Moody, Martha Winbush, and Ada Smith.

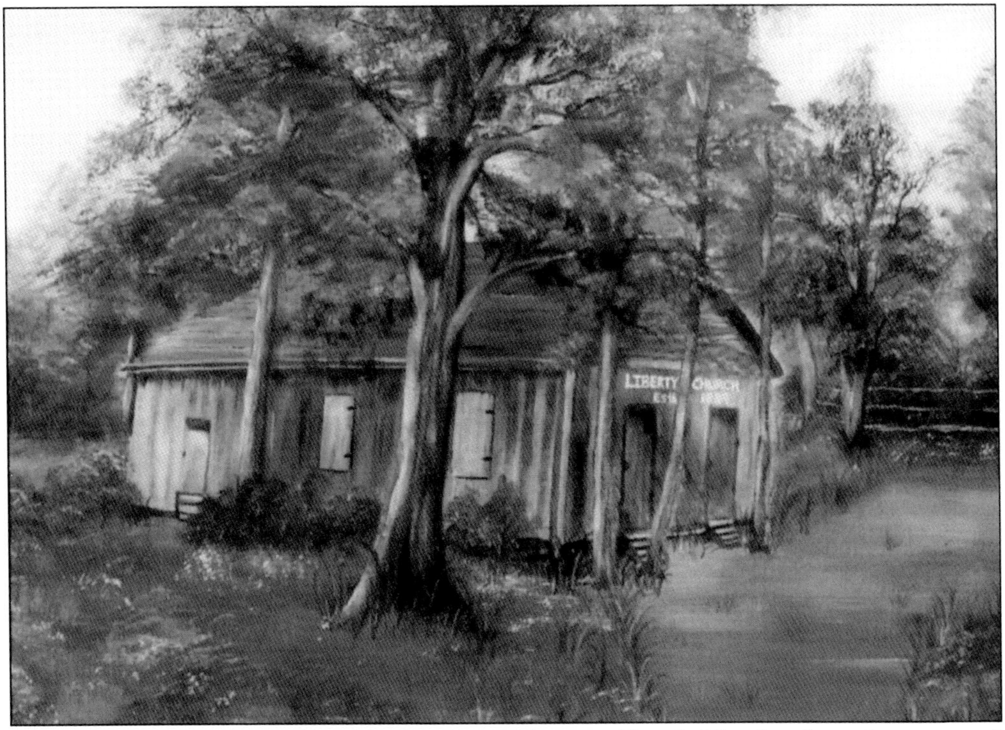

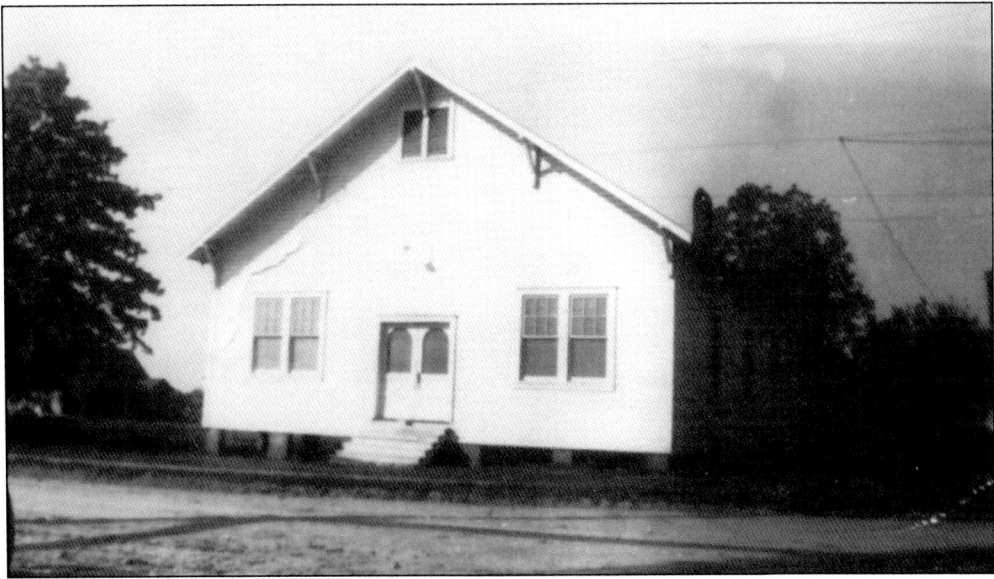

In 1889, T.B. Lindsey donated land for the Liberty Christian Church. The church was later renamed Liberty Church of Christ. Charter members were C.M. Burleson, J.H. Shook, W.W. Shook, Henry Lancaster, J.T. Vaughn, J.C. Johnson, Henry Moore, Jim Carr, T.B. Lindsey, and Willis Burcham. The first elders, appointed in 1895, were C.M. Burleson, J.H. Shook, and J.T. Vaughn.

The Belmont Methodist Church was organized on July 28, 1881, in the Old Valley community, one mile east of Belmont. In June 1892, the church was moved to the New Valley community, one mile north of Belmont. In 1911, it was moved to Third Street, one-half block east of Main Street, in Belmont. In 1922, a new building was erected. (Courtesy of the *Belmont Journal*.)

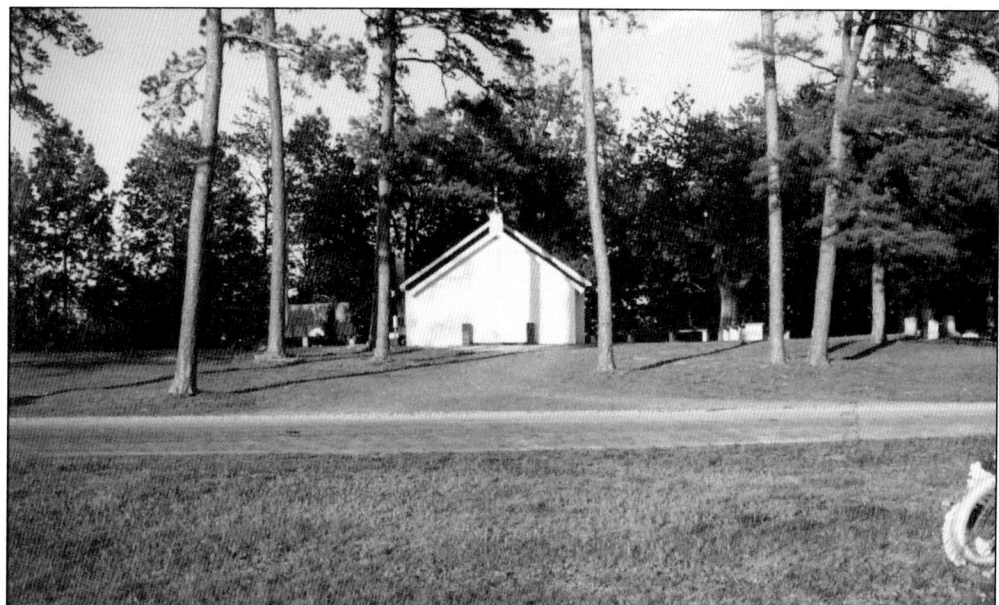

Land was deeded for a school on March 2, 1889, to William S. Smith, Henry Smith, and James Smith, trustees of Fairview School. The deed was signed by J.S. Morris, and the building served as both a school and a church. This building burned, and the church and school were rebuilt separately. The last school year recorded was in 1931. The present church was built in 1951.

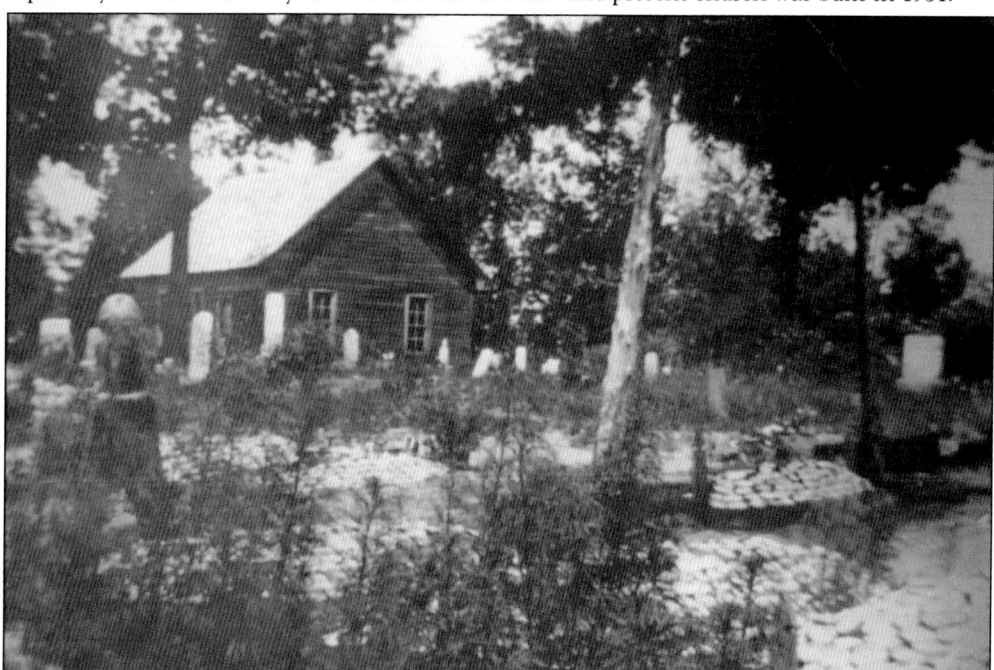

In February 1921, a group of Free Will Baptists erected the New Lebanon Church. Logs were cut and hauled to Charlie White's mill, where they were sawed and then carried back to build the sanctuary. Charter members were Dave P. Rickard, Jack A. Lambert, Martha Howard Lambert, Maudie Lambert Helton, J. Benton Moss, Arthur McCoy, and Kate McCoy. G.P. Mayo was elected as the first pastor.

Burgess Creek Freewill Baptist Church, pictured here, was organized on September 19, 1946, by Rev. G.P. Mayo. There were seven charter members: George and Rosie Lambert, Elton and Emma Nichols, Mattie Bell Strickland, Hazel Gentle, and Arnell Nichols. The land for the original church was donated by the Strickland and Nichols families.

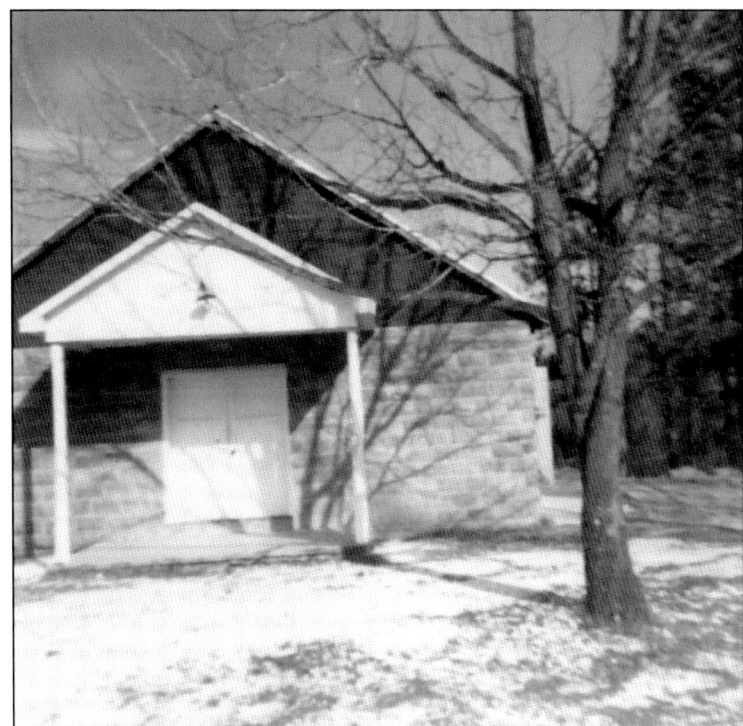

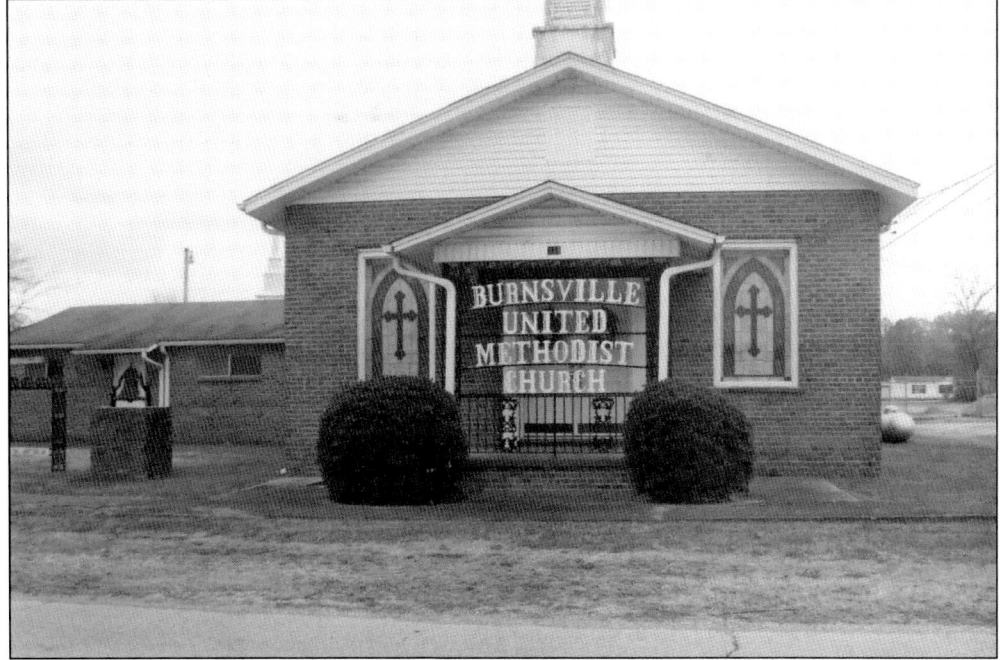

The Burnsville United Methodist Church, built about 1835, had a large membership during the Civil War era. In 1925, the church and business section of Burnsville were destroyed by fire. The only items salvaged from the little white plank church were an antique table, chair, church bell, and some handmade Sunday school furniture. The brick church was erected in the latter part of 1927.

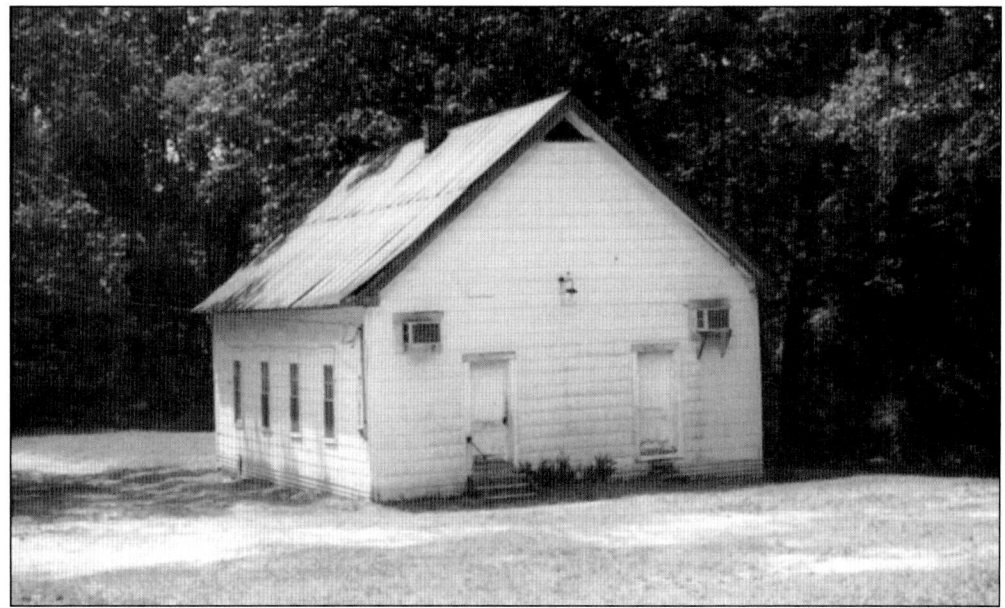

The Mount Pleasant community was settled during the pioneer days. D.R. Kennedy and Mrs. S.H. Smith felt the need for a church, donated some land, and the Mount Pleasant Methodist Church was established in 1889. The total cost of construction was $105.35. The good people of the community raised $104.55, leaving the members owing 80¢.

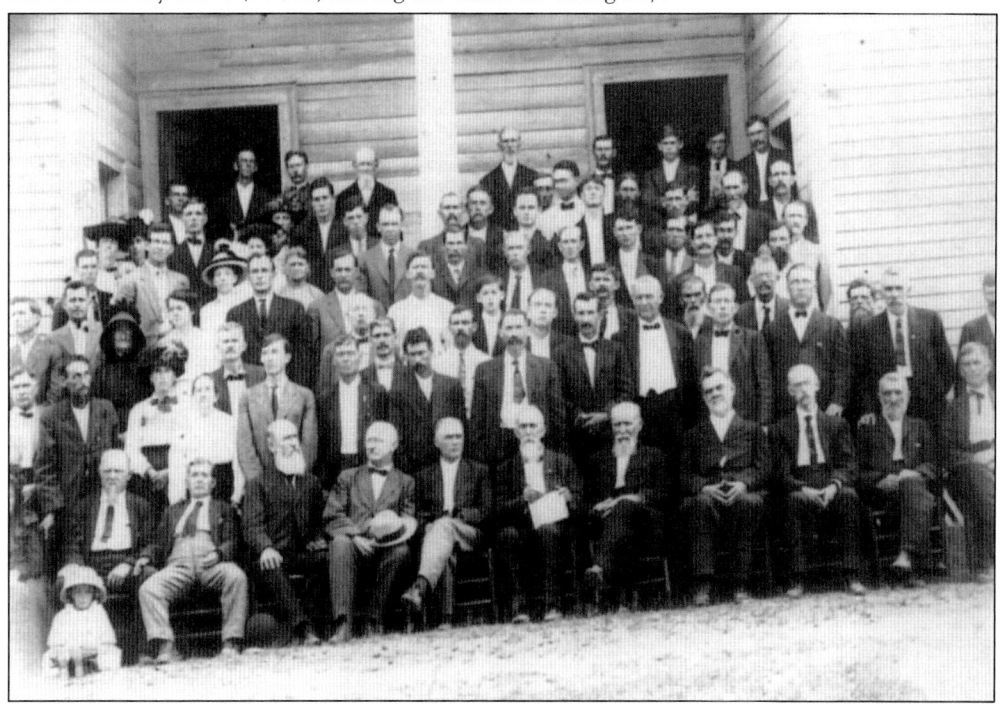

The Tishomingo Baptist Association's 53rd Annual Session met with the Iuka Baptist Church in 1912. Pictured are W.D. Conn, D.J. Akers, G.W. Reid, Mrs. Willard Carmack, Rev. J.D. Franks, G.T. Reid, J.W. Hiett, and J. Houston Reid. The Sunday school had five teachers and 31 pupils. (Courtesy of Jerrell McNutt.)

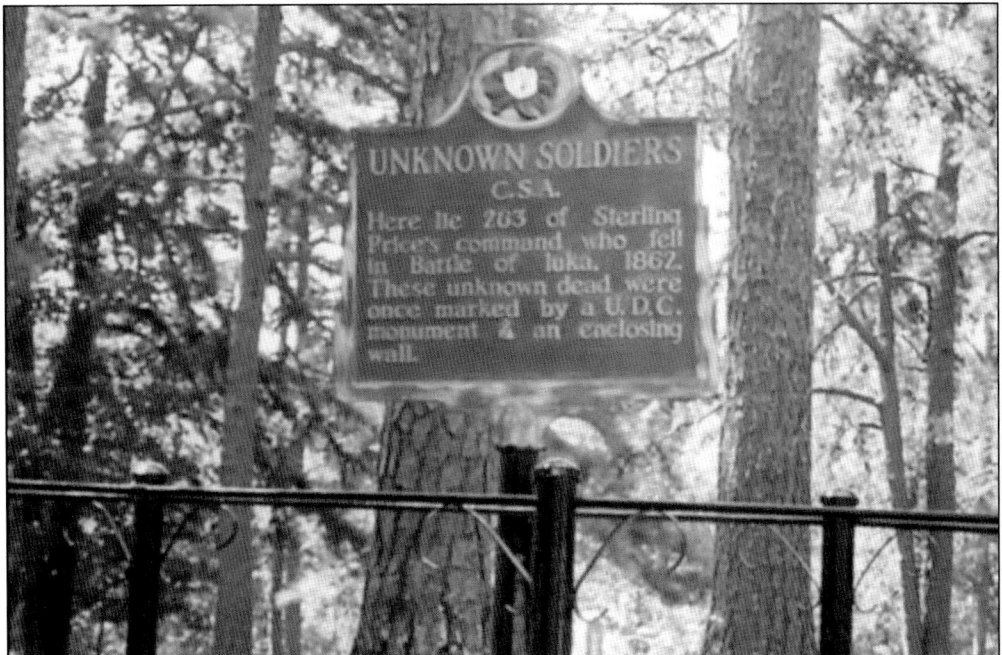

It is believed that the Shady Grove Cemetery opened in 1857 along with the establishment of the town of Iuka. In the northwest corner of the cemetery lies the burial place of 263 Confederate soldiers who died during the Battle of Iuka. They were buried together in a long trench.

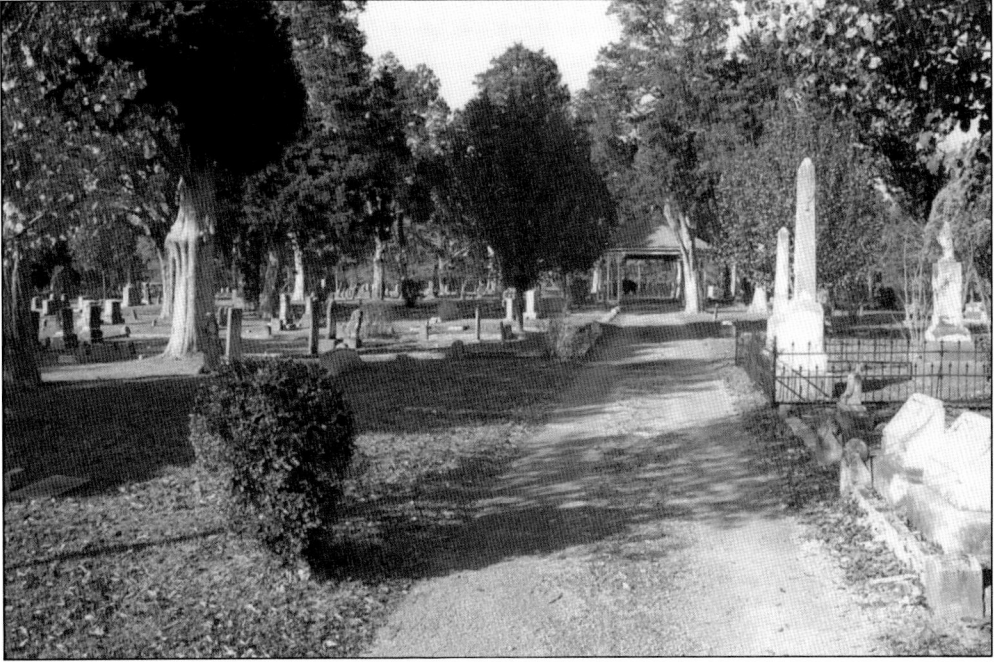

The Oak Grove Cemetery is located on Highway 25 within the city limits of Iuka, Mississippi. Land for the cemetery was deeded to the town of Iuka by Col. Lawrence Moore. The tombstone for former Mississippi governor John Marshall Stone is prominently located in this cemetery. Stone was a resident of Tishomingo County, Mississippi, and a much-loved governor.

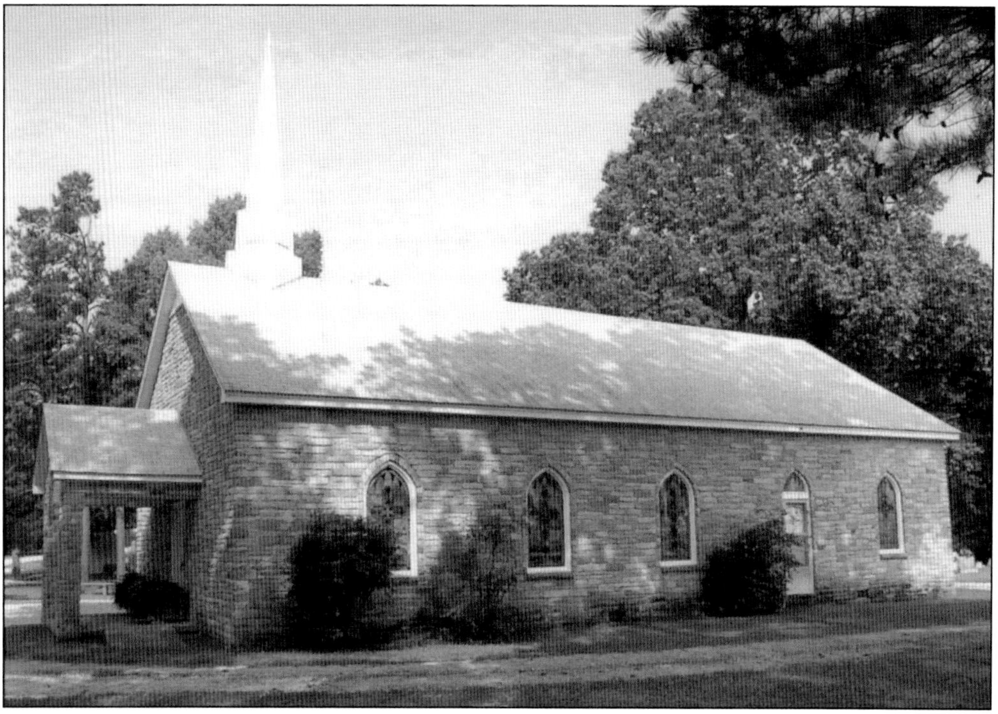

Spring Hill Methodist Church was organized in 1909. There were 14 charter members, including G.C. Stephens, A.W. Millsaps, J.F. Oaks, J.T. Blissitt, A.W. Rast, J.E. Harp, and R.A. Belue. The old Spring Hill School was used as a church meeting place until 1911, when the first church was built. J.T. Blissitt donated the land for the church.

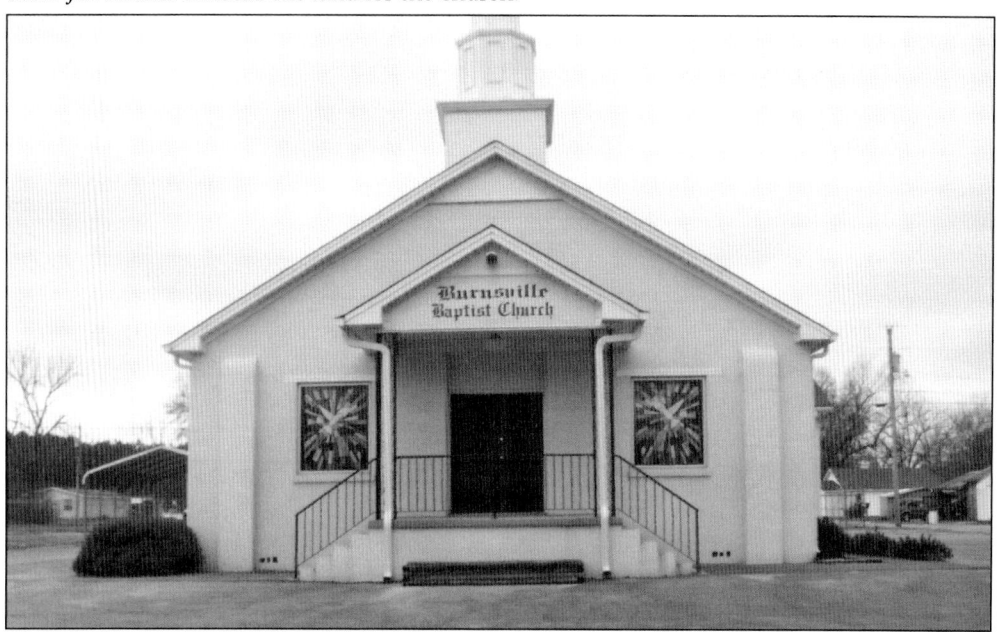

The Burnsville Baptist Church, organized in 1836, was first called Yellow Creek Baptist Church; it was located a half mile north of the present-day Antioch Church. H.M. Cobb donated a lot for the church.

Three

CITIES, TOWNS, AND COMMUNITIES

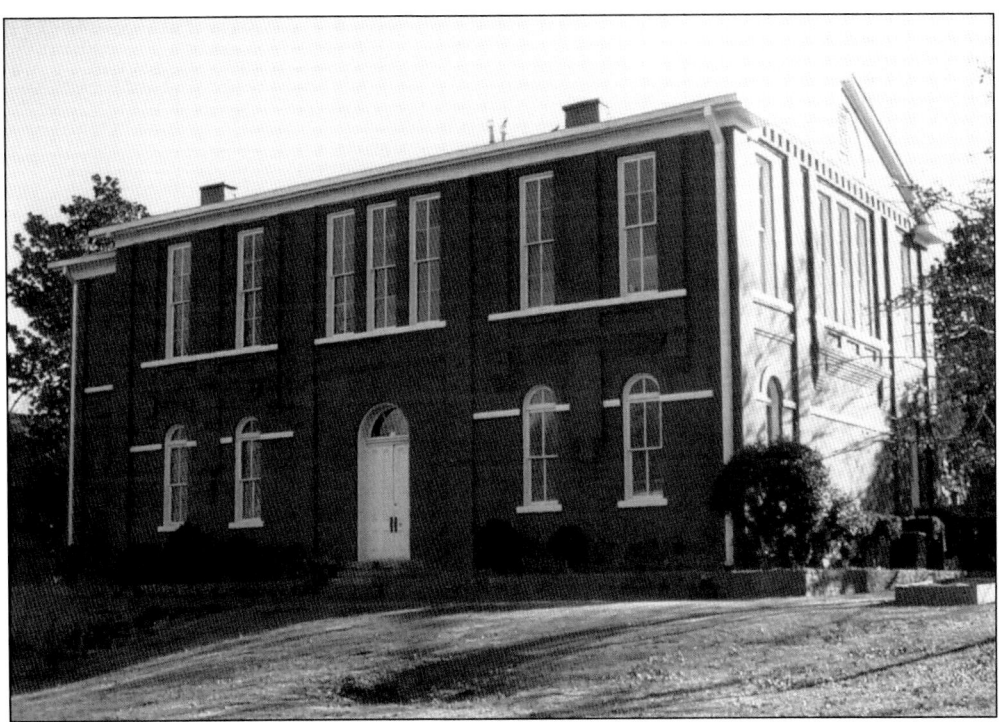

The original courthouse in Iuka was built in 1870 after the division of Tishomingo County into present-day Alcorn, Prentiss, and Tishomingo Counties. A fire in 1886 destroyed the third level, along with all the county's records. The courthouse served as a political center, and various speakers, including James K. Vardaman and Theodore G. Bilbo, were frequent visitors. The courthouse now holds the county archives and history museum.

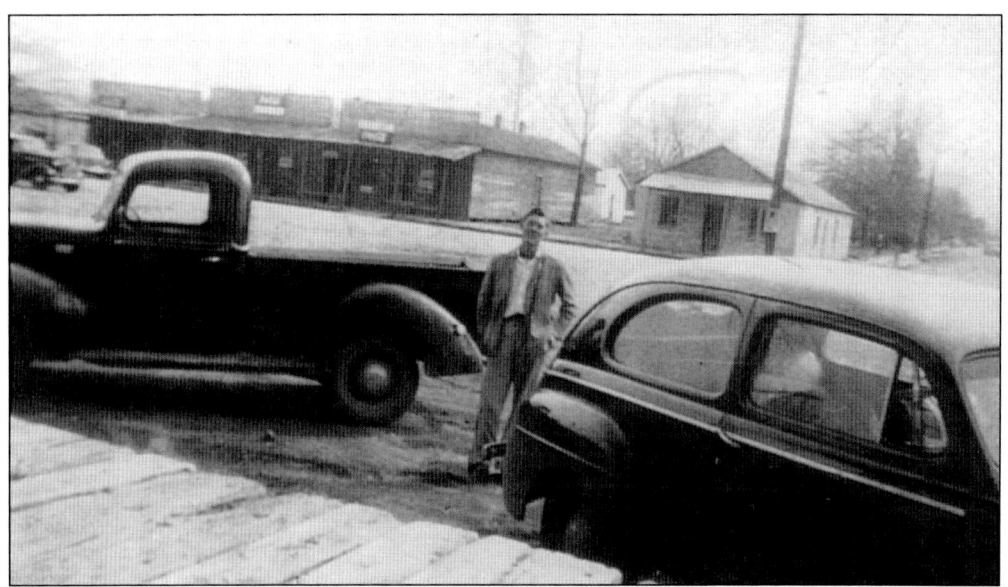

Jeremiah Burns migrated to the Burnsville area with his family in 1832. Pioneer settlers added "ville," so the town became known as Burnsville. Before the Battle of Iuka, Major General Ord, under the command of General Grant, was located in Burnsville. During the Civil War, Gen. Nathan Bedford Forrest also camped in Burnsville, and J.C. Walters was captain of the Burnsville Rifles during the Civil War.

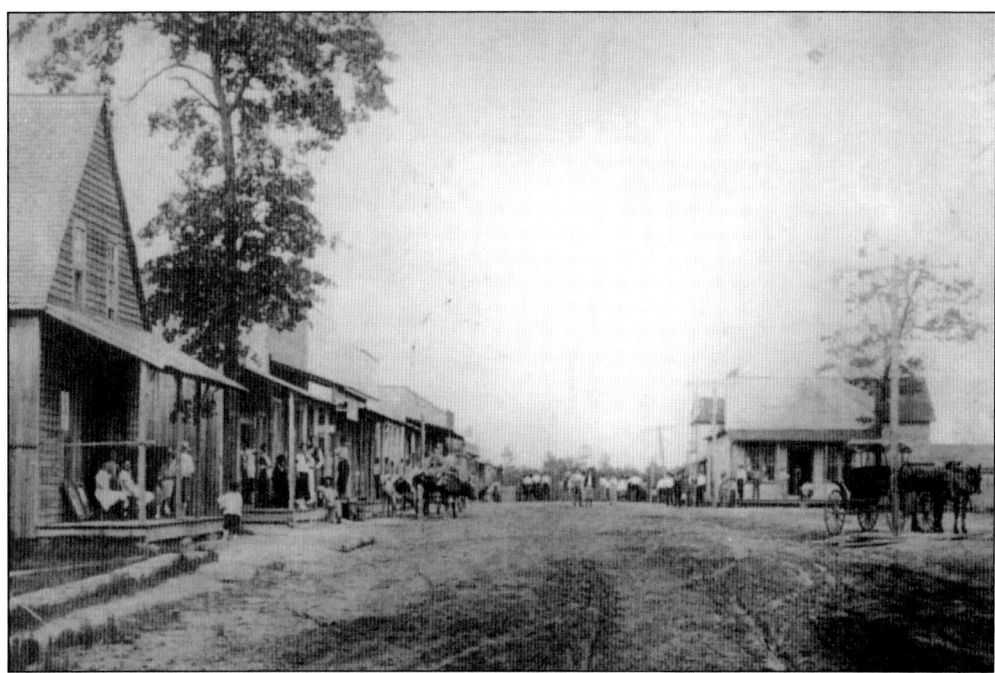

In 1884, Belmont was a settlement called Gum Springs, which boasted a post office. After the Illinois Central Railroad completed its Birmingham Division in 1907, the town grew considerably. It was incorporated as Belmont, meaning "beautiful mountain," on January 22, 1908. Belmont is located about eight miles south of the Natchez Trace Parkway.

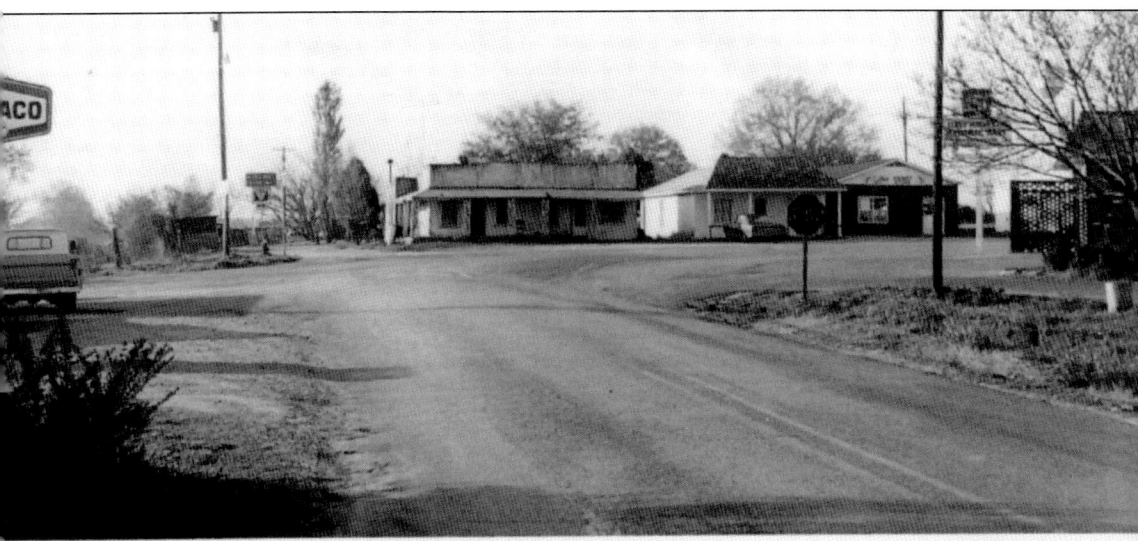

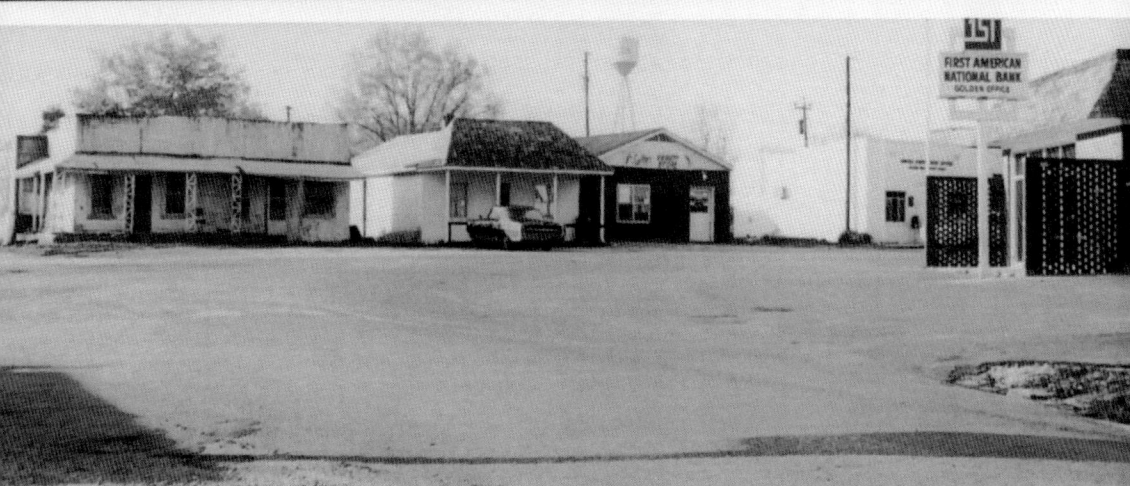

Originally called Wamsley or Wambi, the town of Golden sprang up around a large lumber mill. Most of the inhabitants were employed at the sawmill, and its decline undermined the town's prosperity. The railroad brought new life to the town in the early 1900s, and the town of Golden was incorporated on February 8, 1908. Through the encouragement of Dr. A.E. Bostick, the town of Golden was named after a baby girl, Golden Patrie Wiggins, whom he delivered on January 18, 1908.

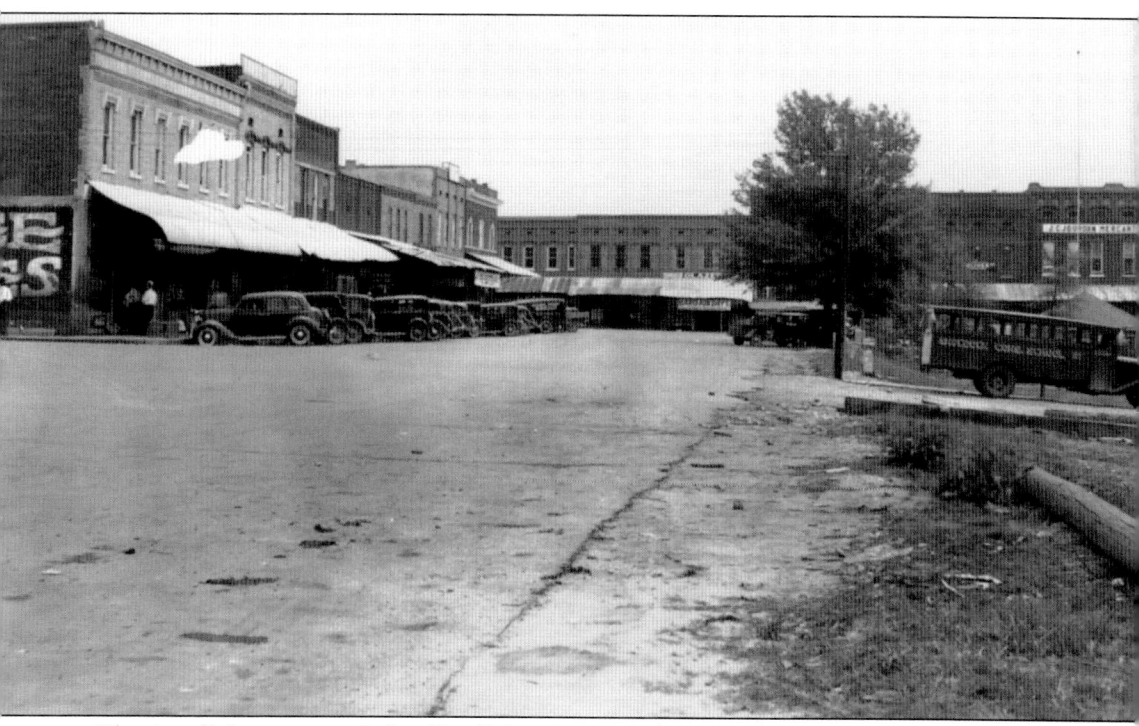

The city of Iuka was named after Chief Iuka, pronounced "eye-you-ka." By the late 1840s, the people of Tishomingo County were acutely aware of the increasing advantages of rail transportation. Railroad officials eventually drove the last spike just outside the limits of Iuka on March 28, 1857, to link the cities of Memphis and Charleston by railway. Iuka, Mississippi, was chartered in 1857 about that time.

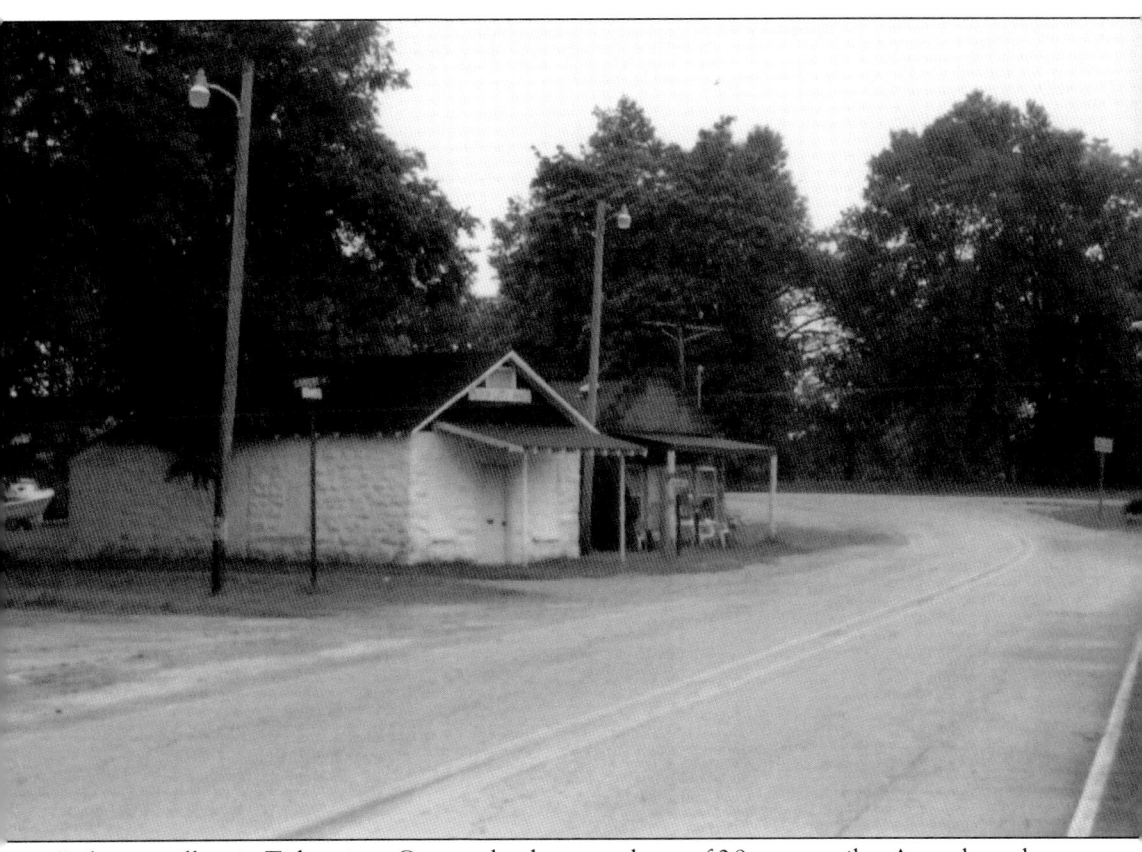

Paden is a village in Tishomingo County that has a total area of 0.9 square miles. An early settler of the area, Thomas Paden, built his home here and called it Castle Garden. It was burned by Union troops during the Civil War, and the area became known as Burnt Mills. When the town was incorporated, its name was changed to Paden.

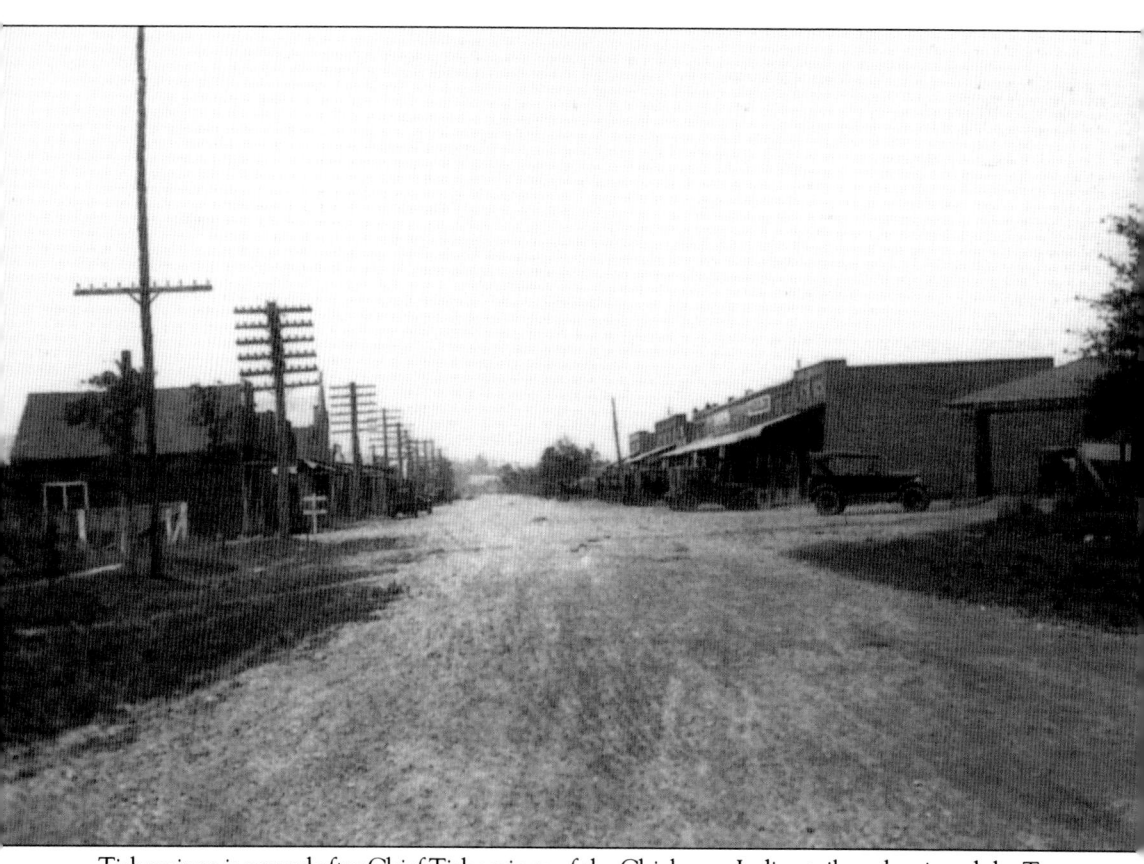

Tishomingo is named after Chief Tishomingo of the Chickasaw Indian tribe, who signed the Treaty of Pontotoc in 1832. History notes that Gen. Andrew Jackson camped at the site of Tishomingo on his way to fight the Battle of New Orleans in the War of 1812. In 1916, a songwriter named Spencer Williams passed through Tishomingo and wrote *Tishomingo Blues*. (Courtesy of Anne Taylor.)

The village of Holcut, named for the Holder and Callicutt families, was founded in 1907. John Martin was the first merchant, and Dr. T.P. Haney Sr. was the first doctor. In 1975, the residents of the Holcut community moved out of their homes and relocated to make room for the future Tennessee-Tombigbee Waterway. Today, a memorial marks the location of the town now abandoned by progress.

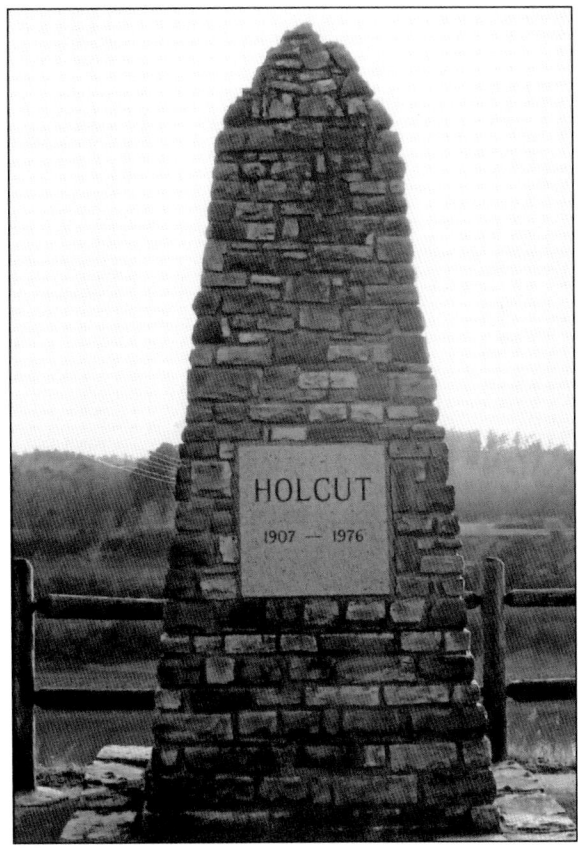

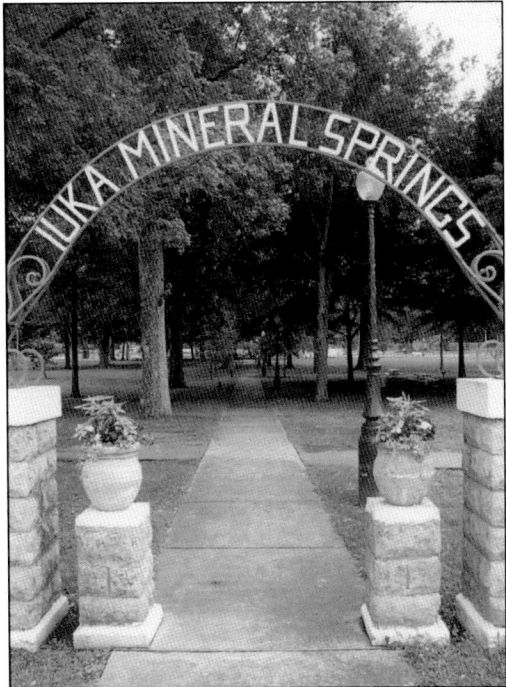

David Hubbard donated 10.5 acres to Iuka to create the Iuka Mineral Springs Park solely as an area for recreation. The mineral waters flowing from the ground became the center of tourism during the late 19th century. Visitors flocked to Iuka for the curative power of the "healing" mineral water. A bandstand, similar to the original, and springhouses still grace the historical Mineral Springs Park.

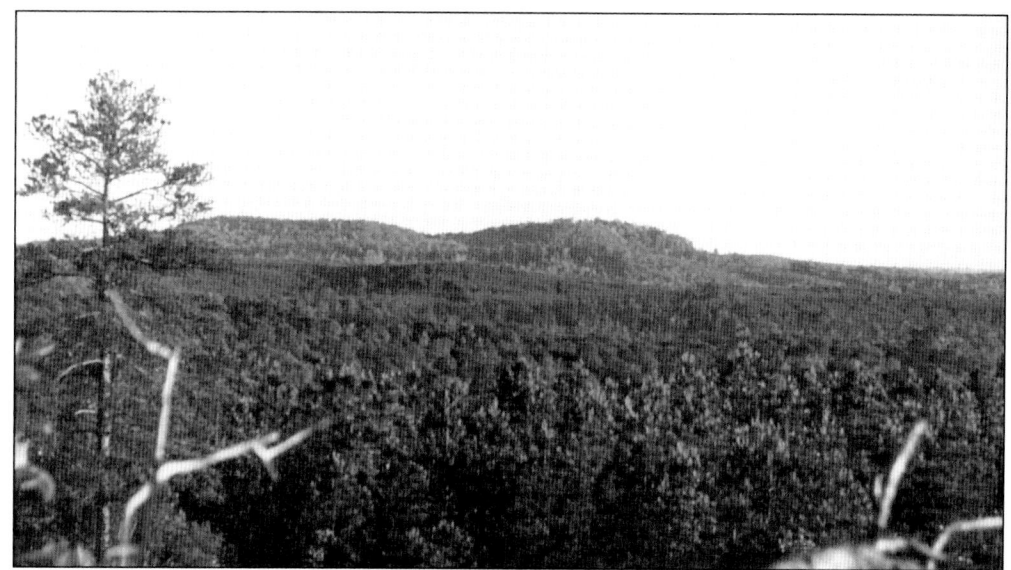

Woodall Mountain is located four miles southwest of Iuka at an elevation of 806 feet above sea level; it is the highest point in Mississippi. According to tradition, Woodall Mountain was called Yow Mountain in the early days before 1878. Woodall Mountain supposedly obtained its name from Zephaniah "Z.H." Woodall, who served as sheriff of Tishomingo County in 1877.

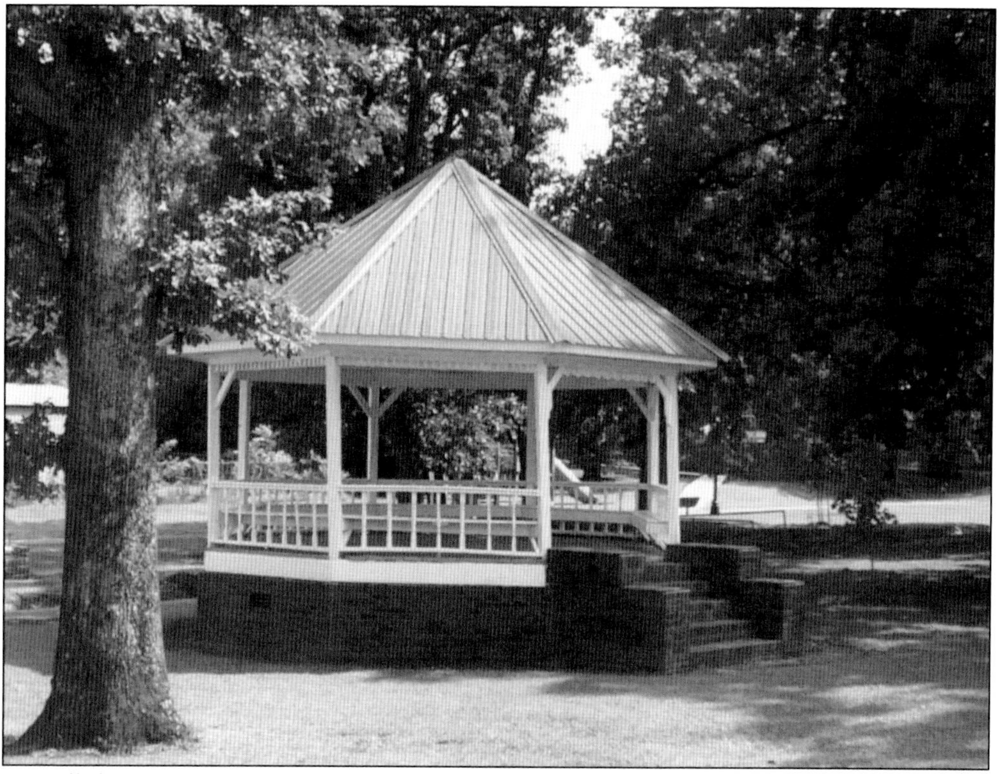

A stroll through Shook Park, also called the Belmont City Park, is a delight to visitors as they listen to the beautiful sounds of the birds and watch the youth play happily on the playground. The park offers space for recreation and picnicking. Pictured here is the colorful gazebo.

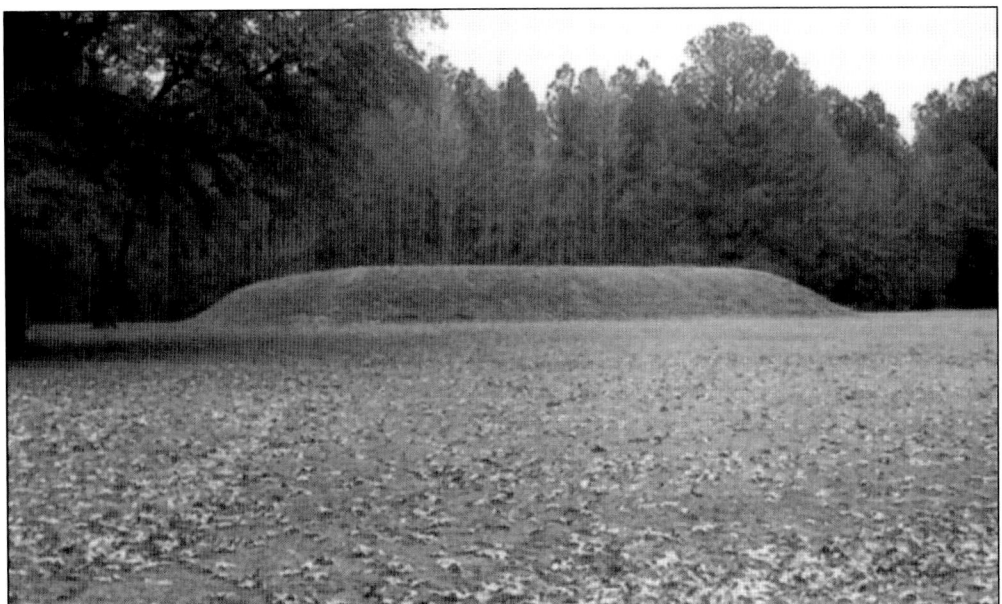

Tishomingo County has three unique sites that are marked near the Alabama–Mississippi border along the historic Natchez Trace Parkway. Bear Creek Mound was a village site occupied as early as 8,000 BC by migratory hunters; they practiced limited agriculture. The nearby fields and streams offered an abundance of nuts, fruits, game, and fish. These people shaped this mound and built a crude temple on its summit to house their sacred images. Cave Spring was a result of solution activity. A long room or corridor was dissolved out of the rock by underground water. Indians may have used this site as a source of water and stone. Tishomingo State Park, the fifth area in Mississippi to be slated as a state park, was selected mainly because of its natural beauty unique to Mississippi.

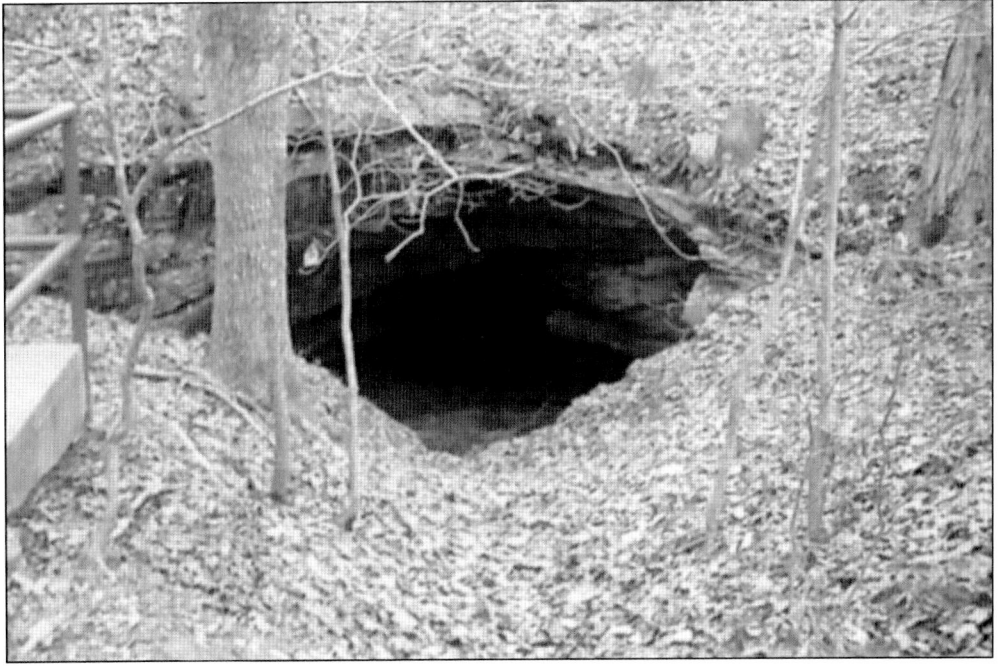

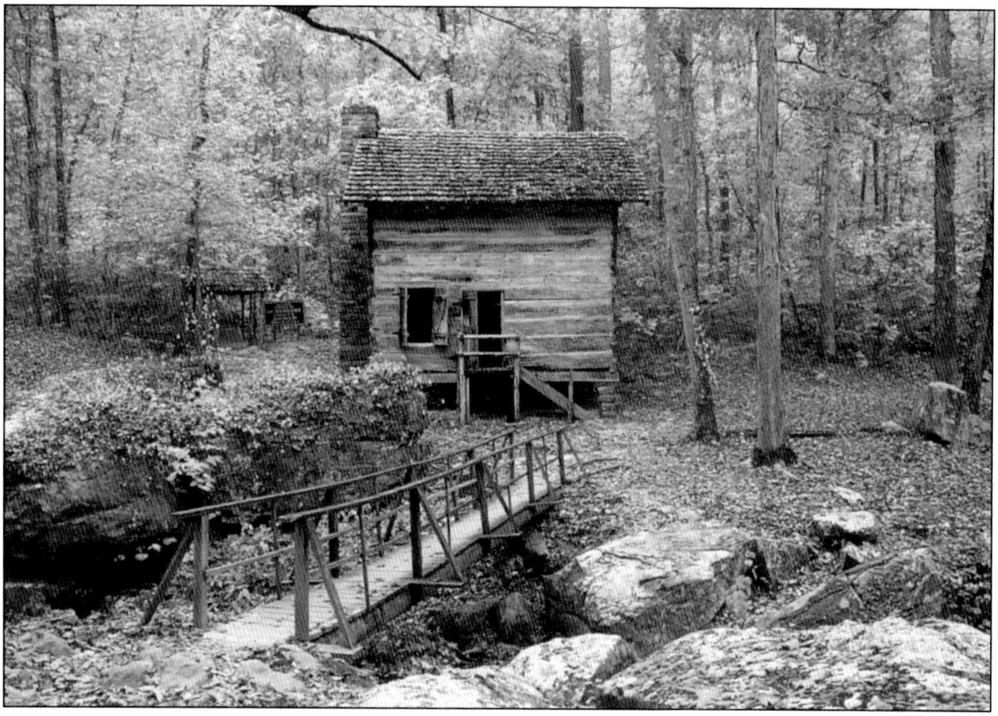

Tishomingo County has two state parks—the Tishomingo State Park and the J.P. Coleman State Park. Tishomingo State Park is widely acclaimed as Mississippi's most beautiful natural area. Many of the park buildings are constructed of the beautiful multicolored sandstone quarried in Tishomingo County. Rocky canyons, hardwood forests, flowering shrubs and trees, and clear streams make this park a nature lover's paradise. Tishomingo State Park is famous for its swinging bridge dating from the 1930s. The native stone and steel-cable bridge crosses high above Bear Creek. In the early 1800s, the Chickasaw Indians roamed these lands, hunting and fishing along the banks of the Tennessee River. It is believed that the spot where the restaurant now stands was a "workplace" frequented by the Indians.

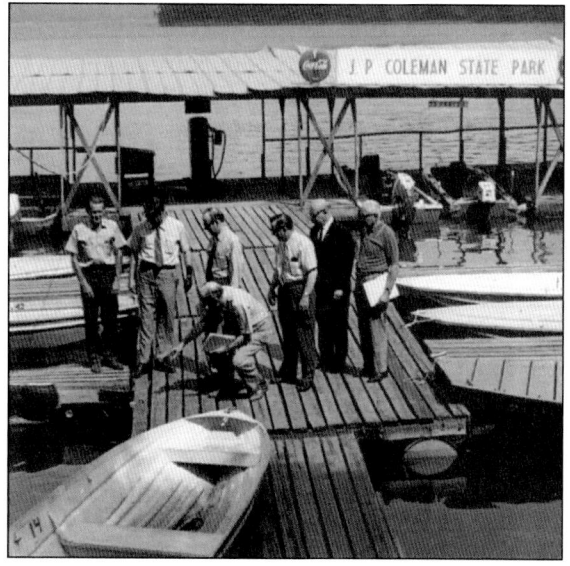

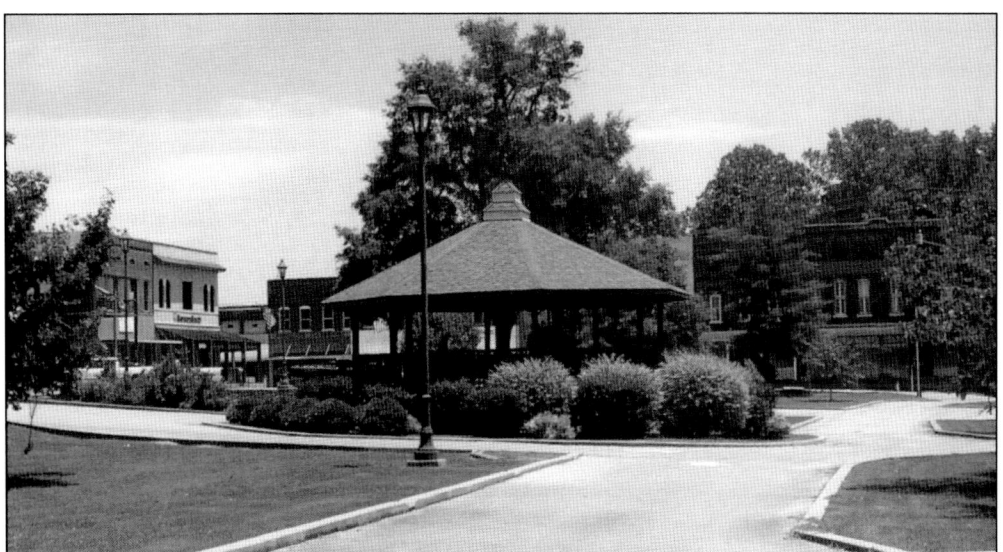

In earlier years, cotton and logs were piled up close to the railroad depot in Iuka for transport by train. Horses and wagons were placed here while families shopped downtown. The animals were given feed bags, and blue jays ate the feed that fell on the ground. Later, the town made a small park with hitching posts, picnic tables, and a gazebo. It was named Jay Bird Park.

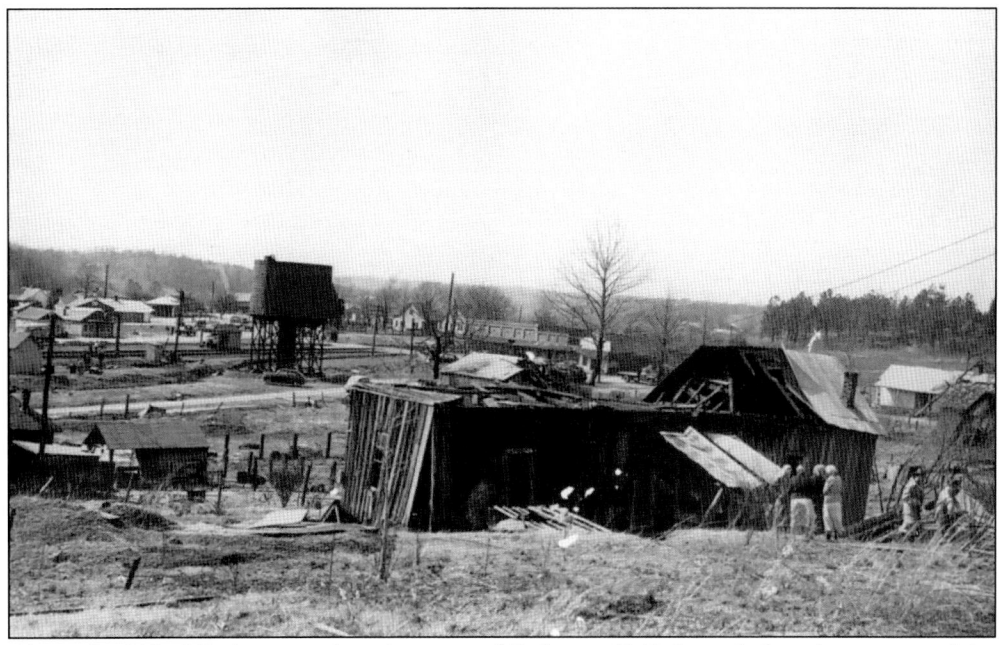

Alexander "Alex" Paden moved to the town of Paden in 1848. Long before the coming of the railroad, Paden built a handsome home, Castle Garden, named for his former estate in Scotland. He used waterpower to operate a cotton gin and make flour, cornmeal, and card wood. In March 1950, a tornado destroyed many homes, the church, and the Masonic building in downtown Paden.

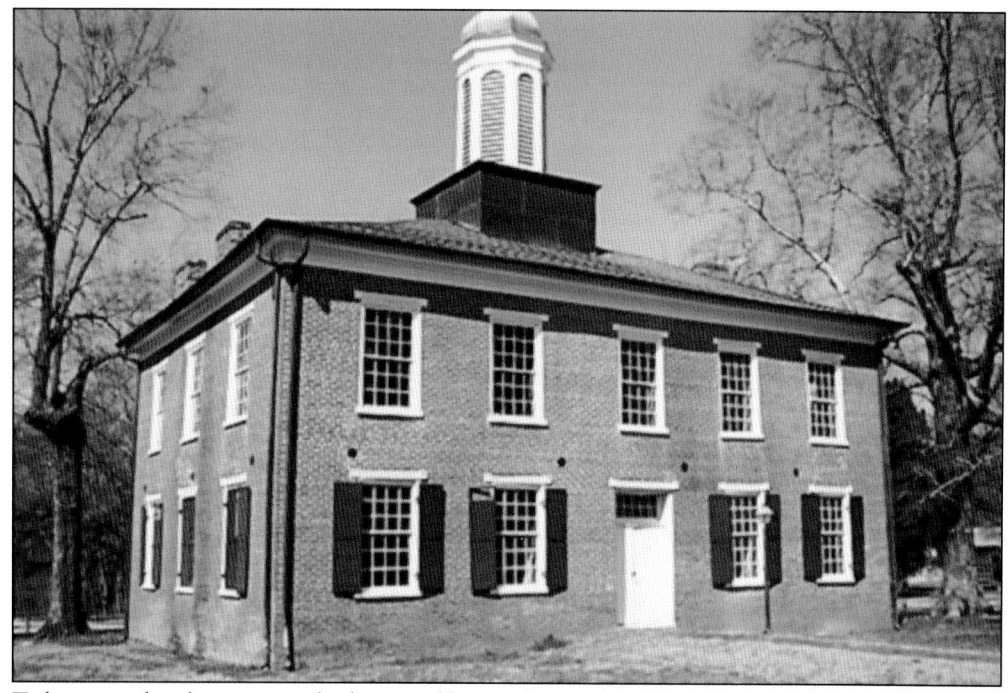

Tishomingo has been given the honor of being the mother county for the three counties that were formed from the original Tishomingo County. At the time of the division in 1870, all three counties built new courthouses. The old Tishomingo County Courthouse at Jacinto, pictured here, remained in the newly formed Alcorn County. It is now a museum.

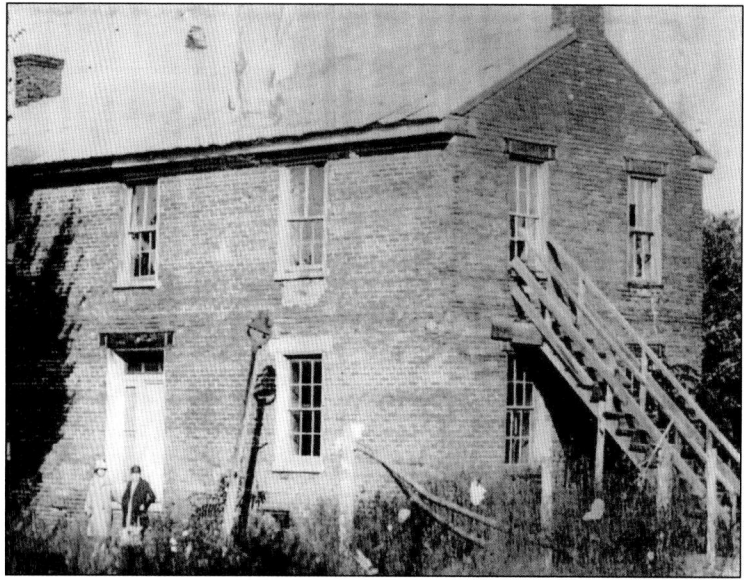

The Tishomingo County Jail, seen here, served at the time when all three counties (present-day Alcorn, Prentiss, and Tishomingo) were one. Based on the size of the building, it was justly built to accommodate the people of this huge county. As was the case with the courthouses, each newly formed county seat built its own jail after the counties were divided in 1870.

Four

CLUBS AND EVENTS

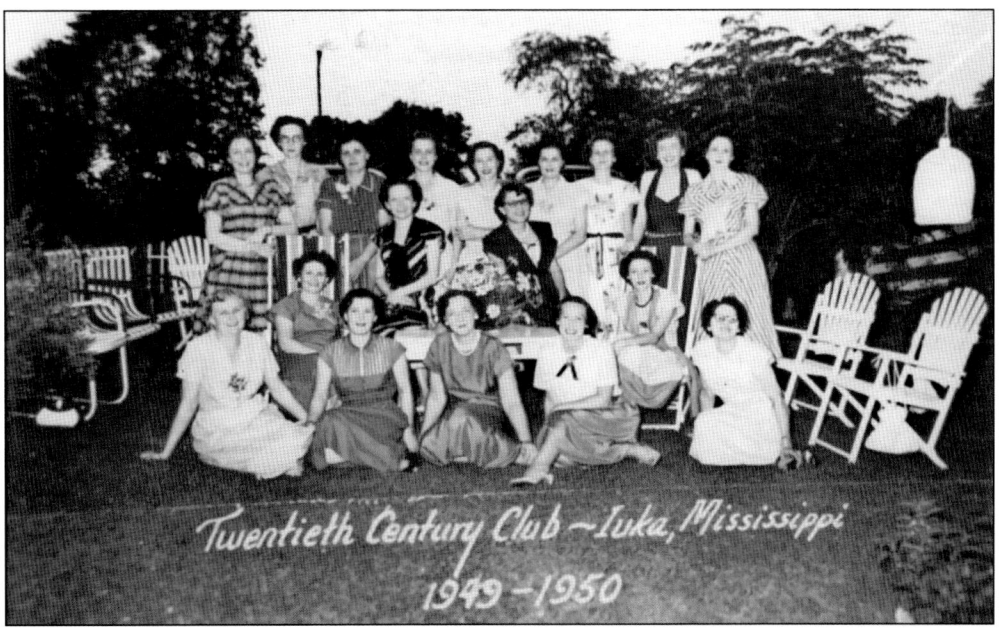

In 1950, members of Iuka's Twentieth Century Club won first place in the national "Build a Better Community" contest sponsored by the Kroger Company and the General Federation of Women's Clubs. A presentation of a $10,000 check was made to the club, which reportedly completed 52 projects in 1949. Club members pictured are, from left to right, (first row) Mrs. Kermit Rushing, Mrs. Austin Drake, Mrs. Nutt Yates, Mrs. Ed Thomas, and Mrs. W.R. "Bill" Jourdan; (second row) Mrs. Nolan "Rip" Pruitt, Mrs. H. F. "Chunky" Chambers, Mrs. Berry Lee Pruitt, and unidentified; (third row) Mrs. O.T. Gaines, Mrs. Neil Harwell, Mrs. Minor Rubel Nixon, Mrs. J.B. Storment Jr., three unidentified, Mrs. P.L. Sweeney, and Mrs. Avon Foote. Joy Robinson, Mrs. J.L. Dean, Mrs. Bryce Kitchens, and Mrs. T.B. Collum are also pictured, though their positions in the photograph are not made clear.

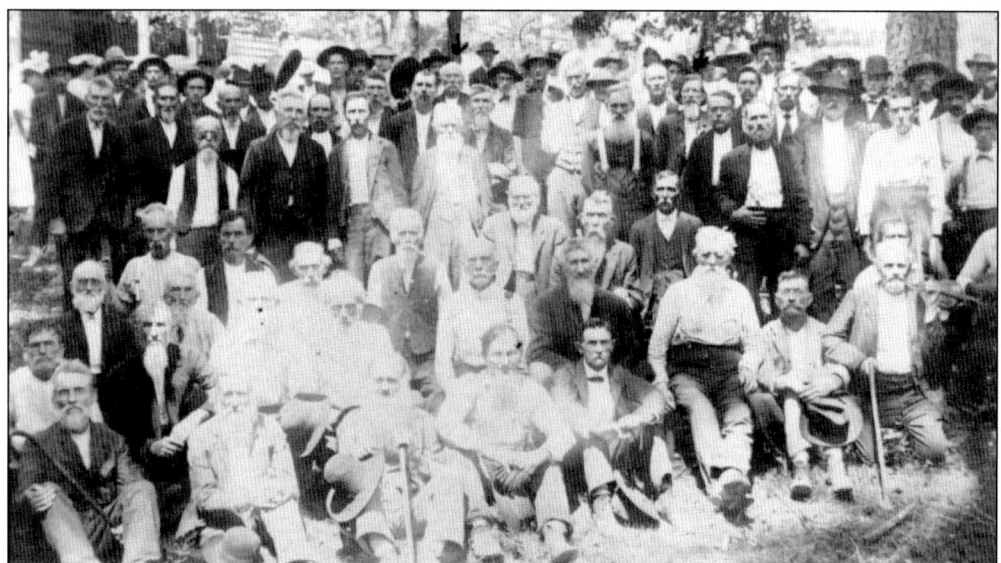

Below the waters of the Bay Springs Reservoir in Tishomingo County lay the remains of a once-prosperous, 19th-century cotton milling community. By the 1970s, only a Masonic lodge, an abandoned general store, and an abandoned bridge remained of the town. Then, in 1979, old Bay Springs became the focal point for the construction of the Bay Springs Lock and Dam. In this picture, lodge members are shown posing adjacent to the Masonic lodge located in the Bay Springs area.

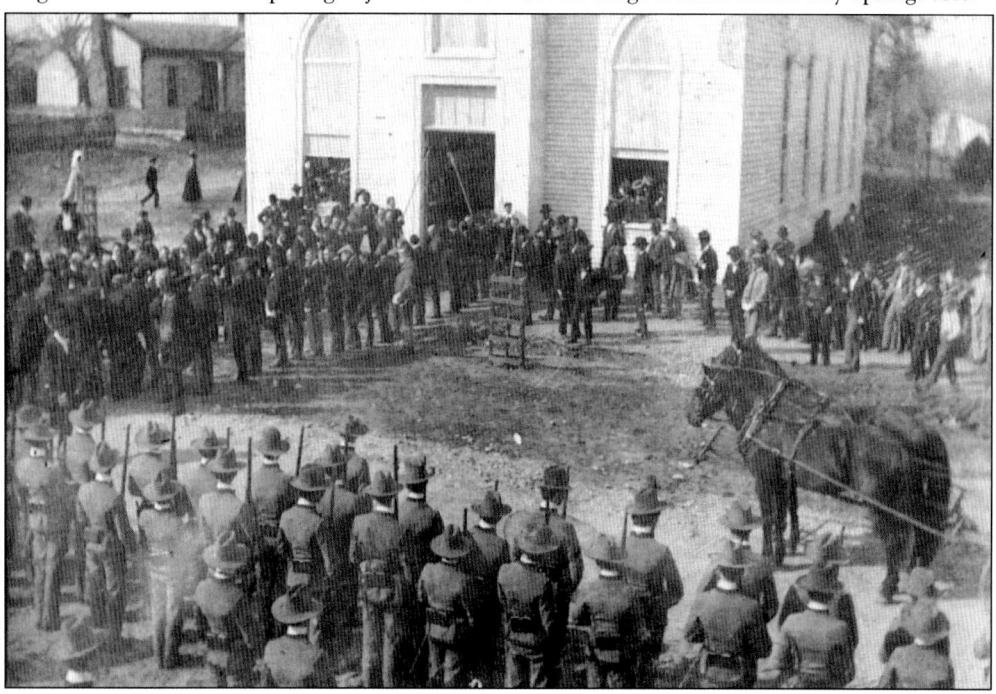

Mississippi governor John Marshall Stone died on March 26, 1900, and was buried in the Oak Grove Cemetery in Iuka. He moved here in 1855 and became a railroad station agent for the Memphis & Charleston Railroad. In 1861, he commanded Company K, 2nd Mississippi Infantry, in the Confederate army. After the war, he was mayor, treasurer, and state senator. Later, he became the longest-serving governor in the state of Mississippi.

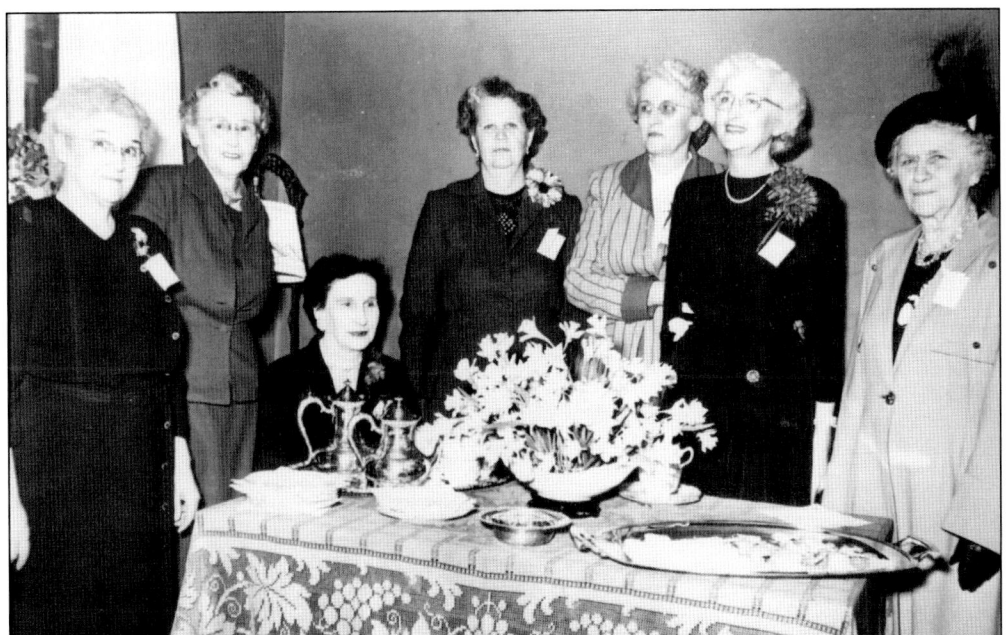

The Thursday Study Club was founded in Iuka by Lucy Rowe. Club members alternated their monthly meetings in various homes throughout the area. Women hosting a tea pictured here are, from left to right, (standing) Mrs. L.F. Carmichael, Mrs. John Allen, Leslie Moser, Beatrice Bostick, Mrs. J.O. Finch, and Lila McDonald. The woman sitting down is unidentified.

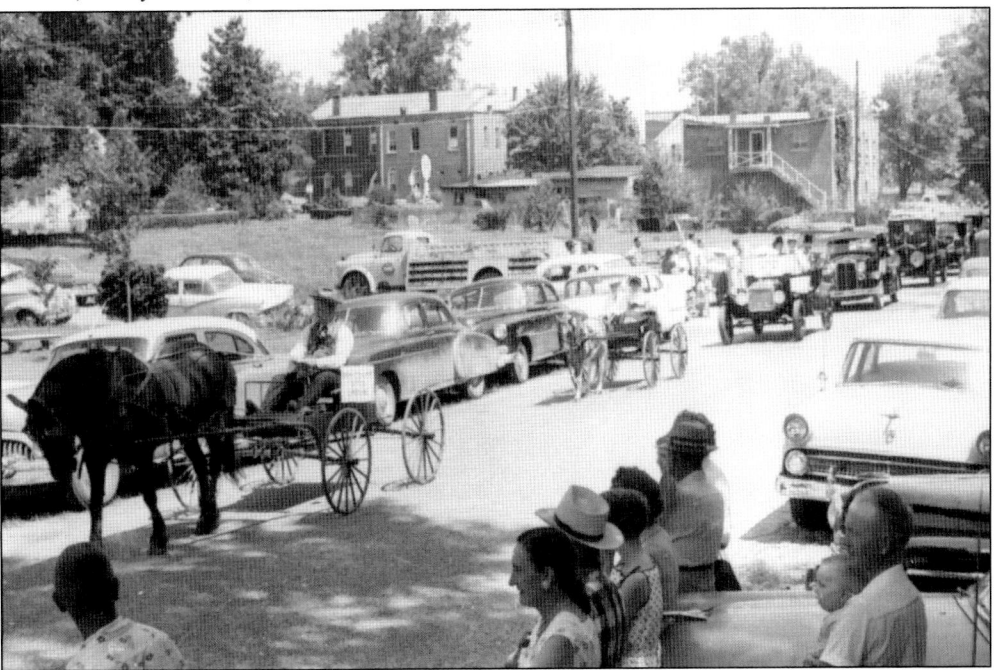

Iuka's centennial was celebrated in 1957 with festivities such as this parade. Onlookers admire the historical types of transportation, including the newer forms, as they watch a horse and buggy lead the parade. Now, in 2012, those new model vehicles that are parked on the sidelines are considered antique today.

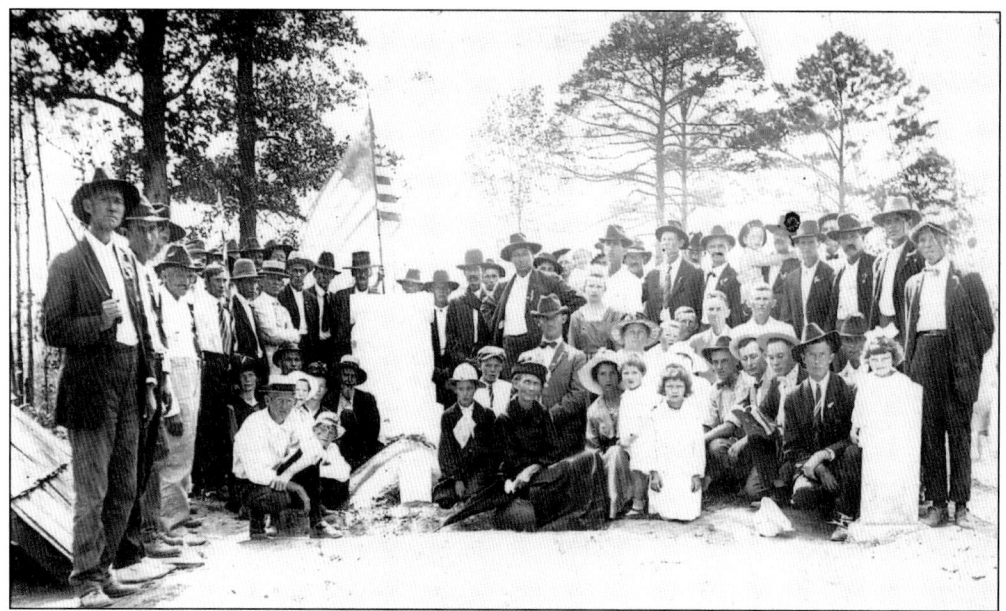

Pictured are Woodmen of the World (WOW) members and friends of James Robinson at the unveiling of the WOW monument. The monument was placed to honor the graves of WOW members buried in the Palestine Cemetery around 1917. Seen here are "Loving" Robinson, Mag Robinson, Lanning Robinson, Ross Robinson, Mr. and Mrs. Dave Beard with children and Grandma Beard, Alice Mayo, Pal Green, Lum Timbes, Rufus Slack, Pate Stephens, Irk Johnson, Maude Searcy, Alfred Lovelace, J.D. Whitaker, Clint Nixon, Homer Bellamy, Lela Timbes, Tom Clark, and Julius Clark. (Courtesy of Hazel Maniscalco.)

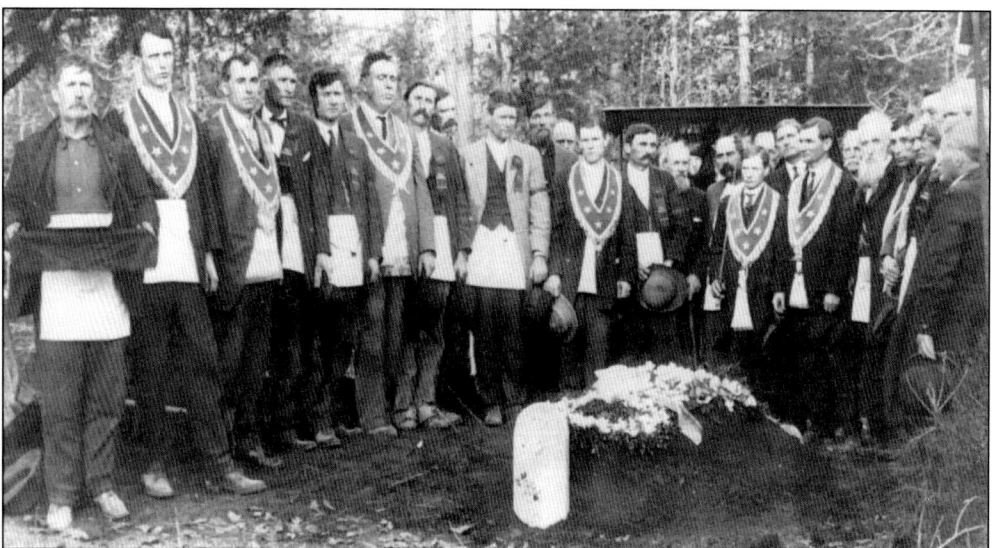

In this photograph are members of the Ada Lodge of Masons at Henry Phelps's funeral in 1918 at the Burnsville Cemetery, including (in no particular order) Dan Lambert, Austin D. Ford, T.L. Hill, Joe Brewer, Dr. Luther L. McDougal, Mr. Hampton, Woodard P. Burney, Ed Woodley, Wesley Marlar, Pink Honeycutt, Walter L. Marlar, O.P. Davis, A.T. Scruggs, Bud Barnes, Willie Norman, Mark Elledge, Ben Davis, two unidentified persons, Charlie Wren, John Henry Nixon, and three unidentified men.

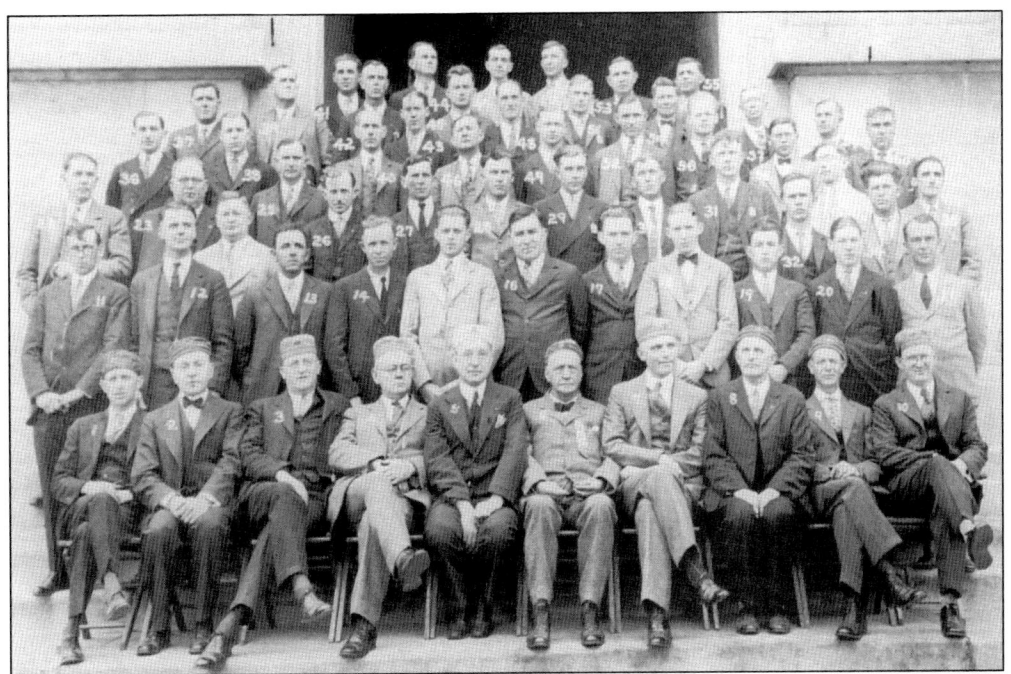

The Joseph W. Power Class, Ancient and Accepted Scottish Rite of Freemasonry, met at Corinth on April 15, 1926. Those pictured (in no particular order) are surnamed Worsham, Scharff, Cooper, Temple, Carter, Rubel, Grant, Holmes, Elledge, McCord, McAmis, Courson, Maxey, McDonald, Jones, Hall, Smith, Weaver, Davis, Gray, Russell, Hyland, Oldham, Page, Corruth, Curtis, Nanny, McKay, Allen, Draper, Tucker, Smith, Conwill, Calhoun, Bingham, Murff, Fry, Spear, Maxedon, Dorsey, Rankin, Nolen, Lester, Filgo, Gibbs, Young, Betts, McDonald, Gaisser, Brown, Bullen, Smith, Johnson, Fugitt, Chase, Pope, Reynolds, Rogers, Spear, Knight, and Cox.

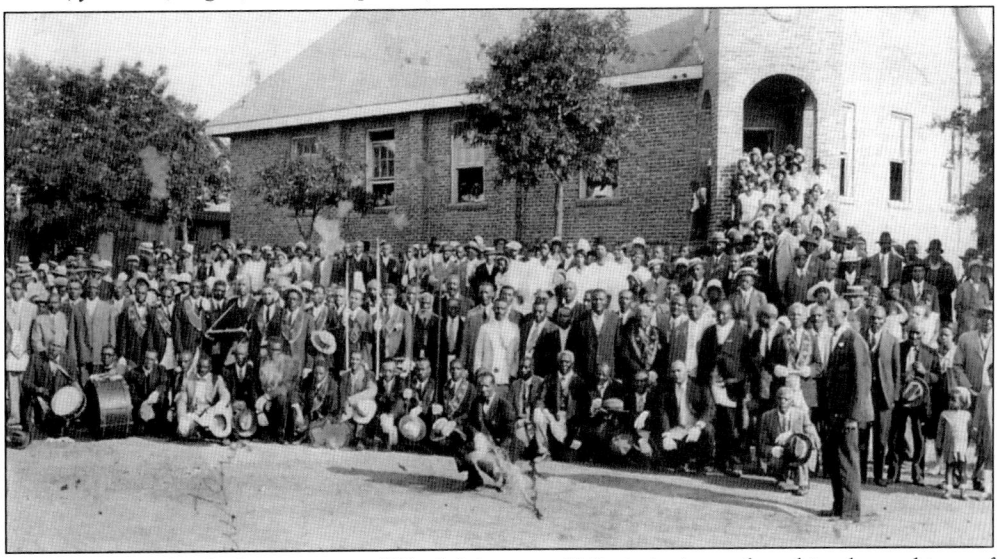

This photograph of a large group of Black Masons of Mississippi was found in the archives of the Tishomingo County Historical & Genealogical Society. The names do not appear with the document. It is believed that there are some Tishomingo Countians included in this photograph. Hopefully, in the future, the identity of these individuals will become known.

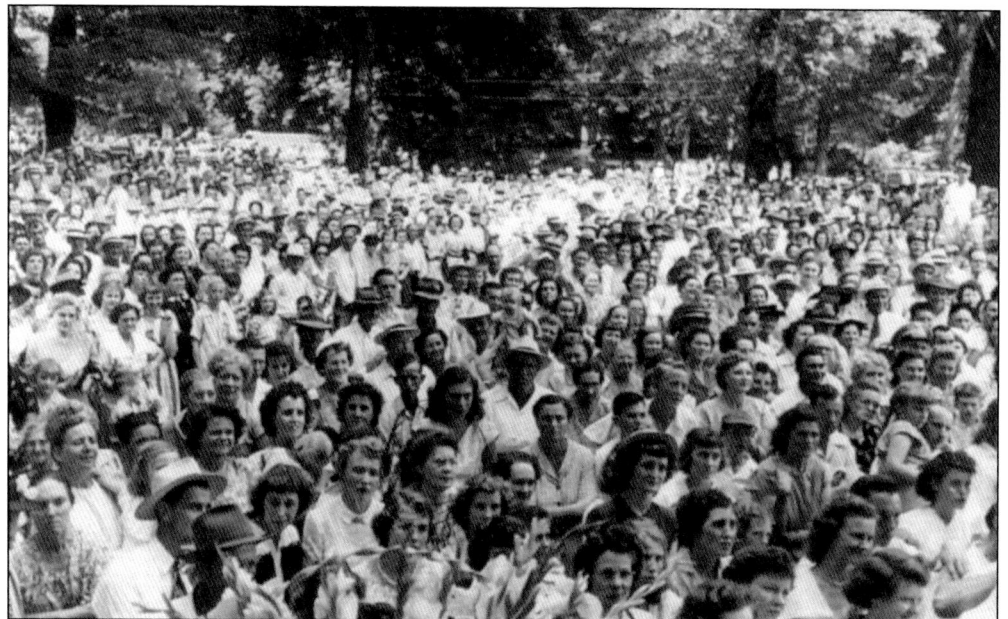

In 1950, the Twentieth Century Club in Iuka celebrated the "Best in the Nation" award for its efforts in cleaning up the town of Iuka and building better recreational facilities. News sources reported that as few as 8,000 and as many as 15,000 people jammed Iuka's Mineral Springs Park for the presentation of the award of $10,000 sponsored by Kroger Company and the General Federation of Women's Clubs. Many dignitaries made speeches complimenting the ladies and the spirit of civic endeavor portrayed by the club.

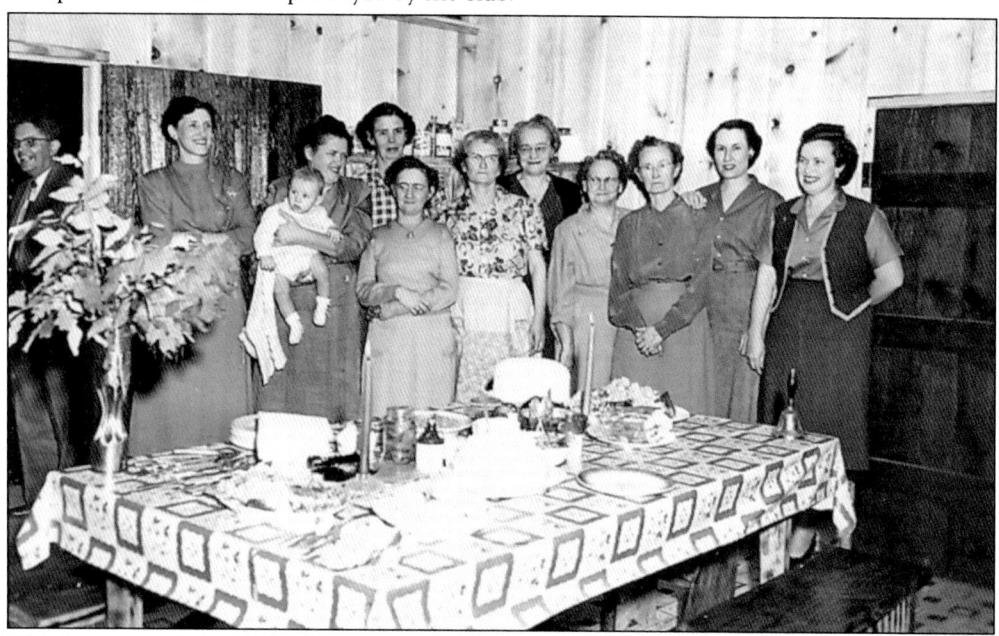

This is a group photograph of women in Tishomingo, Mississippi. Pictured from left to right are Wilma Wright, Mary Tennyson, Illa Trimm, Ruth Fairless, Mrs. Bingham, Lizzie Nettles, Mrs. Whitener, an unidentified woman, Clara Black, and Burma Day. It is not known if this is a church or club photograph. (Courtesy of Anne Taylor.)

Five
COUNTY GOVERNMENT

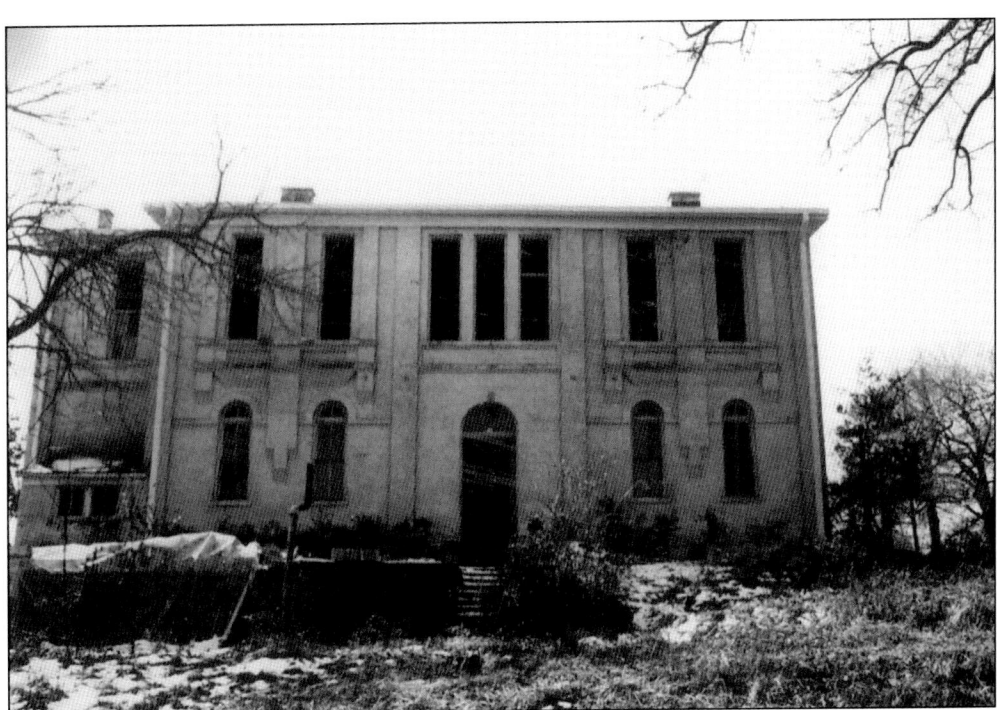

After Tishomingo County was divided into the separate counties of Alcorn, Prentiss, and Tishomingo in 1870, the county seat was moved from Jacinto to Iuka. This is the original Tishomingo County courthouse built in Iuka in 1870. A courthouse fire in 1886 destroyed the third floor, which was not restored as part of the renovation.

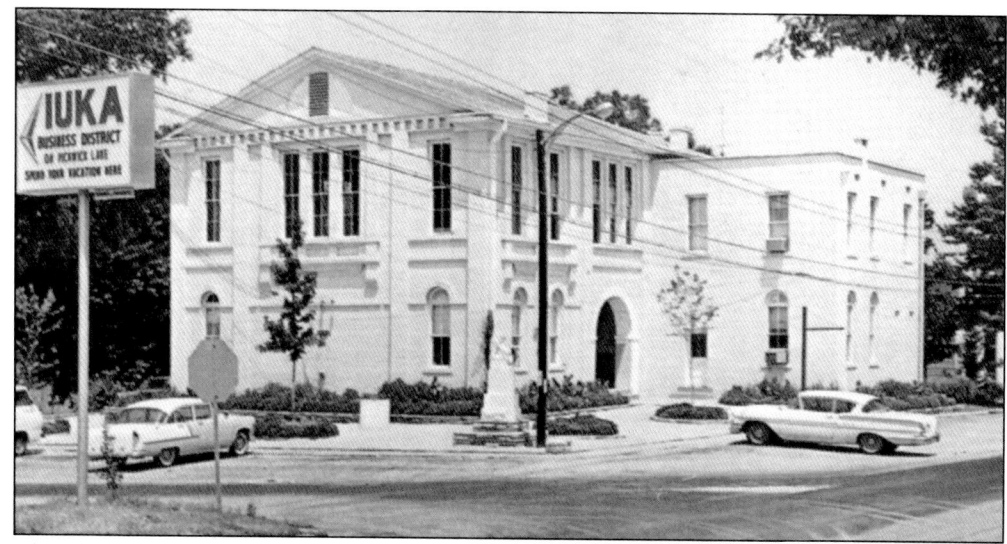
This photograph depicts the newly restored Tishomingo County courthouse, located at 203 East Quitman Street in Iuka, Mississippi. The Tishomingo County Historical & Genealogical Society assumed responsibility for the operation of the historic Tishomingo County courthouse in October 2003. The structure now houses the Tishomingo County Archives & History Museum.

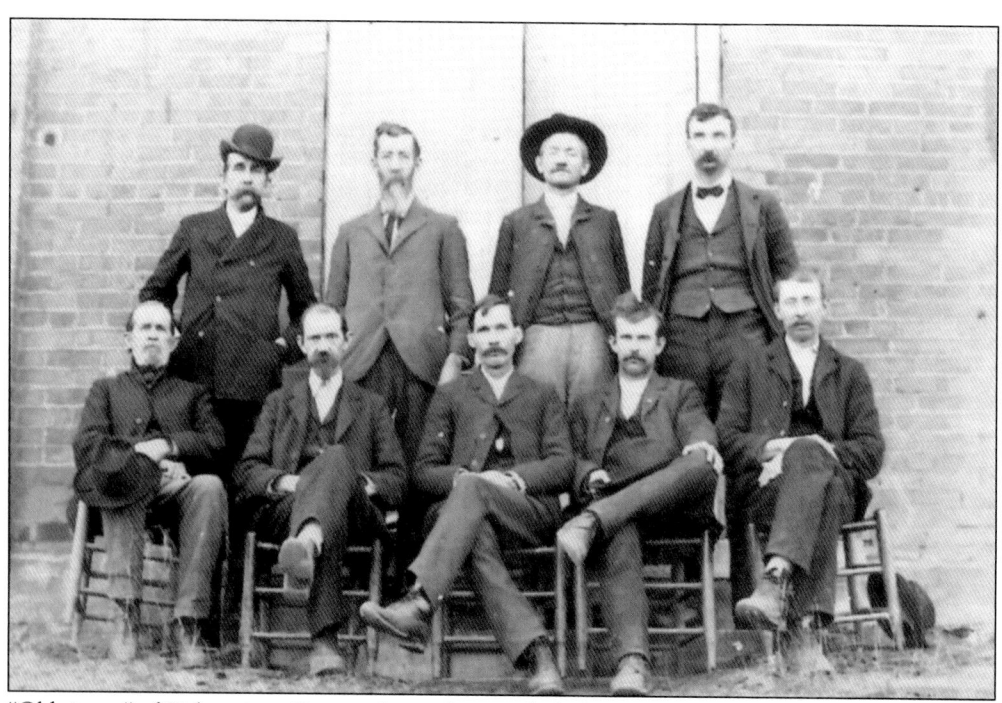
"Old timers" of Tishomingo County shown here include (in no particular order) Bill Nunley, Peter Hubbard, R. Eckols, Mr. Heruige, and Billie Davis. (Courtesy of C.B. Reid.)

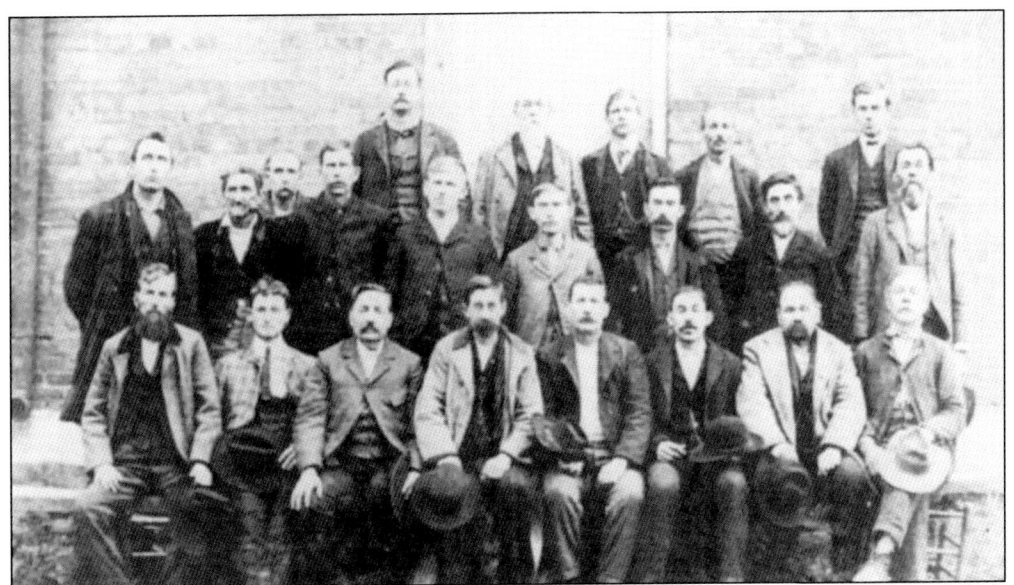

Pictured here are members of two juries convened in Tishomingo County. Jury No. 1, in the center, included C.C. Edmondson, W.C. Bishop, W.A. Broughton Sr., L.D. Hubbard, V.W. Smith, B.L. Hicks, D.L. Glover, J.S. Orrick, J.W. Martin, A.B. Burns, and Ward Paden. Jury No. 2 consisted of Jim Broughton, James Grober, G.A. Clark, W.A. Broughton Jr., G.M. Perry, Joe Dean, Dan Lambert, Billy Dean, Carroll Johnson, Ed Rast, W.A. Sartain, and J.A. Miller.

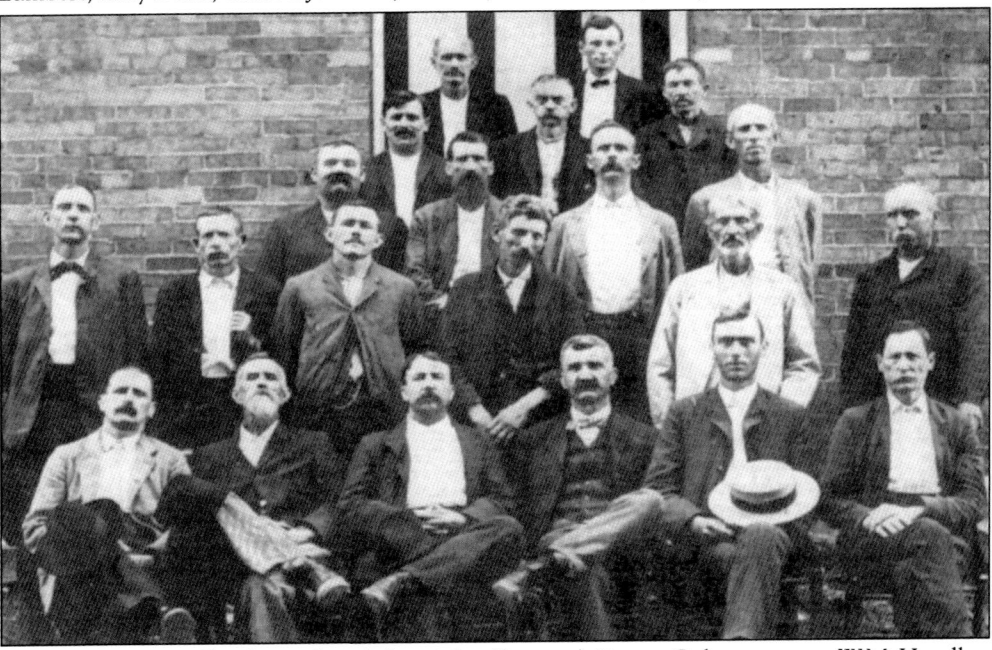

These early 1900s officials are, from left to right, (first row) George Gober, treasurer W.M. Hundley, Sheriff Jim D. Fairless, Rev. Marcus Tumlin, Jesse Jackson, and Mr. Patterson; (second row) county surveyor Byrd Payne; unidentified; first district supervisor John Smith, cotton weigher Finch Scruggs, and two unidentified persons; (third row) Dee Dawson, Bob Lee Marlar, unidentified, and John Robinson; (fourth row) Tom Sprouse and two unidentified persons; (fifth row) Marsh Johnson and unidentified.

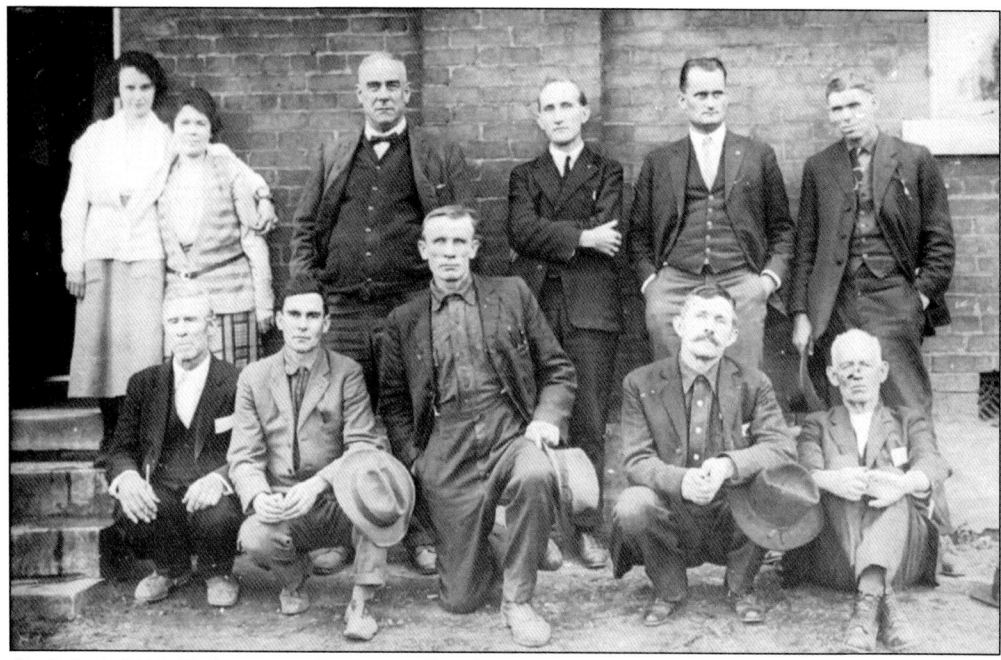

On July 6, 1923, Tishomingo County's officials posed for a photograph. Shown from left to right are (first row) supervisor Russ Arveno, supervisor John Smith, supervisor Dave Pannell, supervisor John Floyd, and supervisor J. H. Mann; (second row) assistant circuit clerk Ollie Adams, chancery clerk Willie Hiett, Sheriff N. L. Phillips, county superintendent of education Joe Epps, county attorney Ernest Ligon, and circuit clerk Paulie Adams. (Courtesy of C.B. Reid.)

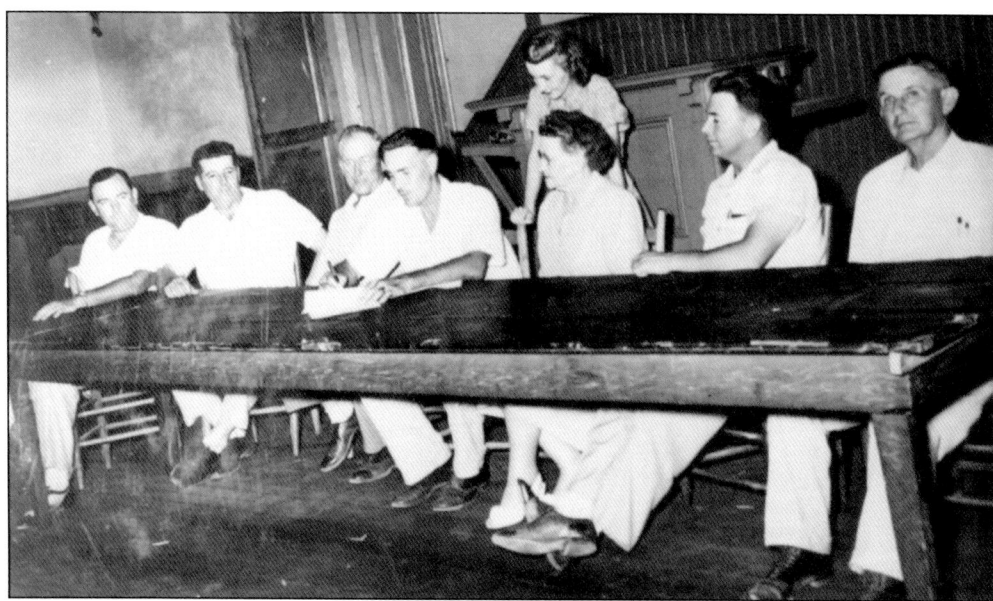

On September 25, 1952, the Tishomingo County Board of Supervisors renewed the contract for the Iuka Public Library at the old county courthouse on Quitman Street. Pictured from left to right are attorney J. Orville "Click" Clark, Herbert Biggs, Lunsford Storment, O.L. Wade, Mattie Fay Allen, unidentified, Russell Bonds, and Bill Gardner.

Six

HISTORIC HOMES AND BUILDINGS

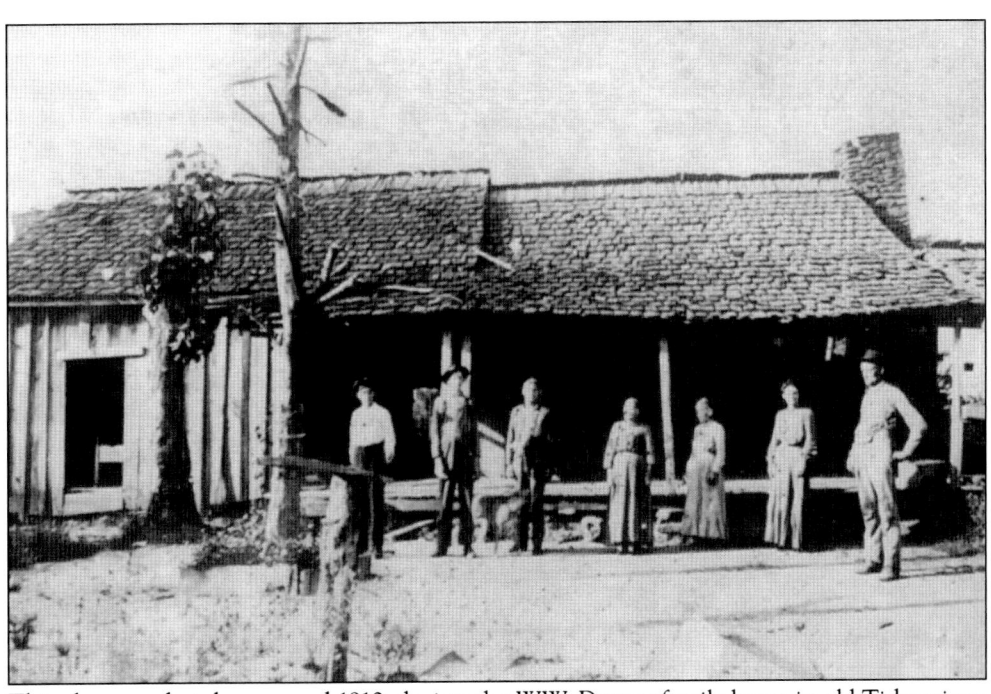

This photograph, taken around 1910, depicts the W.W. Dancer family home in old Tishomingo County. During the late 1870s, the family boarded people traveling through the area and allowed them to stay in their home. On one occasion, the Corinth Bank was robbed following a night's stay of four men believed to be Jesse James's gang.

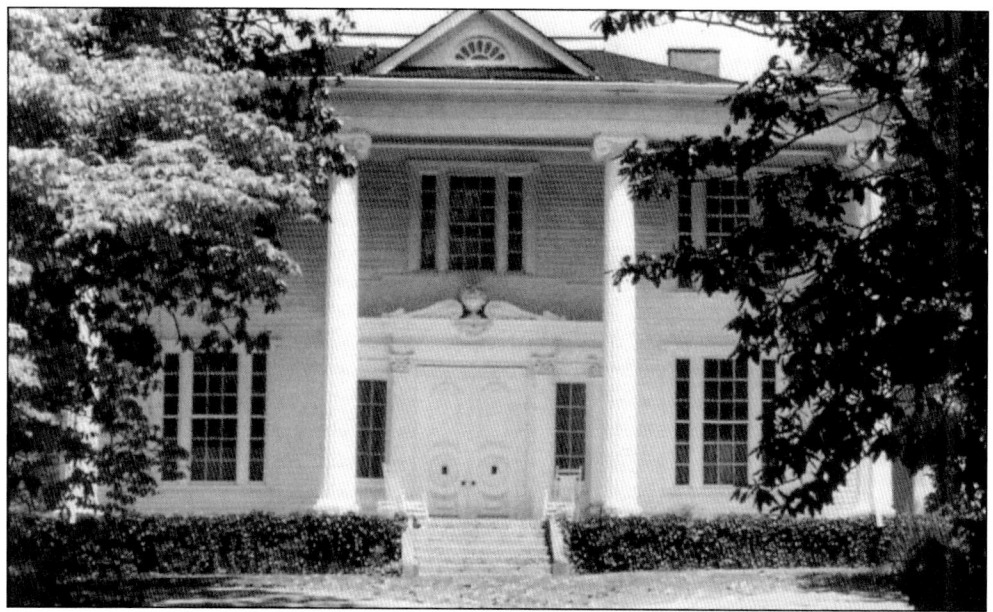

This beautiful home began as a Greek Revival summerhouse and was overlaid with Rococo Revival details from a mansion in Memphis, Tennessee, owned by R.C. Brinkley. It served as headquarters during the Civil War for Gen. Ulysses S. Grant and Gen. W.S. Rosecrans. During the epidemic of yellow fever in Memphis in 1878 an 1879, the Brinkley house opened its doors to the stricken world.

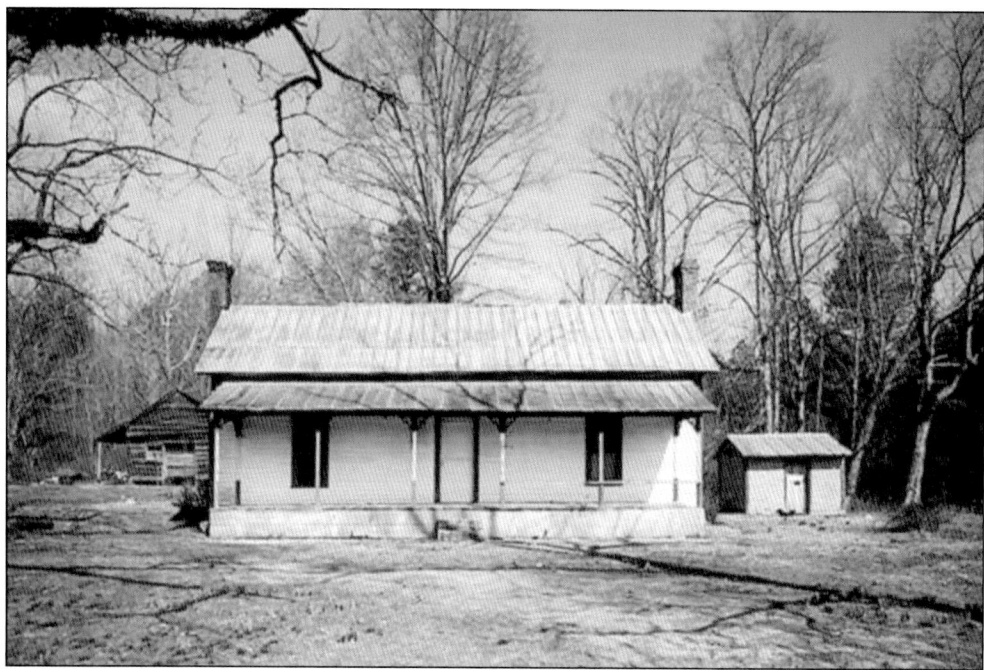

The James Butler House in Tishomingo, built in 1913, is an example of the persistence of 19th-century types of plans and stylistic details in the southwestern part of Tishomingo County. The dwelling was the home of James T. Butler, born in 1855; he was Tishomingo County's oldest citizen at the time of his death in 1957.

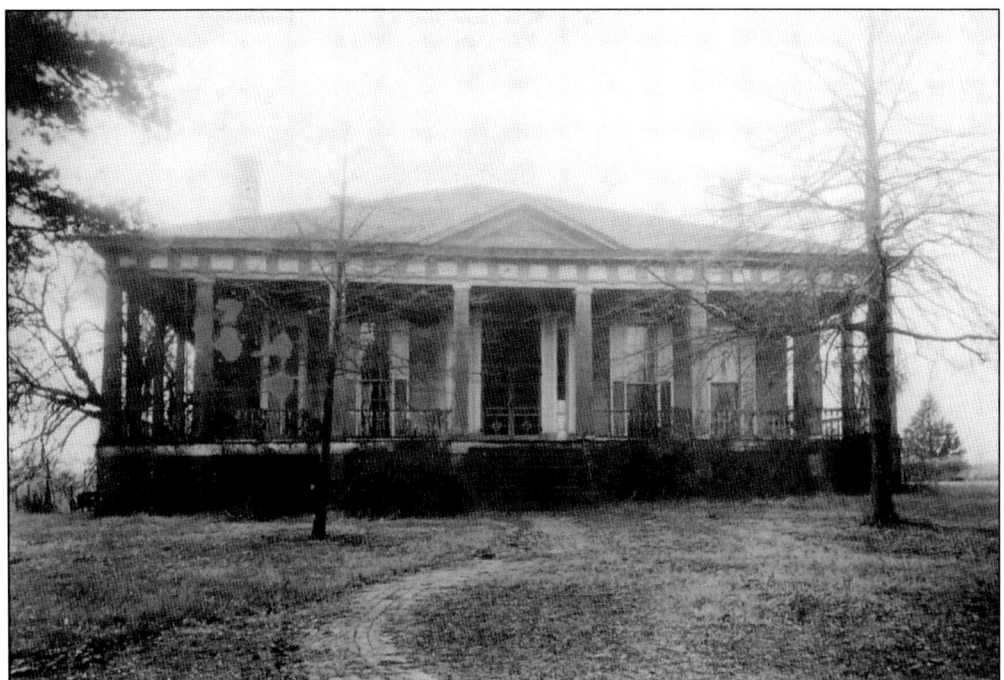

The Tom McDonald home, built before the Civil War, was located where the Iuka Middle School gymnasium is now located. It was torn down in 1962 in order to make way for the construction of the school gym. The McDonald home was the headquarters of Confederate general Sterling Price during the Battle of Eastport. Later, it became the headquarters of Union general William S. Rosecrans.

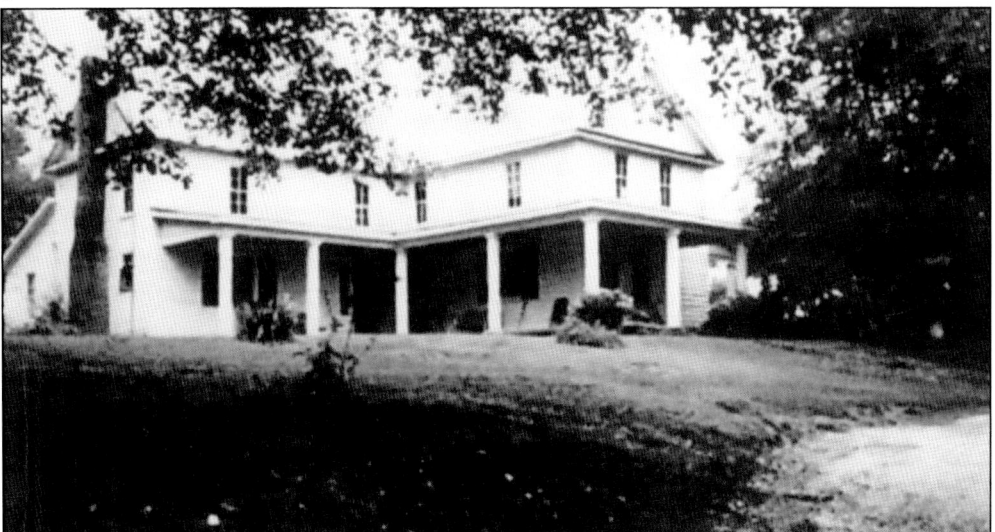

Bryant and Susan (Stokes) Adams left North Carolina and settled in Tishomingo County in 1848. He built a two-room home of logs with a large chimney and fireplace. Additions over the years have given the home three stairwells, four bedrooms, and three porches. Located on Pleasant Hill Road, it is the oldest homestead still standing and has been lived in continuously by various members of the Adams family. Three generations of Adams family descendants visit the home yearly.

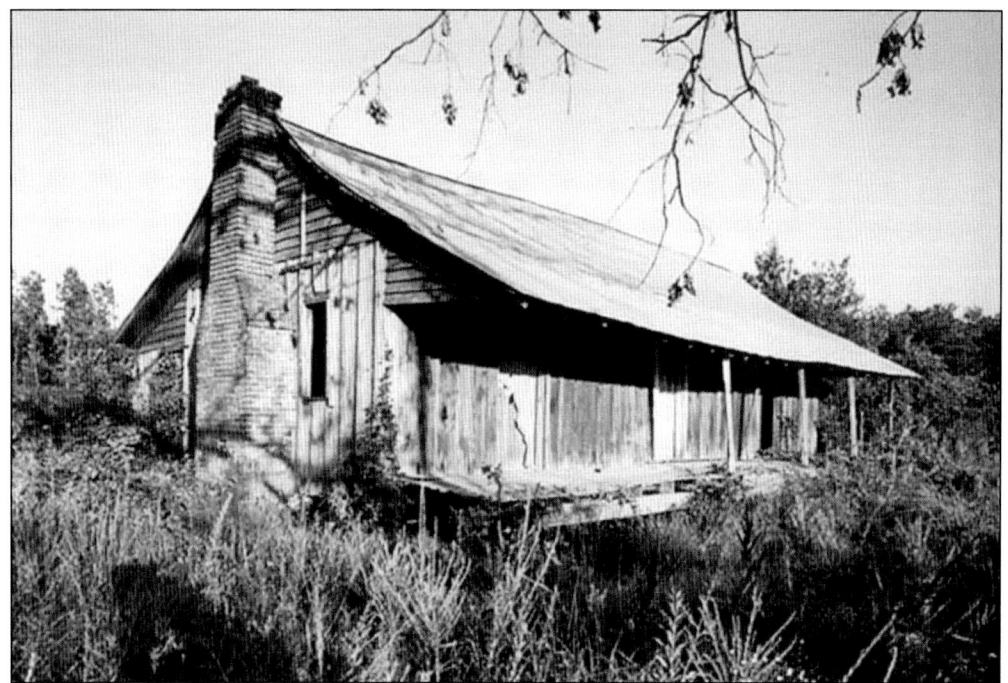

This home, built in the 1890s near the Old Natchez Trace, was a two-room house with an open central passage. The house was the home of the Billie Eaton family. Mr. Eaton taught at the Billingsley School until his death in 1907.

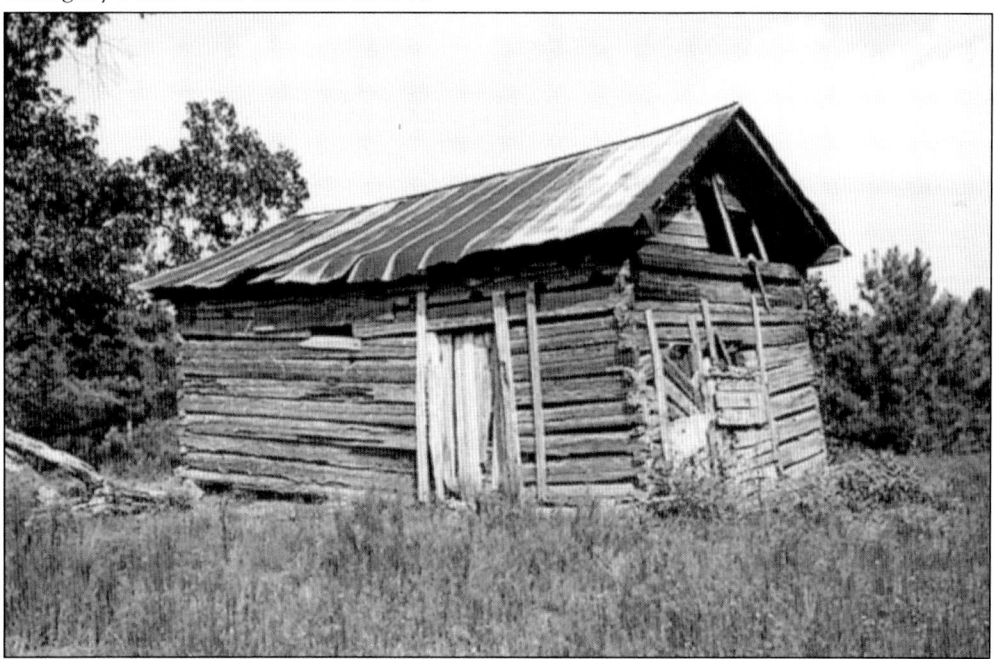

The A.L. Riddle House may have originally been used as a schoolhouse after the Civil War. This log structure was moved to its present site in 1919. In a warranty deed dated September 6, 1919, A.L. Riddle received the property on which the structure is located from his father, W.C. Riddle, for the sum of $500.

Seven
MILITARY

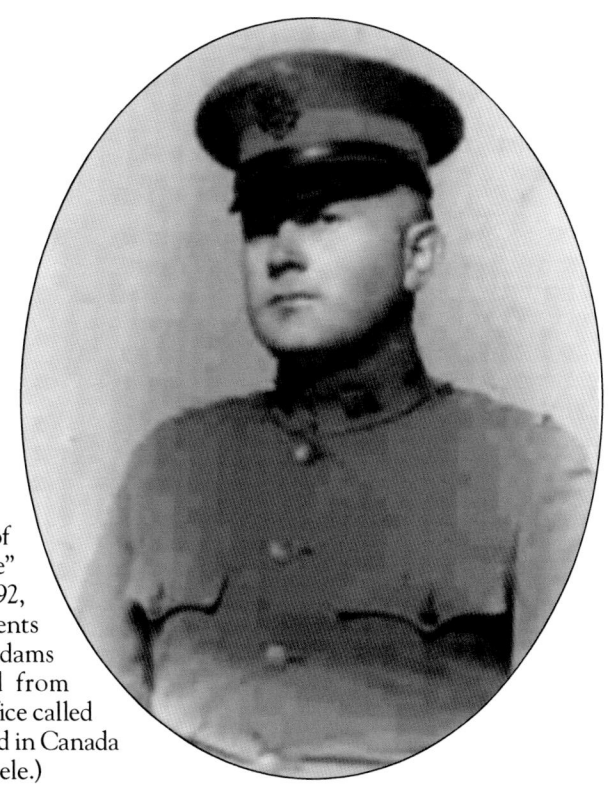

Lee Alfred "Webster" Adams, son of David Andrew and Dorothy Ida "Dollie" (Welch) Adams, was born on July 9, 1892, in Tishomingo County. His grandparents John Quincy and Candis (Brooks) Adams purchased land west of the road from Tishomingo to Belmont near a post office called Hill Side. Webster, as he was called, died in Canada in 1939. (Courtesy of Mary Lou Mergele.)

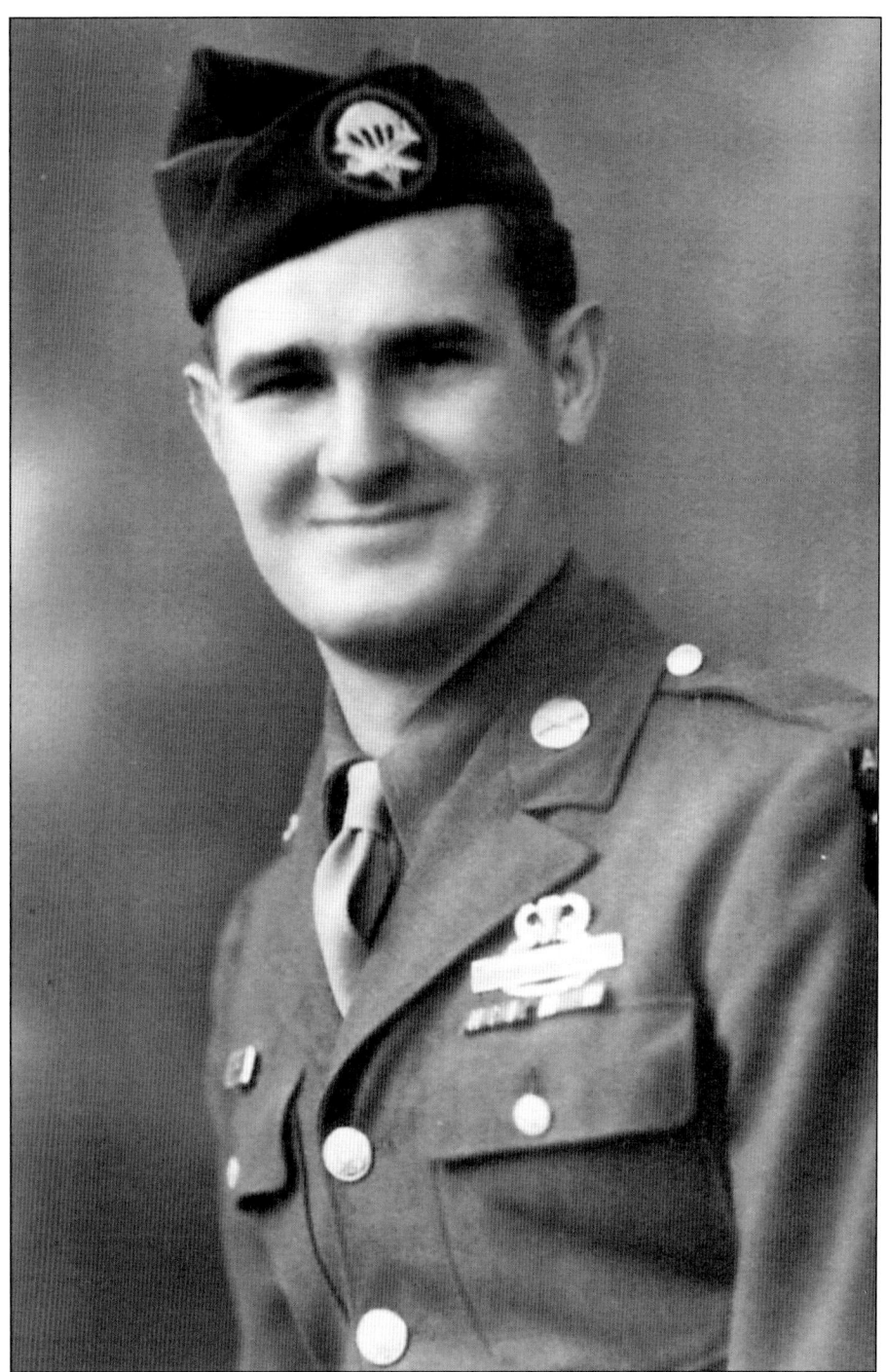
Oliver Wendell Anglin, son of Robert Huey and Eva (Epps) Anglin, was born on August 3, 1919, in Tishomingo, Mississippi. Drafted into the US Army, Oliver entered the military at Camp Shelby, Mississippi, and took basic training at Fort Benning, Georgia. He was shipped to Europe with other soldiers in the airborne unit and participated in the Battle of the Bulge and the Battle of Bastone in Belgium. (Courtesy of Virginia Anglin.)

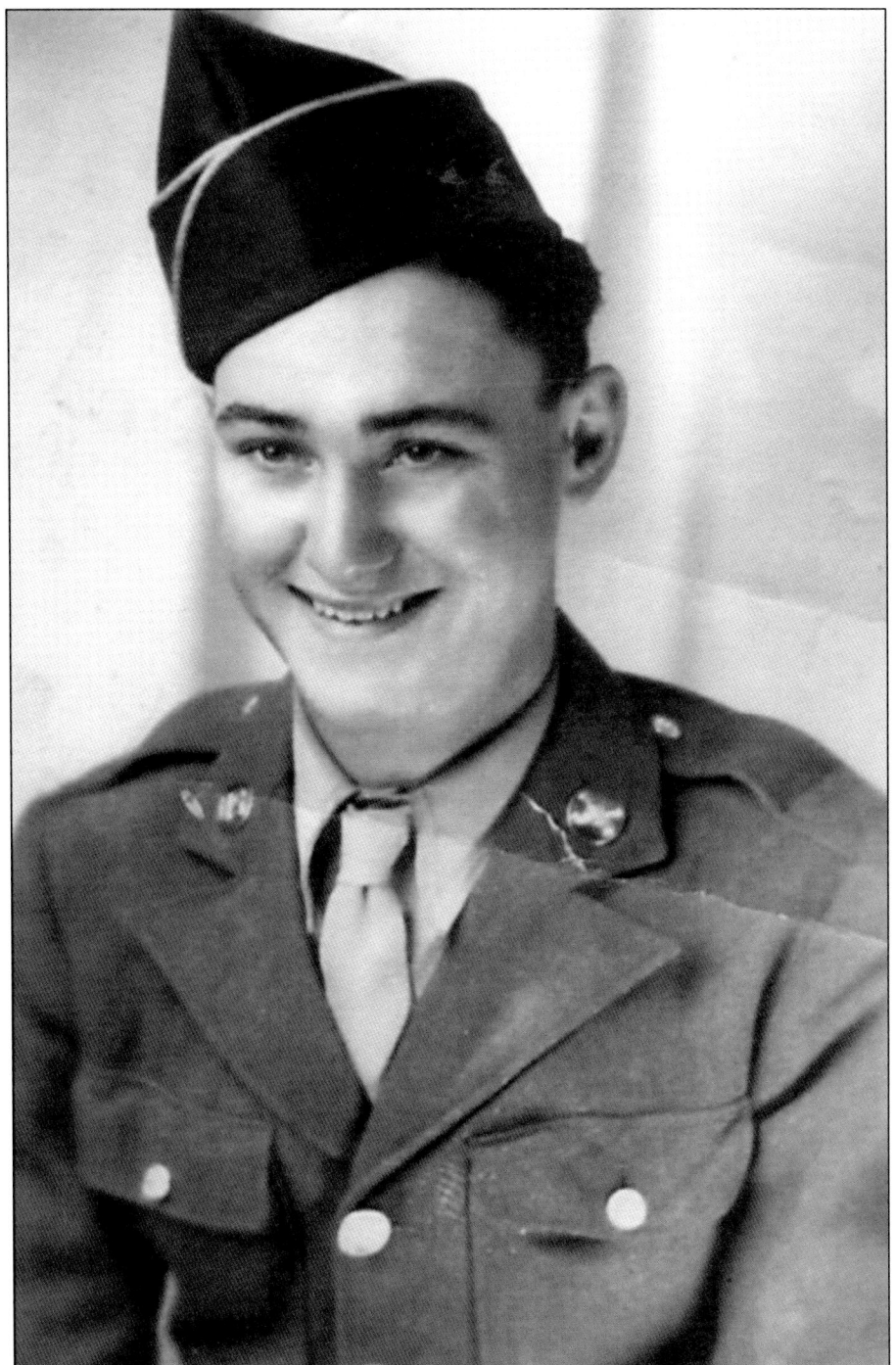

Pfc. Wayburn Forrest Anglin, son of Robert Huey and Evie (Epps) Anglin, served in the US Army during World War II. Born January 22, 1925, he was killed in action on October 26, 1944, and is buried in the Henri-Chapelle American Cemetery in Hornburg, Belgium. A memorial stone was placed in his honor in the Lindsey Cemetery where his parents are also buried. (Courtesy of Jennifer Anglin Phifer.)

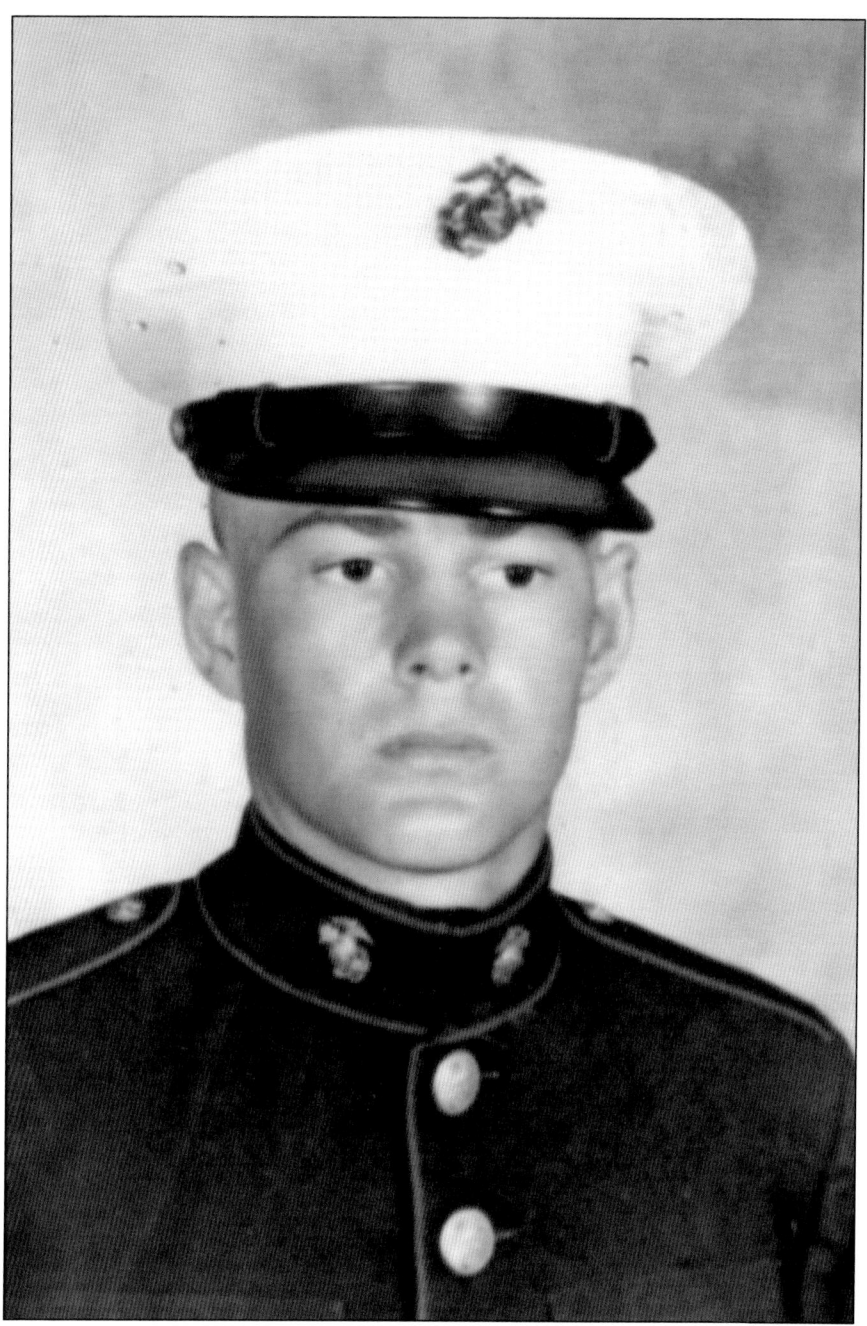

Larry Wayne Daniel, son of Felix Edward "Ed" Daniel and Littie Mae (Borden) Daniel, was born on April 30, 1955, in Tishomingo County, Mississippi. He attended Tishomingo High School. At age 18, he voluntarily joined the US Marines and served proudly in the Vietnam War. Following the war, he married and had two children. On March 9, 1988, he died in Prentiss County, Mississippi, as a result of a motorcycle accident. He is buried at Snowdown United Methodist.

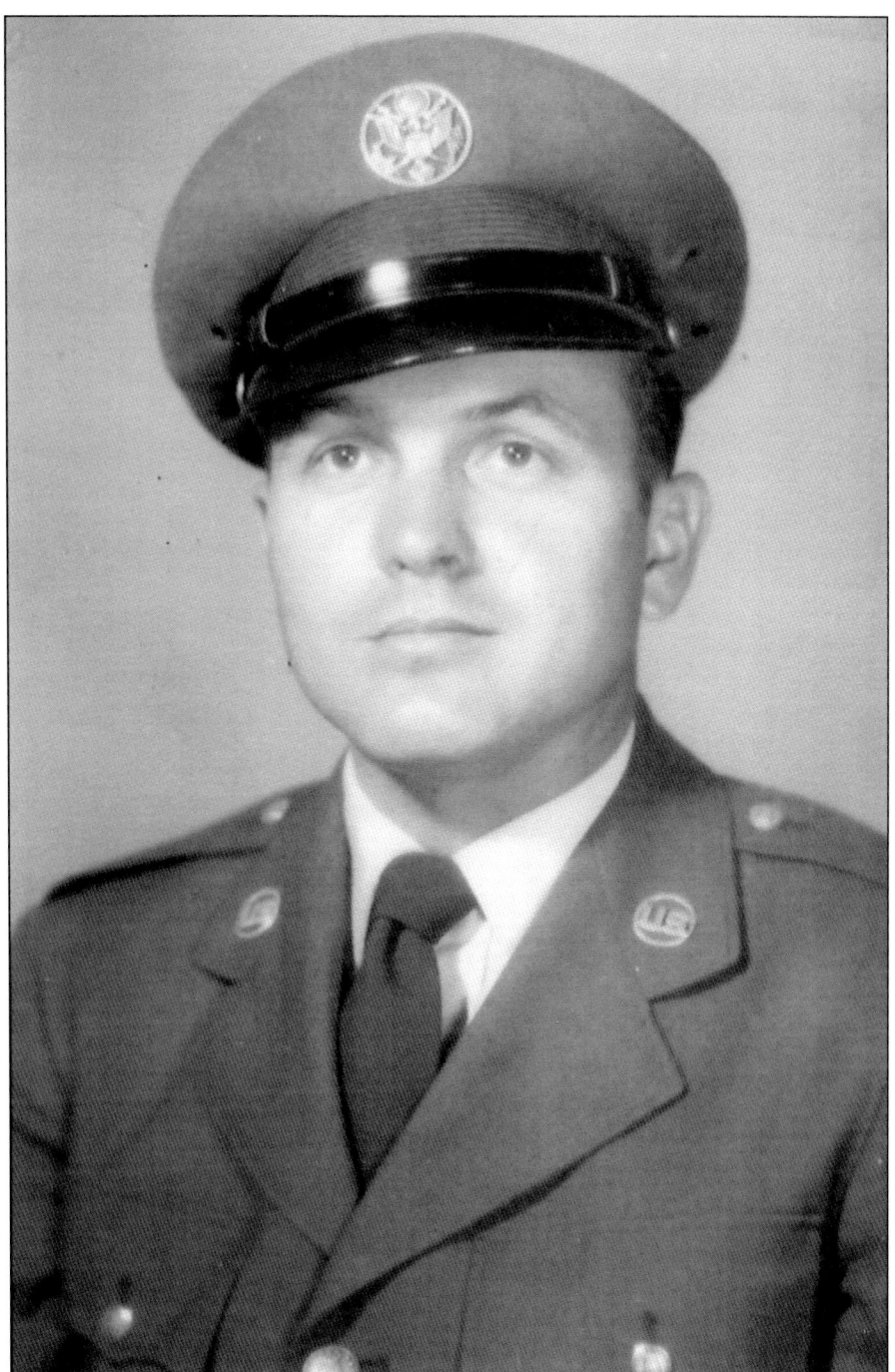

Charles Byram, son of Charles Samuel and Mable (Wetzel) Byram, was born in Dennis. He entered the US Navy during World War II and was stationed at President's Island, where the construction of the destroyer USS *Lowry* (DD 770) was completed. Charles left the Navy but soon joined the US Air Force. He trained as a jet mechanic on the B-47 and was stationed at Walker Air Force Base, where he spent the rest of his military service in the Strategic Air Command. (Courtesy of Charles Byram.)

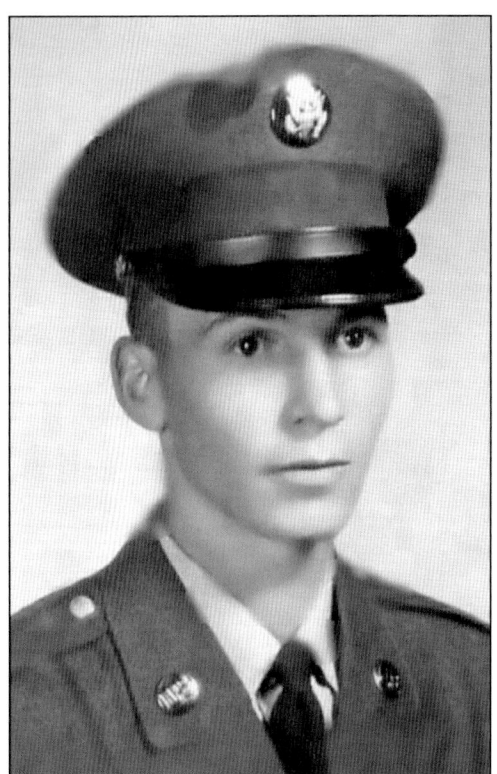

Steve E. Bostick, son of Leland Adel and Martha (Daniel) Bostick, was born in Tishomingo County. He graduated from Burnsville High School. At 18, he voluntarily joined the US Army and served in Korea. After retiring from the US Corps of Engineers, he returned to his home in the South Crossroads community. Steve and his wife, Martha, had two children. (Courtesy of Wanda Bostick Little.)

Weldon M. Hanks, son of Virgil and Cora Hanks, was born in 1923. He trained as a pilot on the B-24 Liberators at Westover Field, Massachusetts. During World War II, Weldon served in the 788th Bomb Squadron, 467th Bombardment Group. He was killed in the line of duty on December 25, 1944, in Belgium and is buried in the Henri-Chapelle American Cemetery in Hornburg, Belgium.

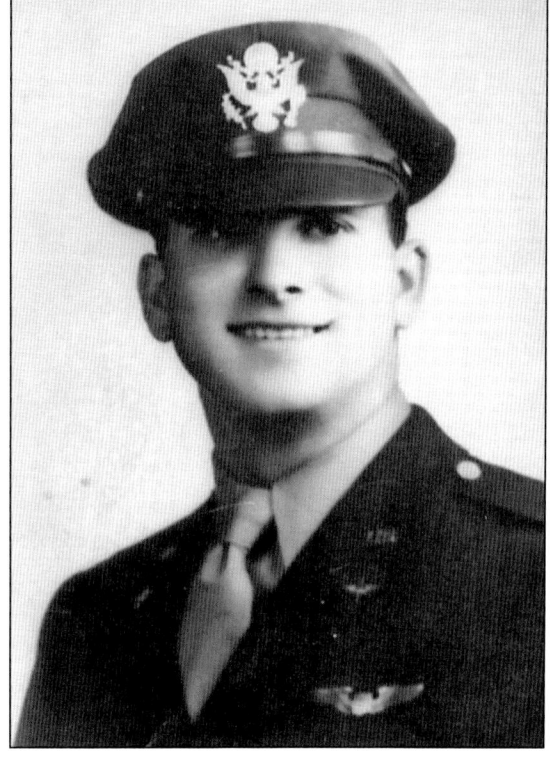

Hassell Tulon Holder, son of Fred Owen and Ola (Jourdan) Holder, was born in Paden. In the US Army, he was assigned to the 1259th Combat Engineers Battalion in January 1945. Hassell and his fellow soldiers were sent to Camp Shanks, New York, and boarded a ship headed to Europe on April 18, 1945. (Courtesy of Hassell T. Holder.)

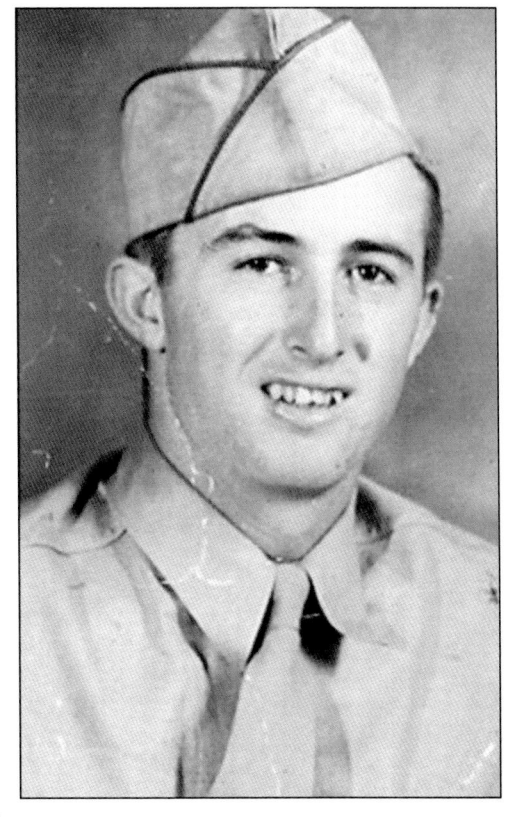

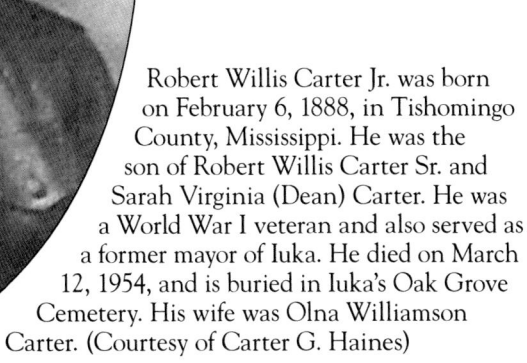

Robert Willis Carter Jr. was born on February 6, 1888, in Tishomingo County, Mississippi. He was the son of Robert Willis Carter Sr. and Sarah Virginia (Dean) Carter. He was a World War I veteran and also served as a former mayor of Iuka. He died on March 12, 1954, and is buried in Iuka's Oak Grove Cemetery. His wife was Olna Williamson Carter. (Courtesy of Carter G. Haines)

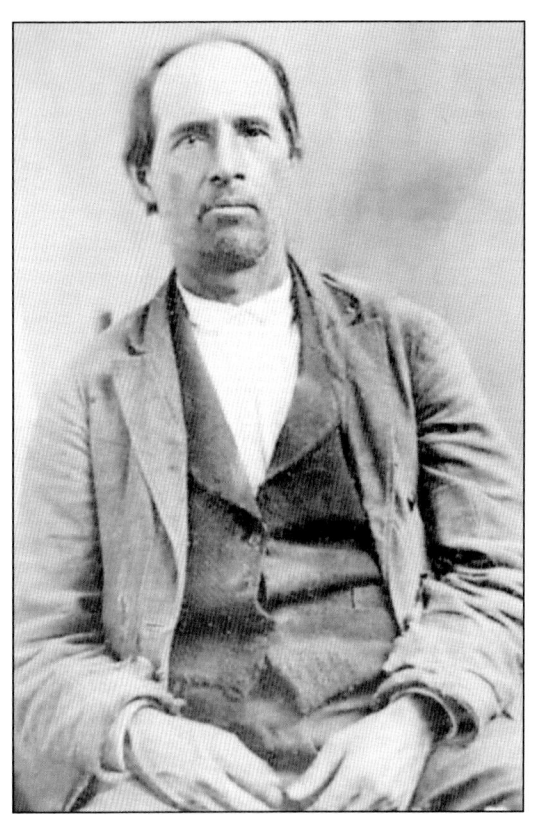

John Bailey Daniel, son of Obediah and Sally (Smith) Daniel, was born in Tennessee on November 30, 1831, and died on June 9, 1908. He lived in Tishomingo County during his adult years. He served in the 9th Tennessee Infantry, CSA, during the Civil War. His clothing in this photograph is reportedly prisoner-of-war attire. (Courtesy of Wanda Bostick Little.)

Preston Nyal Malone, son of Curgus Earnie and Dora Lucille (James) Malone, was born in Belmont on January 27, 1929. He was drafted into the US Army and participated in combat infantry training at Camp Chaffee, Arkansas, and heavy field artillery training at Fort Sill, Oklahoma. He was then assigned to the Army's 2nd Infantry Division and sent to Korea. (Courtesy of Preston Malone.)

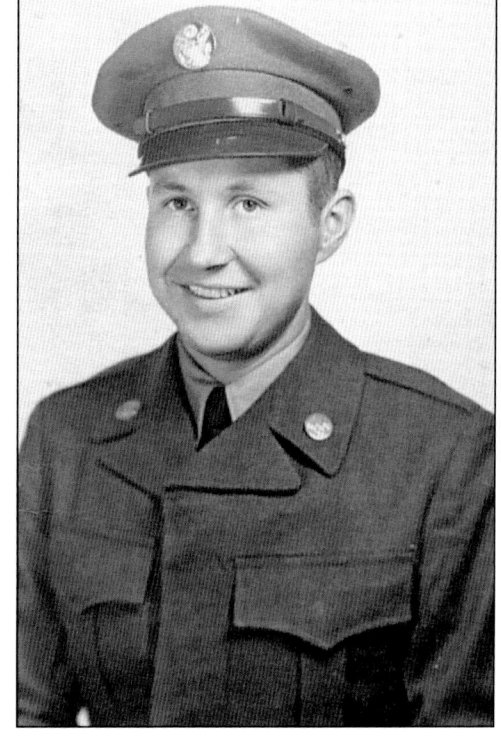

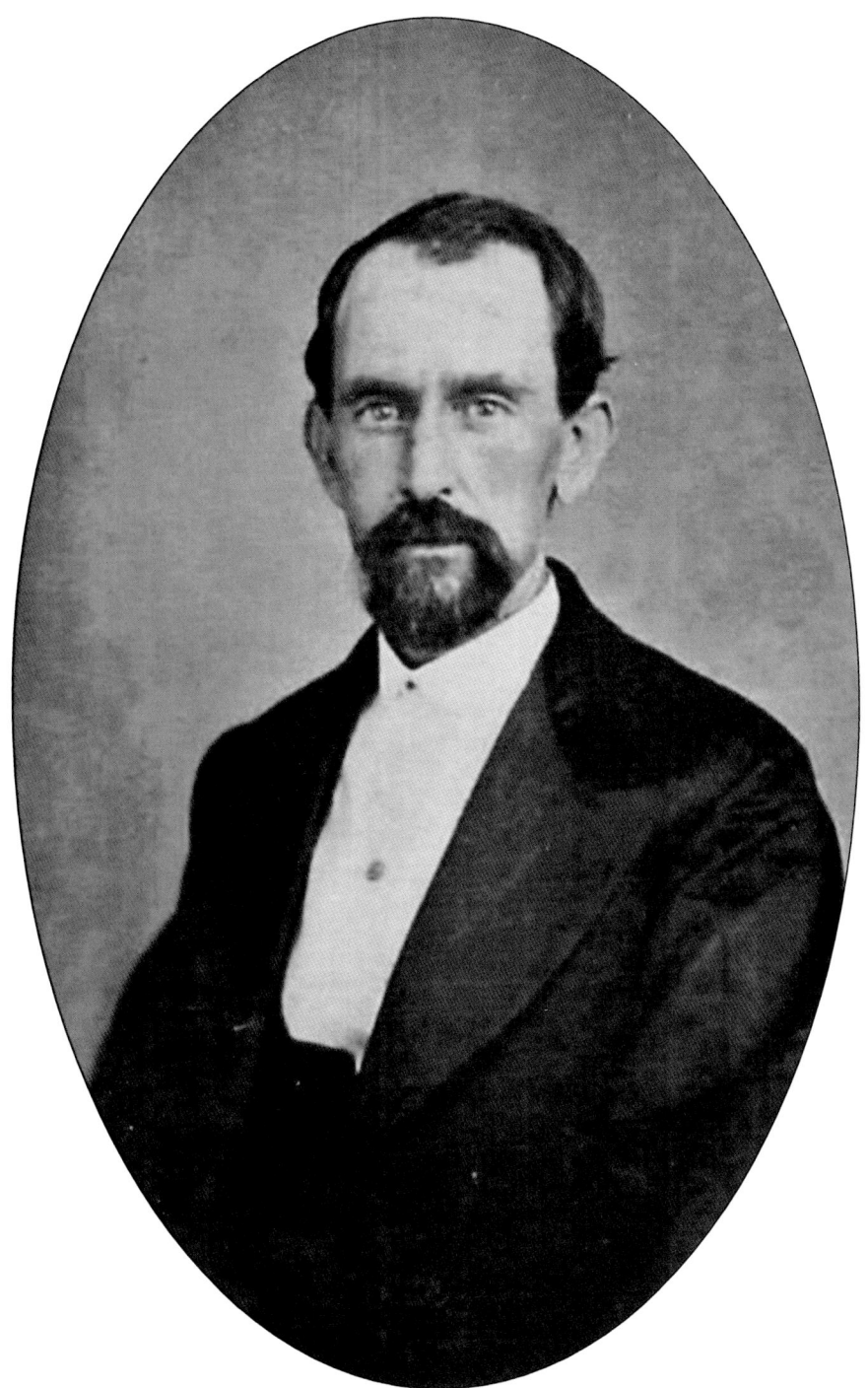

Capt. Calvin J. "C.J." Hyatt was born in January 1833 in Lauderdale County, Alabama. He served as a captain in the 11th Alabama Cavalry, Company A, CSA. C.J. married Mary Thomas Price on August 2, 1863, and after her death in 1883, he married Ida Lee White in 1885. He served as president of the Bank of Iuka from 1889 until his death in March 1897. He is buried in the Oak Grove Cemetery in Iuka, Mississippi.

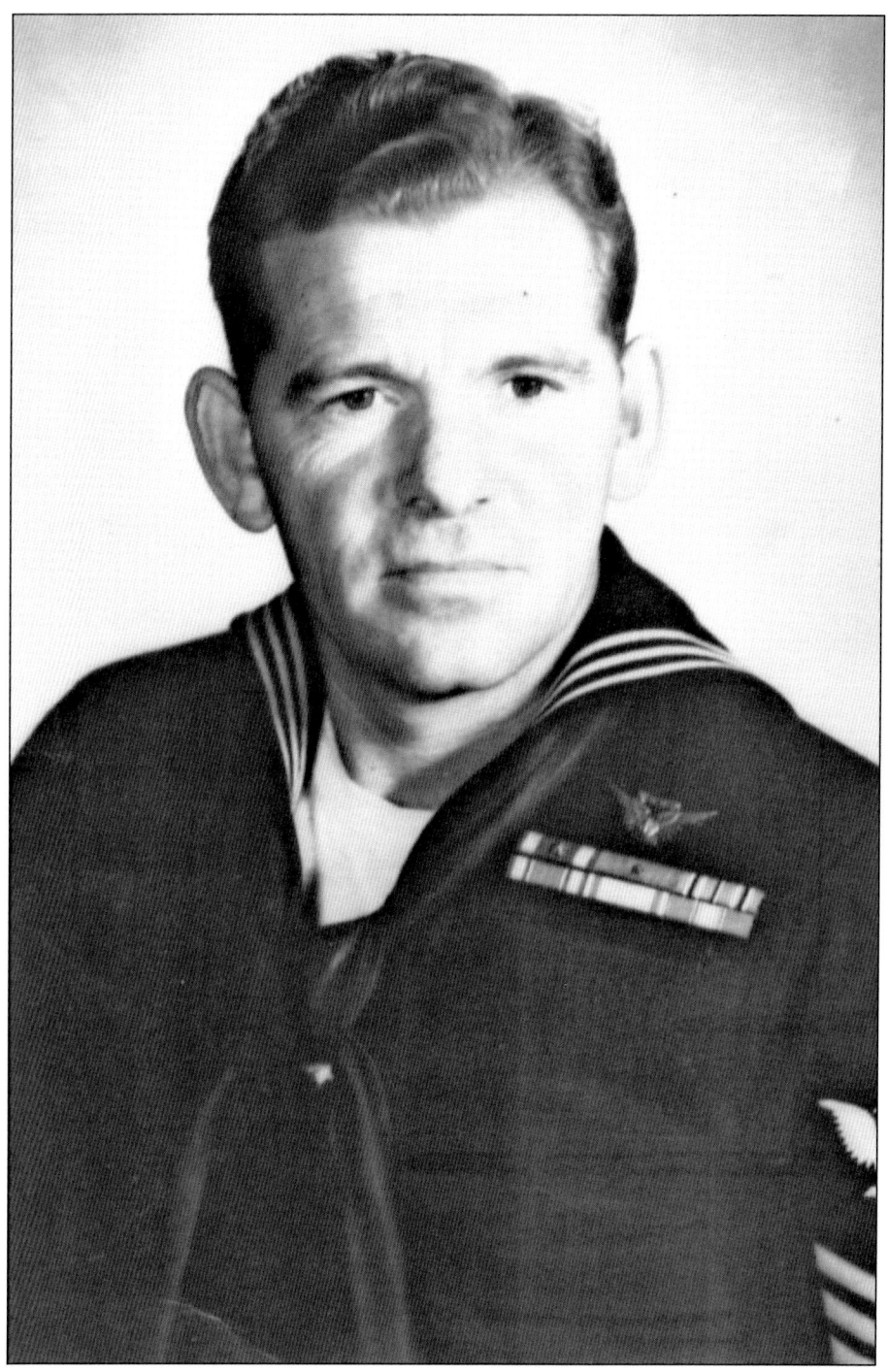

Robert M. "Bob" McAlister of Tishomingo was born in 1925 to Andrew and Eva McAlister. The US Navy sent Bob to photography school in Pensacola, followed by aerial gunnery school and photographic squadron training. He served as a Navy photographer until 1968. His career also included serving as the official summer White House photographer at the *Newport Daily News* in Rhode Island for Pres. John F. Kennedy from 1961 to 1963. (Courtesy of Robert M. McAlister.)

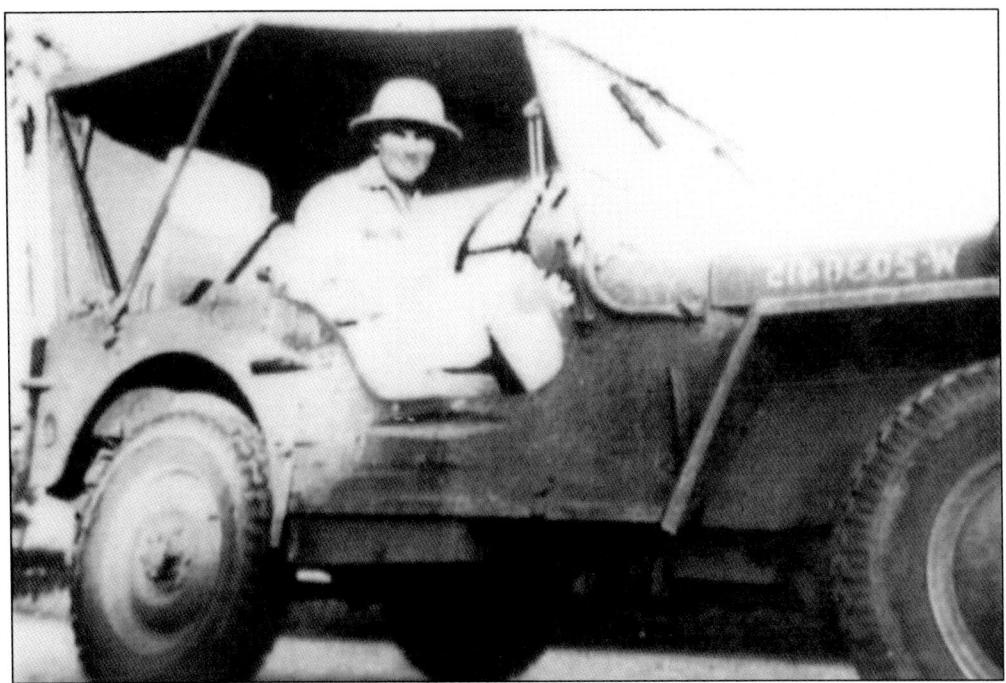

Ershell Jerome McNutt, son of Lula May Skinner and Thomas Nebraska McNutt, was born in Dennis in 1915. Ershell McNutt enlisted in the US Army instead of waiting to be drafted. He was trained as a rifleman and assigned to the 100th Infantry Division. After World War II, Ershell rejected several offers to study for a doctor of philosophy degree in favor of marriage. (Courtesy of Jerrell L. McNutt.)

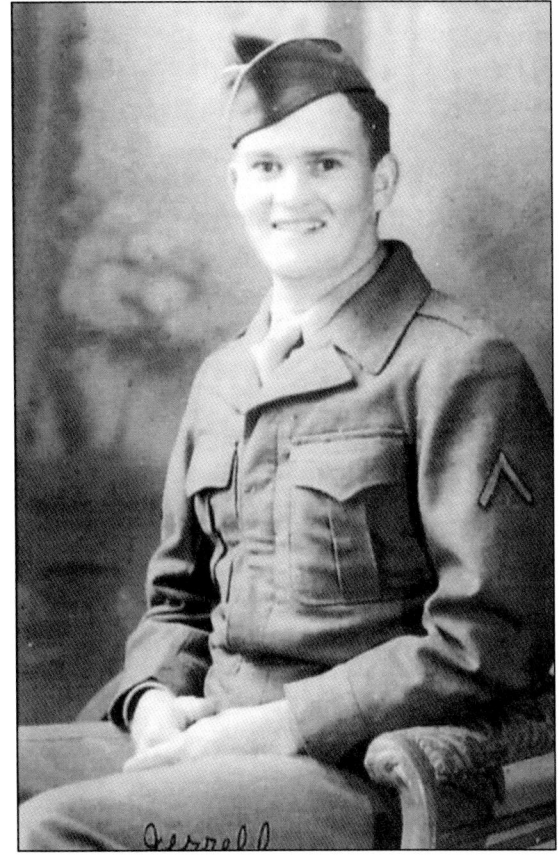

Jerrell L. McNutt, son of Lula May Skinner and Thomas Nebraska McNutt, was born in Dennis in 1926. In 1945, Jerrell was drafted into the US Army and shipped to Korea. His duty in Korea was with the Army of Occupation, which was responsible for rounding up Japanese soldiers and sending them back to Japan. (Courtesy of Jerrell L. McNutt.)

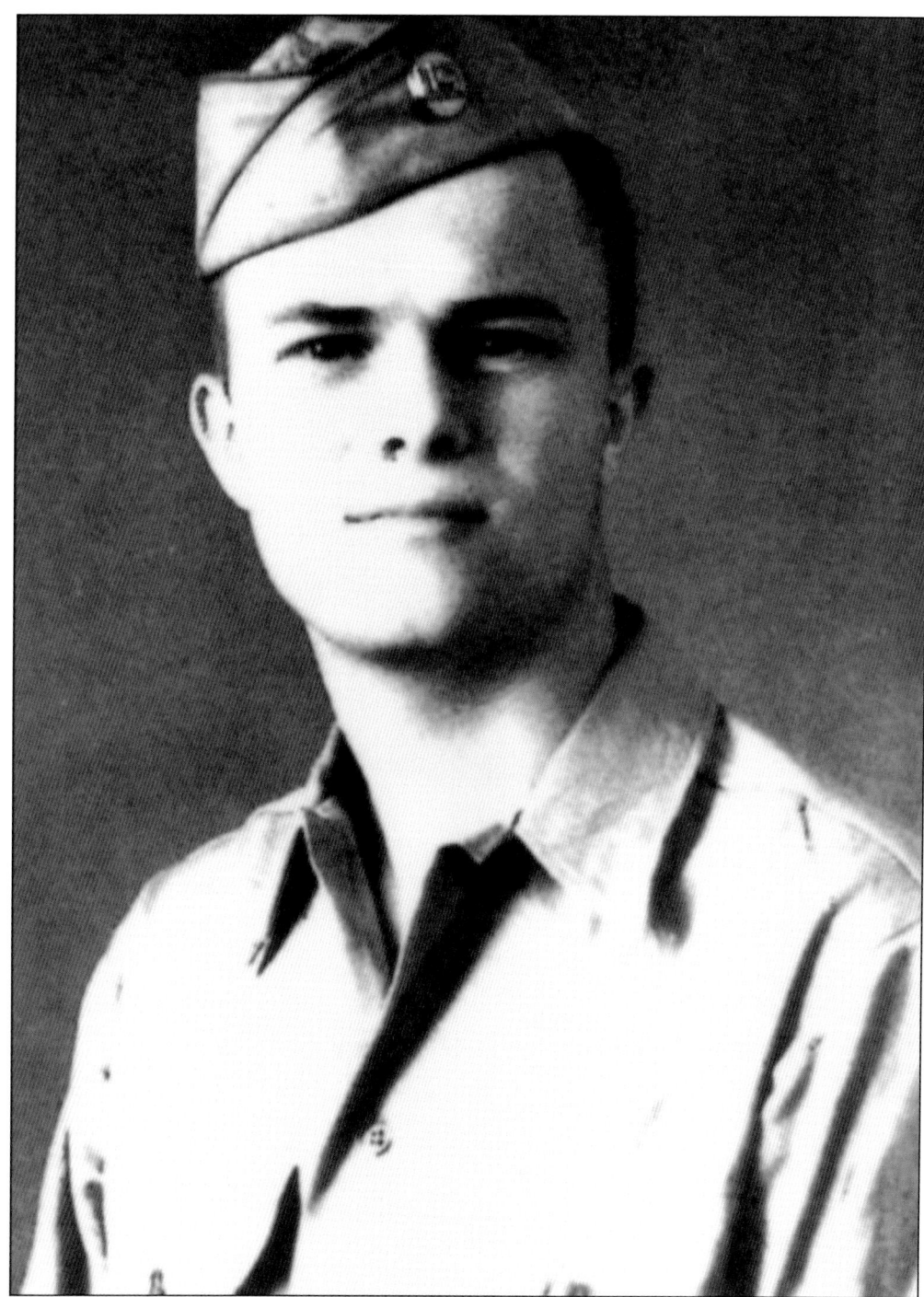

Orville Van McNutt, son of Lula May Skinner and Thomas Nebraska McNutt, was born in Dennis in 1923. Orville volunteered to train at Mississippi State University to be a radio operator. He served overseas with the combat engineers across North Africa, Sicily, and Italy. Orville, his five brothers, and one brother-in-law all served in World War II at the same time. (Courtesy of Jerrell L. McNutt.)

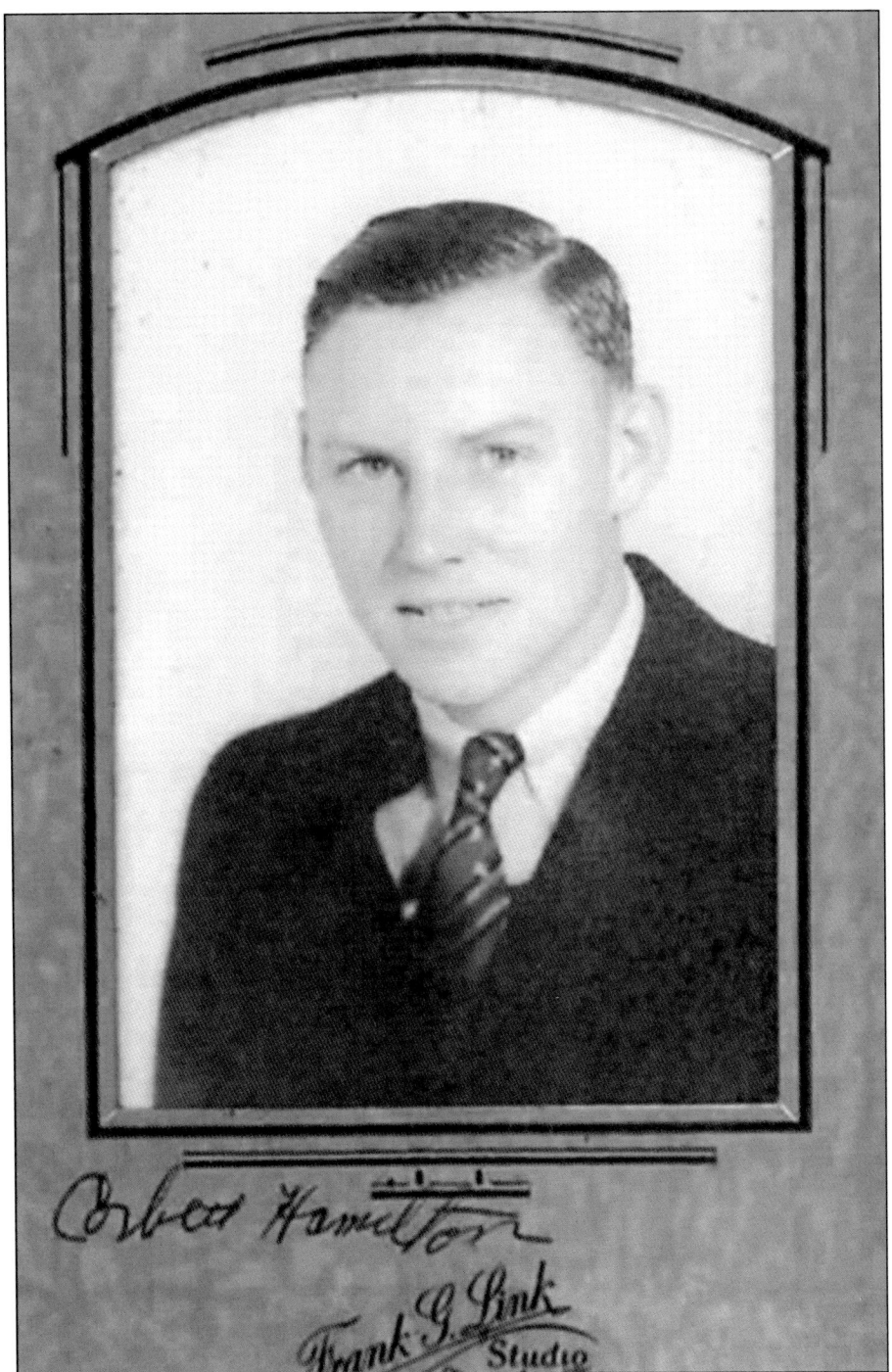

William Corbett "Ham" Hamilton served as a bombardier with the 561st Bomb Squadron, 388th Bomb Group in the US Army Air Corps, based in England. During World War II, Ham flew 25 of his allotted 25 bombing missions over German-occupied Western Europe in B-17 bombers. On his 25th mission, he was shot down over Kiel Bay in Germany. Captured, Ham remained a German prisoner of war until mid-April 1945.

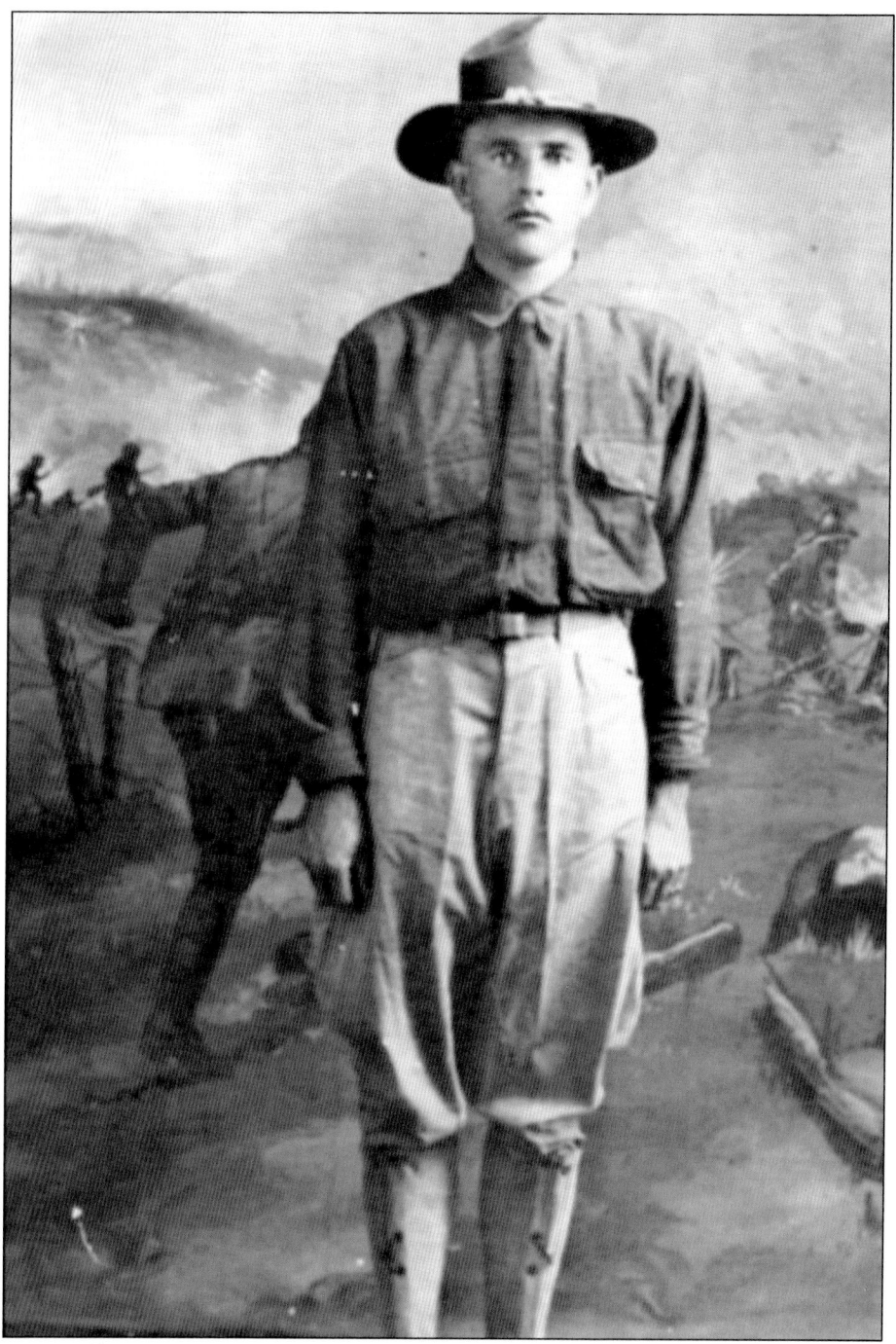

Milton Candler Sprouse Sr., son of Hosea S. Sprouse and Nancy Jane Thomas, was born in Tishomingo County, Mississippi, on July 19, 1896. He enlisted in the Army on August 30, 1918, and was assigned to the 71st Engineers, Washington Barracks, D.C. With a Scruggs cousin, Milton was on a boat nearing Paris, France, when the war ended. The soldiers were returned home and honorably discharged on December 5, 1918, after three months and five days of military service.

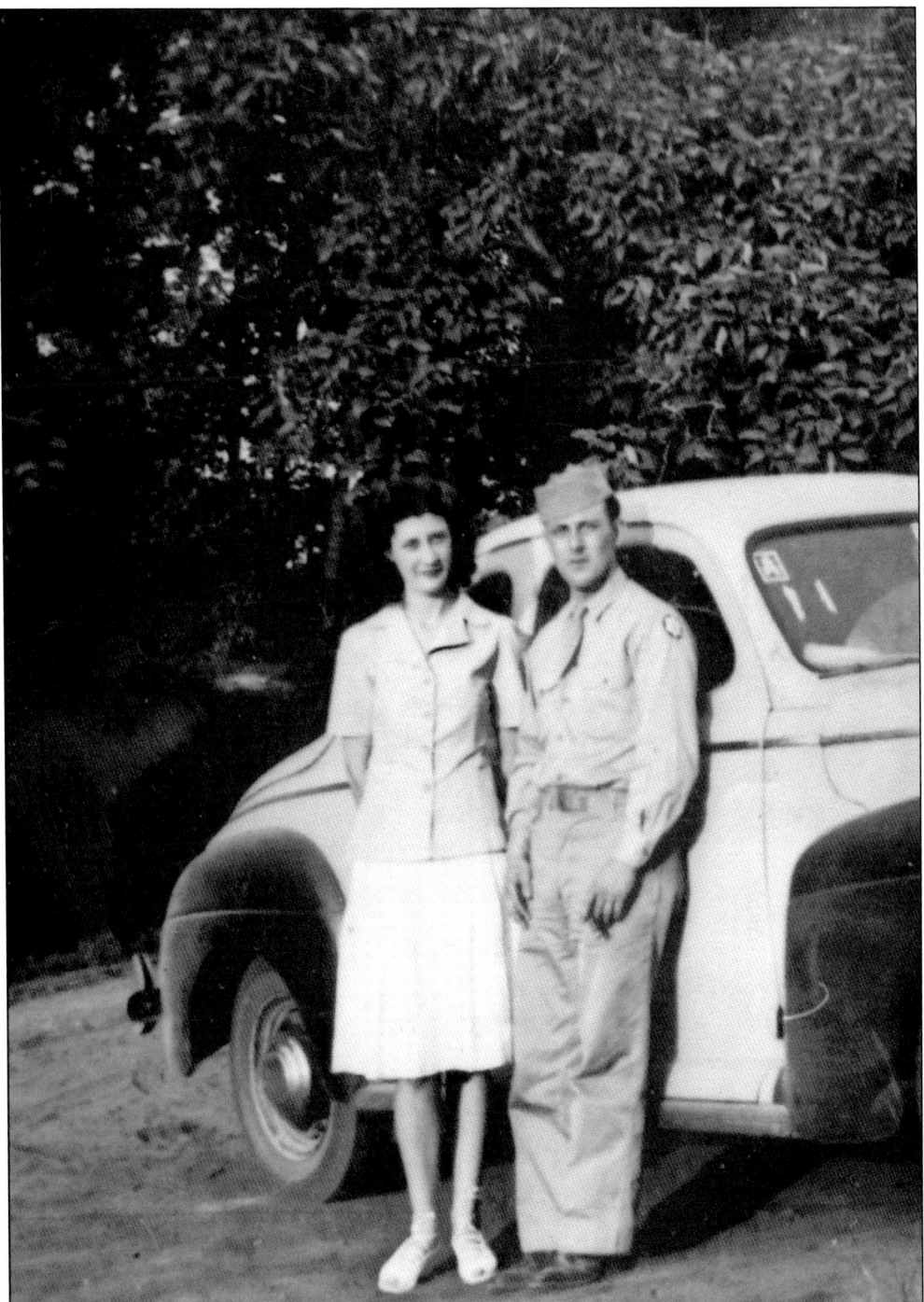

Horace Delton Nelson, son of James Jefferson and Hester (Hill) Nelson, was born in 1913 in Tishomingo County. After his military service, Delton became interested in the cattle business, and one day, while attending an auction in Tupelo, the auctioneer failed to show up for work. Delton immediately asked for the job. He was successful at his first attempt and was faithful to the cattle trade for many years afterwards.

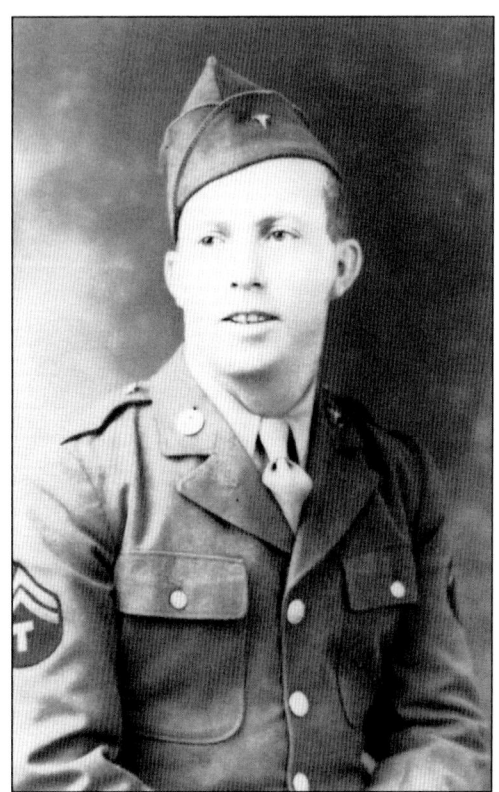

James Tulon Nelson, son of James Jefferson Nelson and Hester (Hill) Nelson, was born in 1923 in Tishomingo County. Tulon Nelson married Doris Graham Haines. Tulon died on August 31, 1987, at the Veterans Administration Hospital in Memphis after a brief illness. He was 64 years old. He was a Methodist, a retired salesman for Falstaff, and a World War II veteran. (Courtesy of Bobby G. Nelson.)

Merle L. Nelson, son of James Omer and Altye (Callicott) Nelson, was born in 1924 in Holcut. In 1944, Merle received his wings and served in the Air Force during World War II. He remained in the Reserves until 1953. During his Reserve years, he served in the Korean Conflict. He also taught young cadets to fly single-engine planes and B-25s while stationed in Lubbock, Texas.

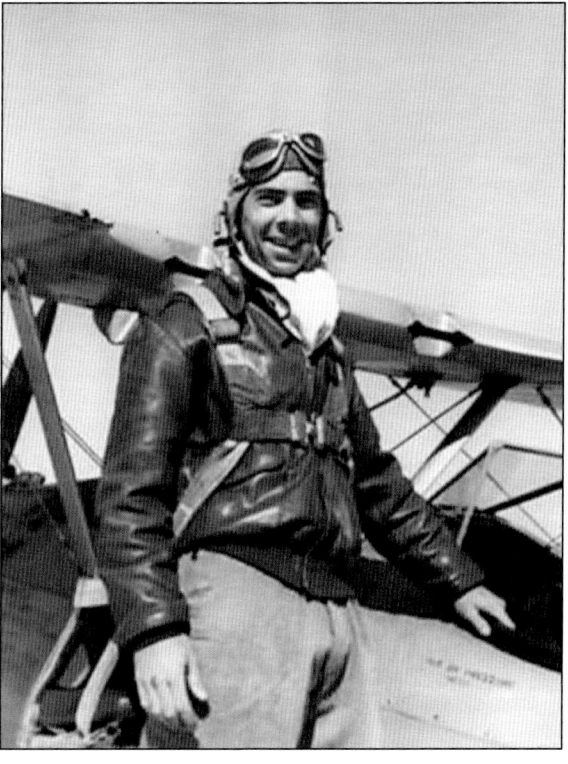

Pictured are Merle L. Nelson (left) and Omer Callicott Nelson (right). These sons of James Omer Nelson and Altye (Callicott) Nelson both served in the US Air Force. Merle served in World War II and the Korean War, and Omer served in three wars—World War II, the Korean War, and the Vietnam War—and flew in the Berlin Airlift in 1948. Omer flew 97 combat missions and logged 568 combat hours in Korea. During his military career, Col. Omer Nelson accumulated more than 10,000 hours of flying time. Merle received his "wings" in 1944 and saw action with the 13th Air Force in Manila, The Philippines, Okinawa, Japan, and Polywain. He was a pilot with the responsibility of flying "Billy Mitchell's" B-25s.

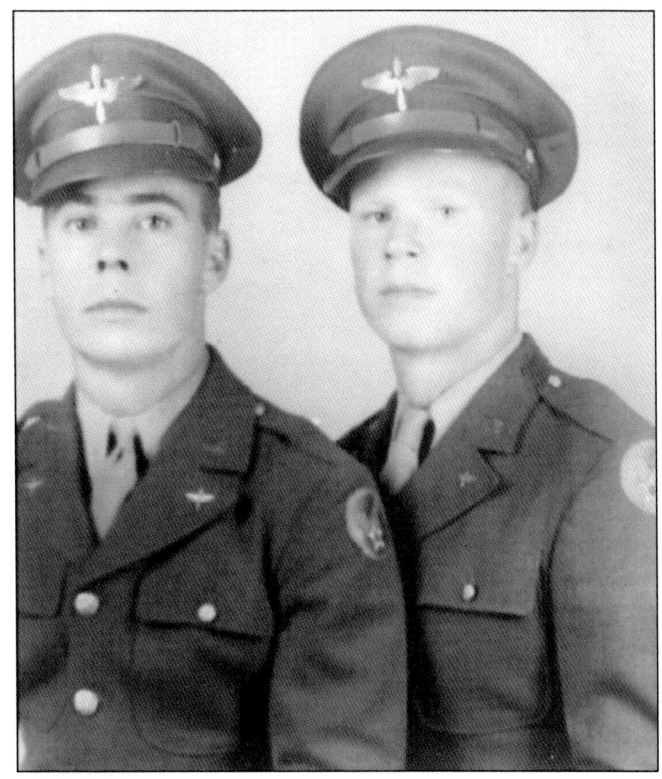

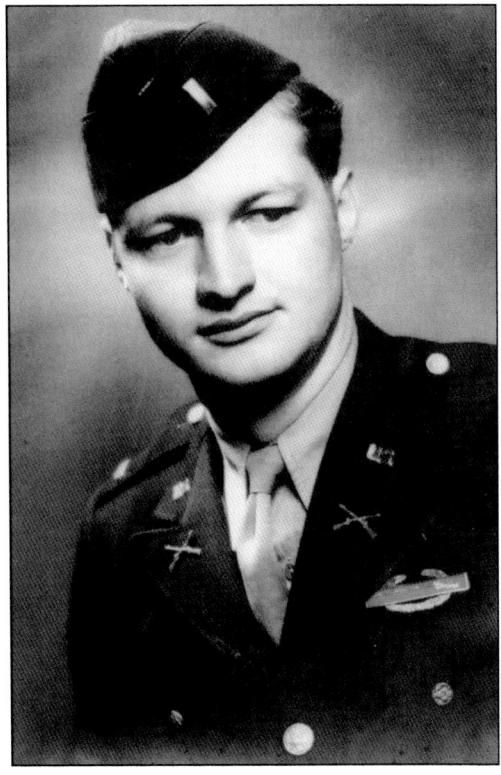

William R. Nettles Jr., son of William R. and Lizzy Nettles, was born in Tishomingo in February 1923. He was an ROTC graduate from Mississippi State University and graduated as a second lieutenant in 1944. William was assigned to Company A, 273nd Infantry Regiment, 69th Infantry Division. He entered combat in Belgium and moved through Germany. William's last major battle was at the City of Leipsig.

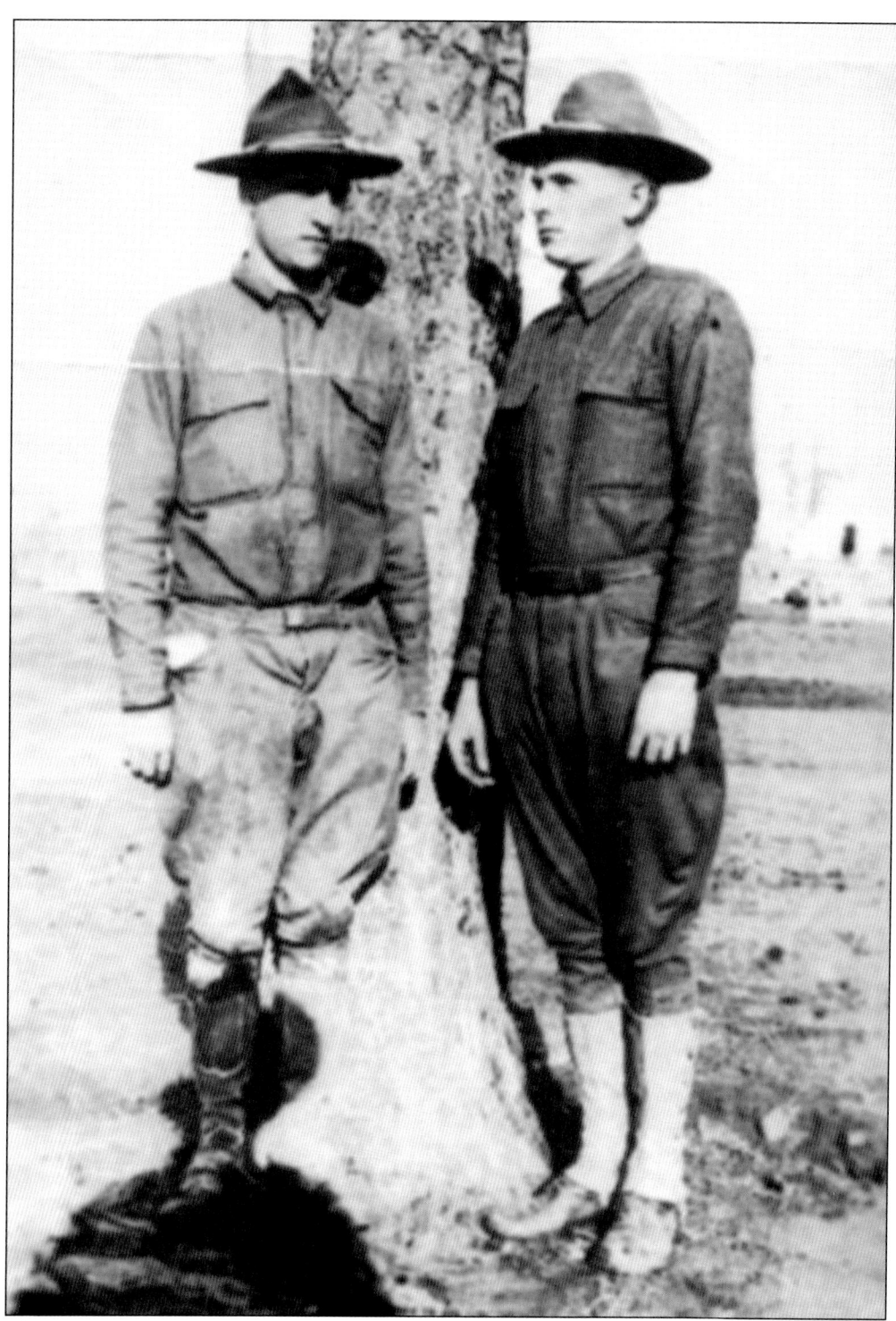

These veterans of World War I are Pauly Hale (left) and Samuel Sylvester "Vester" Daniel (right). Vester was born on March 2, 1892, the son of John Monroe "Munn" and Sarah "Sallie" T. (Lambert) Daniel. He married Minnie Pearl Millsap. No other information is known about Hale.

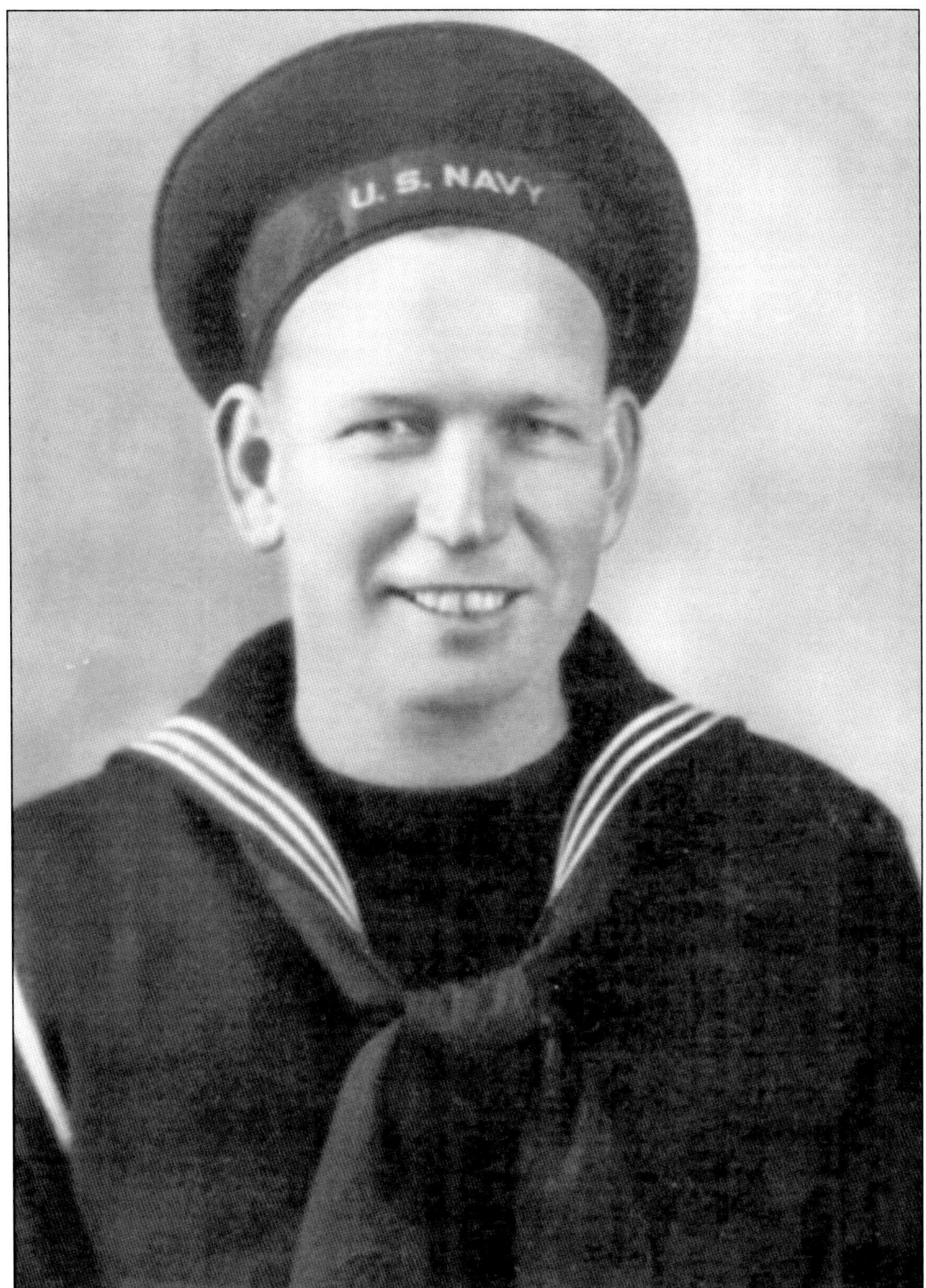
Guy Cleston Newcomb, son of Charles Anderson and Emma (Whittemore) Newcomb, was born in Leedy in 1914. When the Japanese bombed Pearl Harbor, Guy was working on a construction job near Paducah, Kentucky, as a welder and sheet-metal worker. He quickly joined the US Navy. Guy served in the Quartermaster Corps and was shipped to the American Samoan Islands. (Courtesy of Lessie M. Newcomb.)

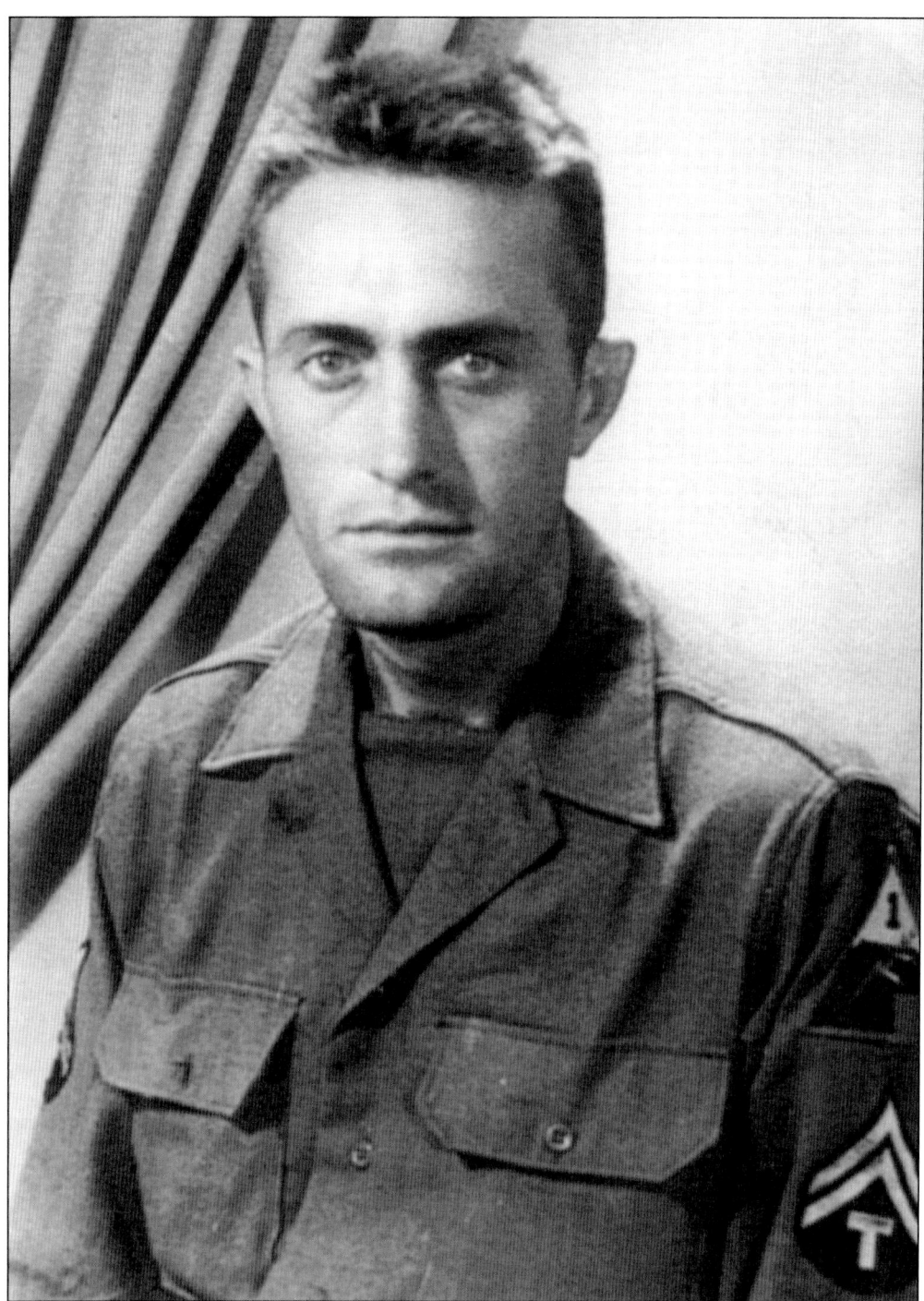

Walter Ellis Paden, son of John William Boone and Minnie (Millner) Paden, was born in Golden in 1914. He was assigned to serve as an ammunition handler with the 5th Army in North Africa and Italy. Walter also served as a tank driver and drove from Salerna, Italy, through Anzio, Rome, the Po Valley, and the Apennine Mountains near the Swiss border. (Courtesy of Reba Inez [Collier] Paden.)

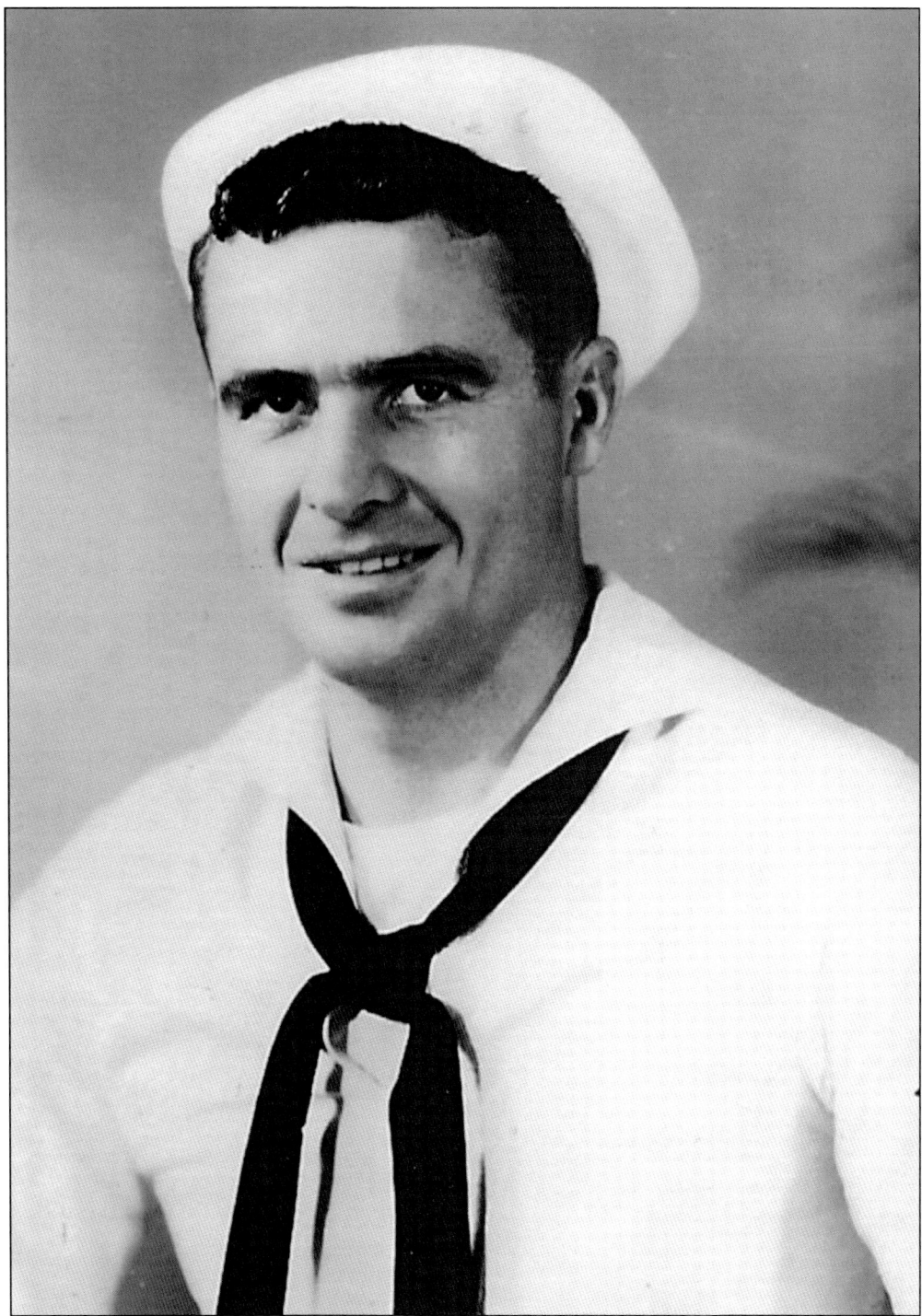

James Bryan Pounders, son of Myrtle Russell and James Riley Pounders, was born in 1931 in Tishomingo County. The US Navy assigned James to a supply ship, the USS *Diphda* (AKA-59). James bid for a position as barber after a year aboard ship and served in that capacity for the remainder of his naval career. (Courtesy of James B. Pounders.)

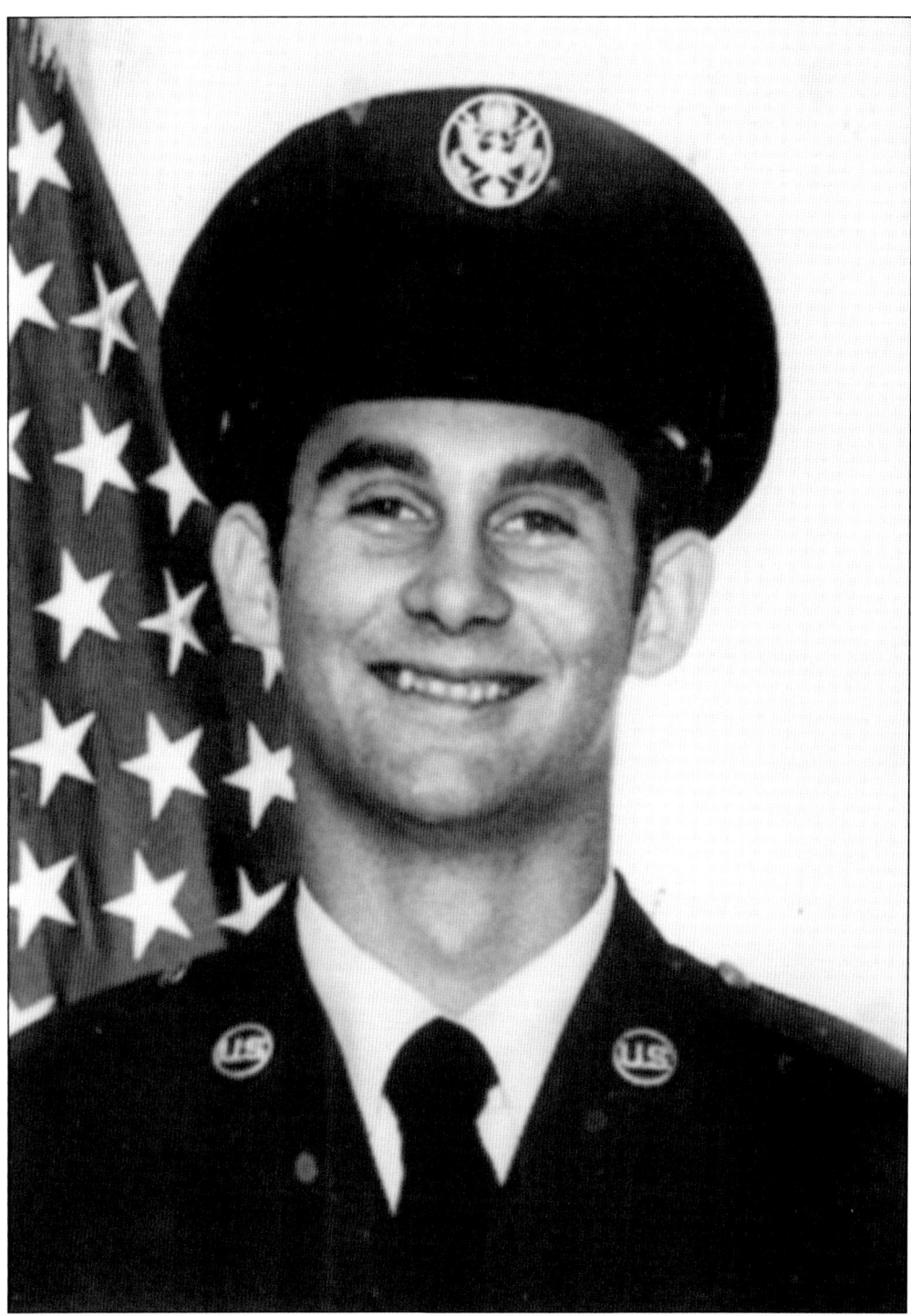

Terry Dell Parsons, son of O'Dell and Imogene (Moore) Parsons, was born at the Cosby Hospital in Iuka in 1958. Terry joined the US Air Force and was trained in electronics at the Lacklin Air Force Base in San Antonio. He was later sent overseas to Korea for training exercises. Terry has lived in Tishomingo County his entire life. He married Alisa Vaughan.

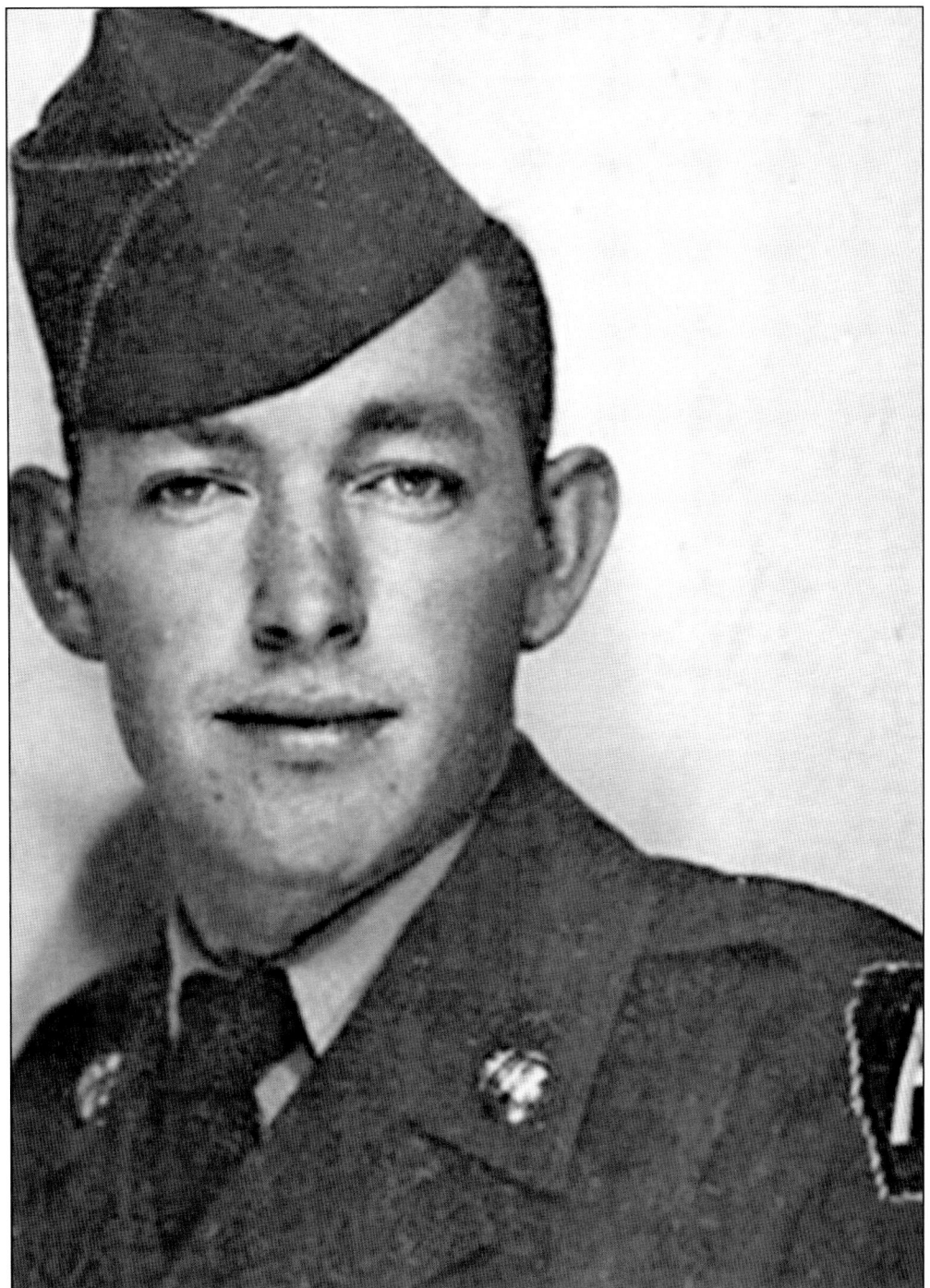

Carley E. Puckett, son of Roman B. and Emma (Ham) Puckett, was born in Tishomingo County in 1933. He was drafted into the US Army during the Korean War, assigned to the 151st Engineer Combat Battalion, and was deployed to replace troops already stationed in South Korea. His company's mission in South Korea was to build and repair bridges and roads. (Courtesy of Carley E. Puckett.)

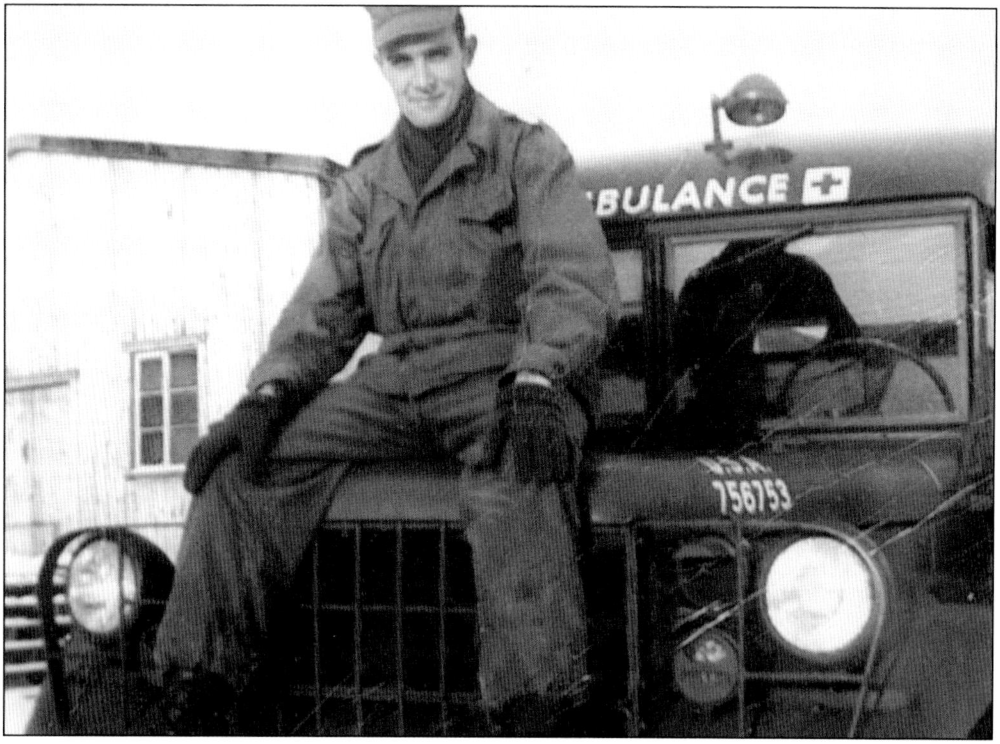

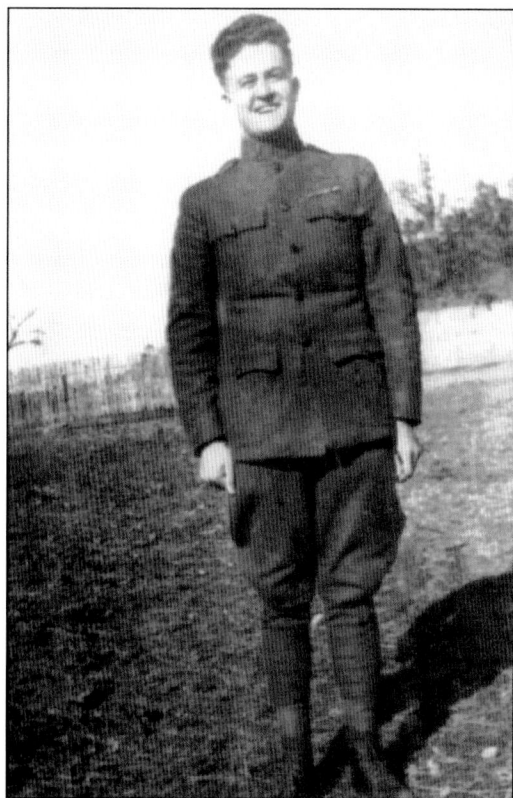

William A. "Billy" Rushing, son of James Richard and Georgia May (Blakney) Rushing, was born in Tishomingo County in 1926. Billy was drafted into the US Army, trained as a medic, and shipped overseas to Germany during the Korean War. He was married to Mary Nash, and they had one son, Bill. Billy left Tishomingo County to find work, but in 1988, he retired in Burnsville.

Charles Edmund "Charlie" Smith was born on September 19, 1896, in the old "section house" by the railroad track in the Oldham community near Iuka. He was the son of the late James Thomas and Mary Ann (Archer) Smith. He was the last surviving veteran of World War I in Tishomingo County. Charlie was honored and recognized on many occasions for his service to his country. He served in World War I under Gen. John "Blackjack" Pershing on the "Border Patrol." He celebrated his 102nd birthday before his death in 1998.

William Riley "W.R." Smith, son of David Samuel and Margaret "Peggy" (Wright) Smith, was born in 1821 in Tennessee. He was in Company A, 2nd Mississippi Infantry, CSA; however, due to chronic illness, he was medically discharged and never saw combat. W.R. Smith was deputized one night in Burnsville to assist Sheriff Beall in capturing the Jack Davenport gang. He died in Burnsville in 1903.

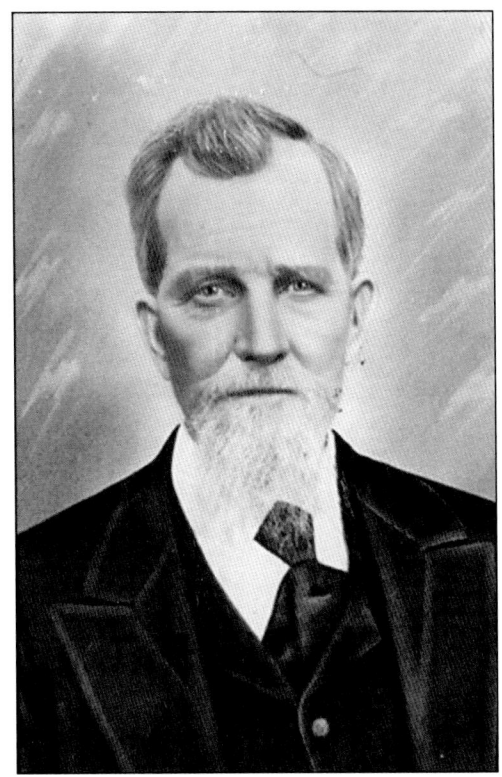

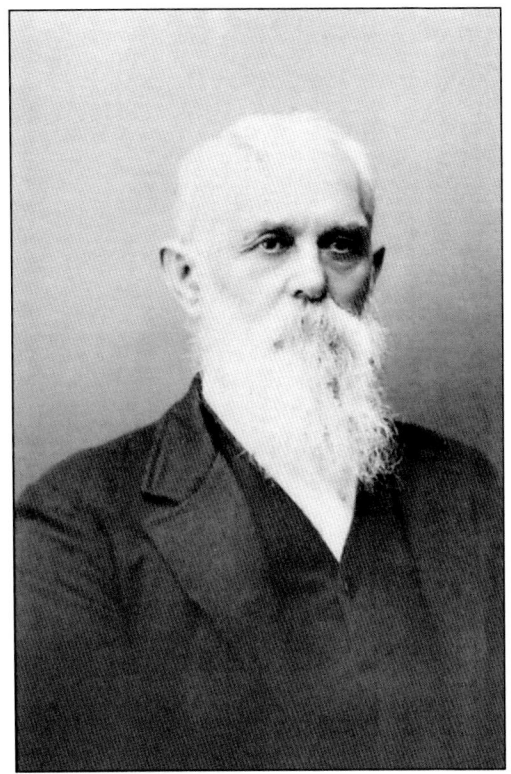

Henry James Williams, son of Wiley and Louisa (Johnson) Williams, was born in 1831 in Tennessee. He enlisted in the Confederate army in 1861, served in Browne's Company, Tennessee Light Artillery Battery, and was listed as a corporal in Company D, 2nd Alabama Light Artillery Battalion. He lived in Franklin County, Alabama, and later moved to Iuka in the 1900s. He was buried in Iuka's Oak Grove Cemetery.

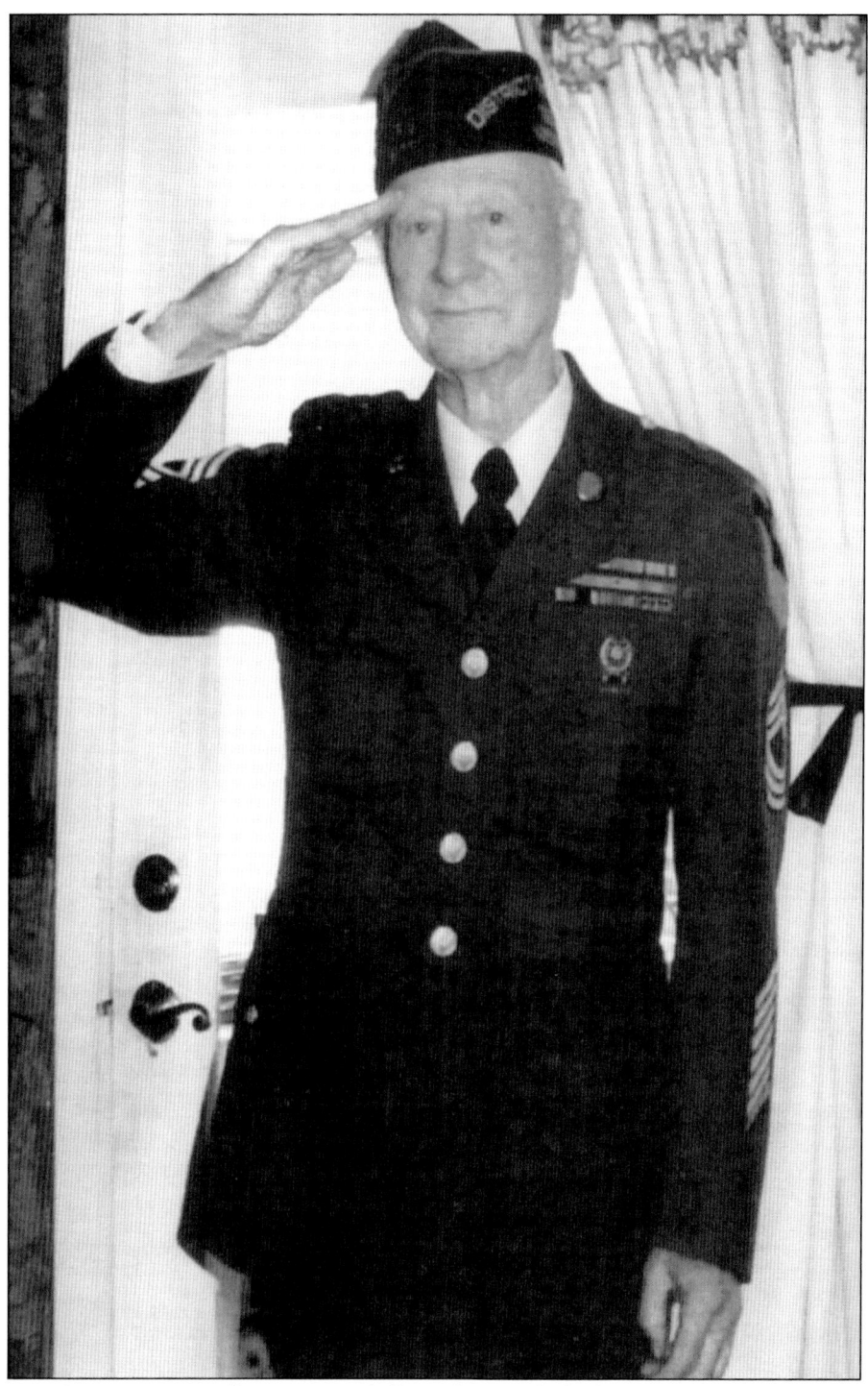

Born in Belmont in 1919, Delbert H. Stamphill was the son of Charles A. and Lila (Reno) Stamphill. Delbert served in England, Normandy, France, Belgium, Holland, Germany, and Korea. He was a prisoner of war during the Korean War, returned to the United States on a prison exchange, and then returned to Korea again to keep fighting. He served 32 years in the military.

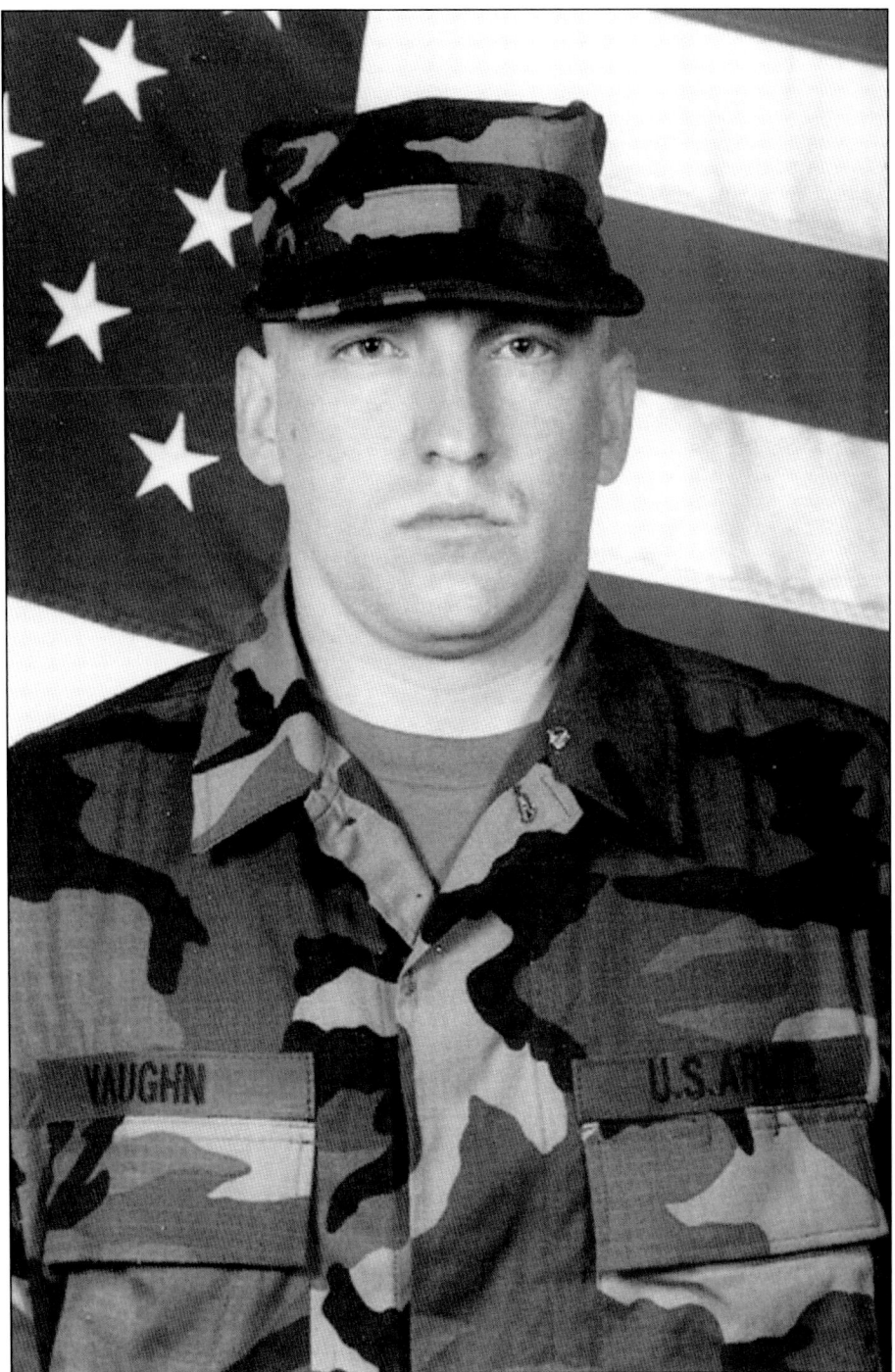

Jason W. Vaughn was the son of Walter and RaNae (Smith) Vaughn. Jason was assigned to the 3rd Brigade, 2nd Infantry Division and drove the Army's new Stryker. He was killed by an IED on May 10, 2007, near Baqubah, Iraq. Five years after his death, the Iuka Post Office was renamed the Sergeant Jason W. Vaughn Post Office in honor of Tishomingo County's only casualty in Operation Iraqi Freedom. (Courtesy of RaNae S. Vaughn.)

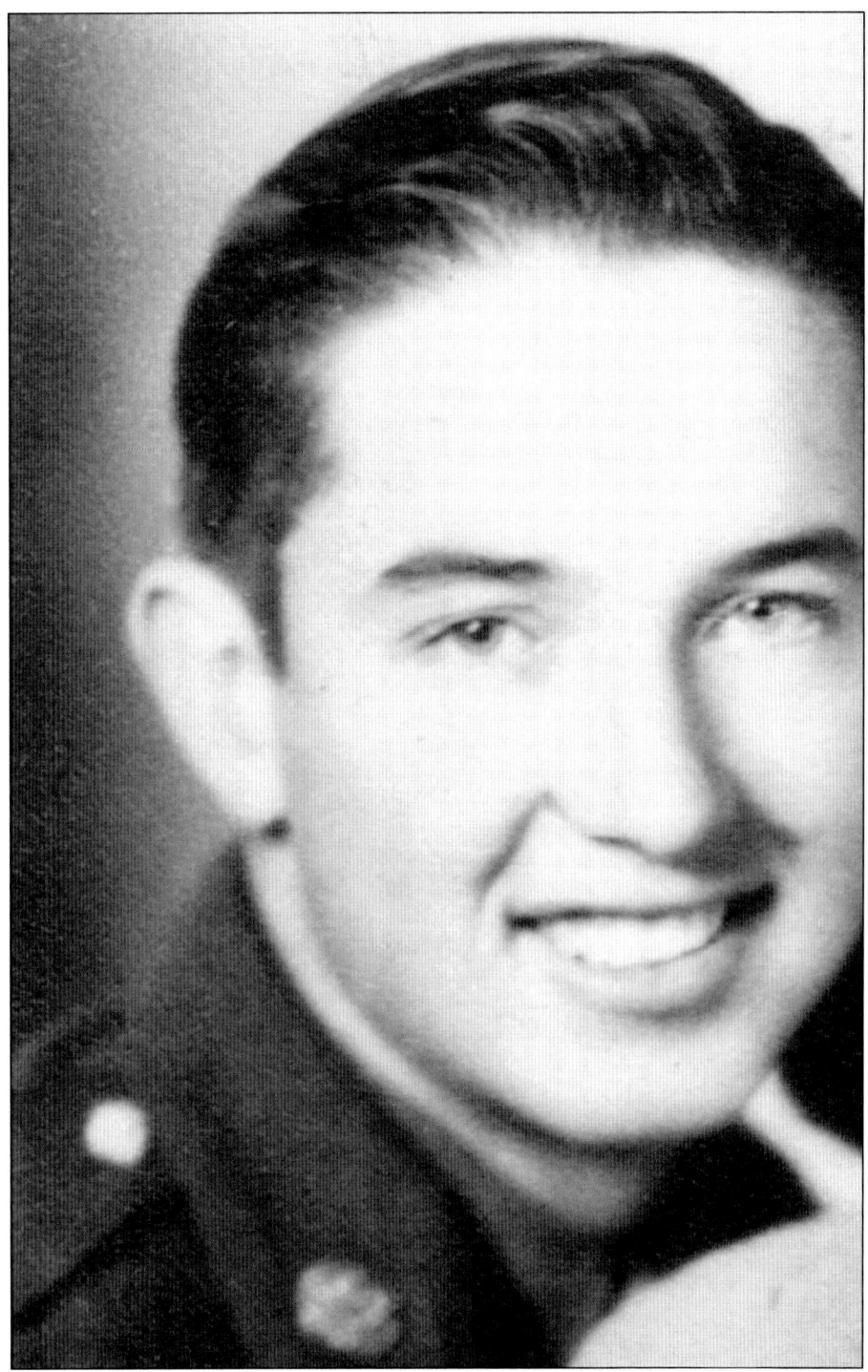

James Lon Weathers, son of Early Marshall and Mae Pearl (Bonds) Weathers, was born in Iuka in 1926. He was drafted into the US Army at the age of 18. After his training, he was assigned to the 86th Infantry "Blackhawk" Division and spent the majority of his time in Germany and France. (Courtesy of J. Don Weathers.)

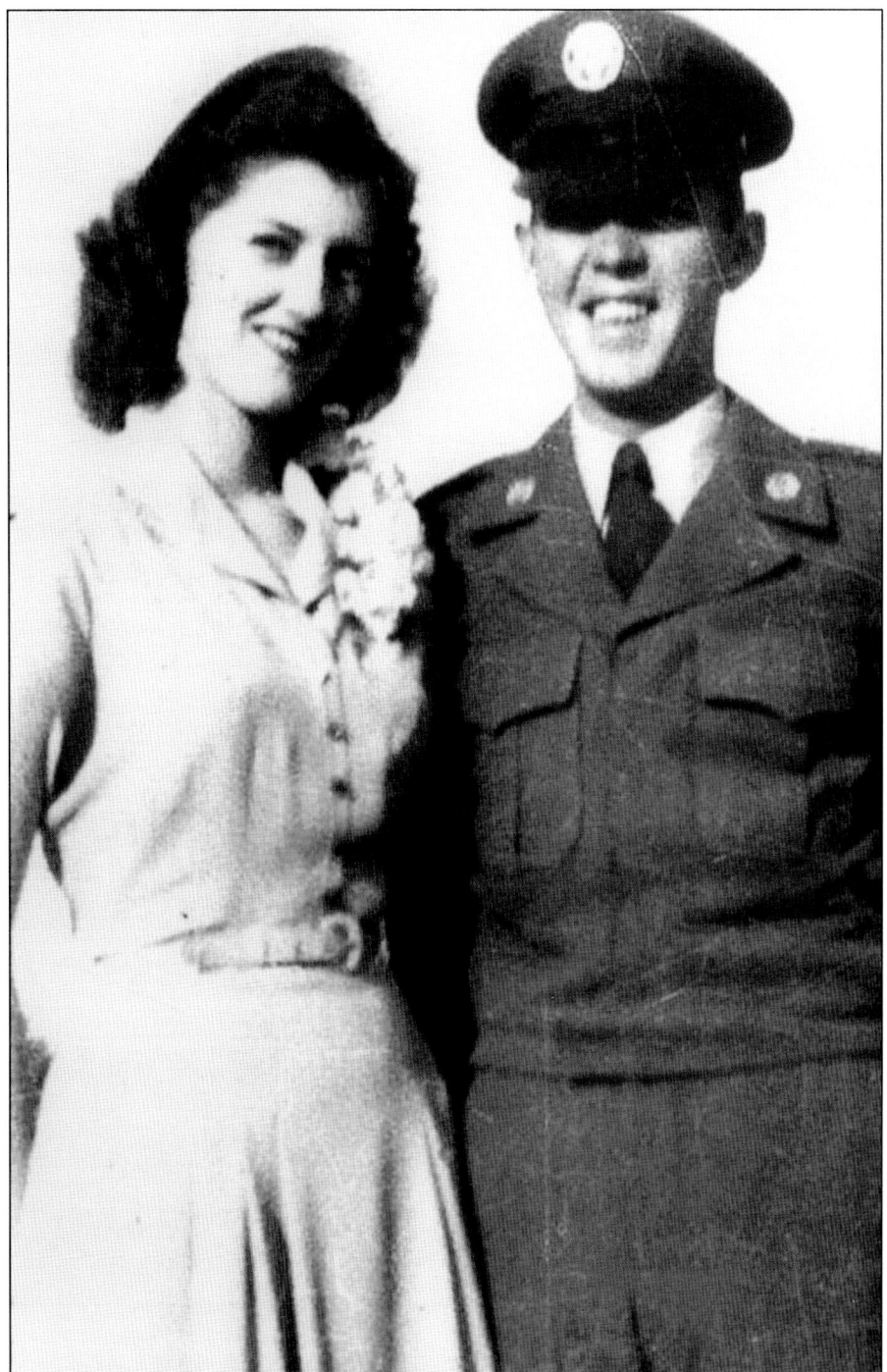

Victor Earl "Vic" White was born in Haleyville, Alabama, in 1931. His parents, Victor and Evelyn, raised him in Burnsville. Vic entered the US Air Force during the Korean War and received on-the-job training as a payroll and records clerk at Lackland Air Force Base. After Vic was honorably discharged in 1955, he attended technical school and worked his way up in the computer services business. (Courtesy of Vic White.)

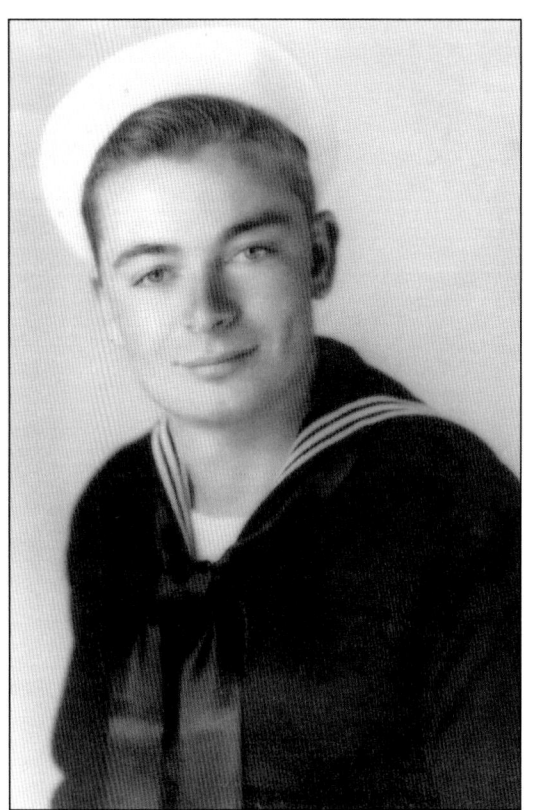

James Clay Whitfield, son of Walter Smith and Georgia Gertrude (Seago) Whitfield, was born in 1923 in Burnsville. Clay was drafted into the US Navy to fight in World War II. He was classified as seaman first class aboard the USS *William C. Cole*, an escort ship. He served in the South Pacific and participated in the Battle of Iwo Jima. (Courtesy of Charlotte [Whitfield] Vines.)

Neal Monroe Wiginton, son of Cratie Lee and Virga (Dickinson) Wiginton, was born in Dennis in 1920. He was assigned to the USS *Cimarron* and the USS *Appalachian*. His company was engaged in the following operations: Tokyo Raid, Midway, Guadacanal Tugi Landings, New Georgia Occupation, Wake Island, Marshall Island Operations, Truk Island, Marianas Island Operations, and the Palau Island Operation. (Courtesy of Dolores [Wiginton] Hutcheson.)

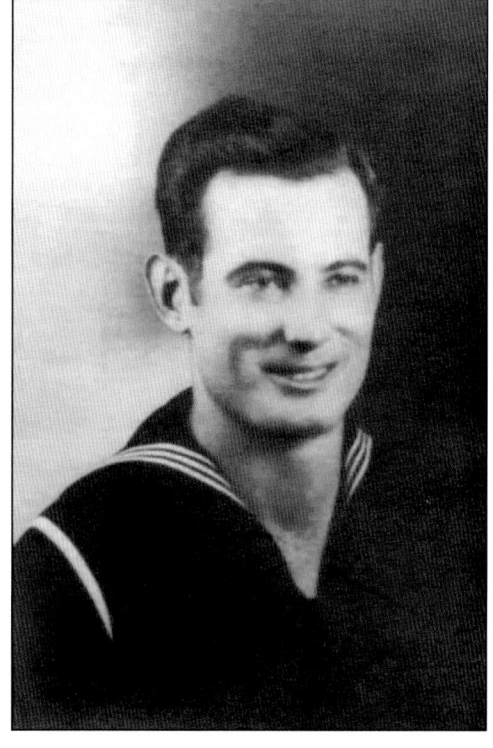

Eight
SCHOOLS

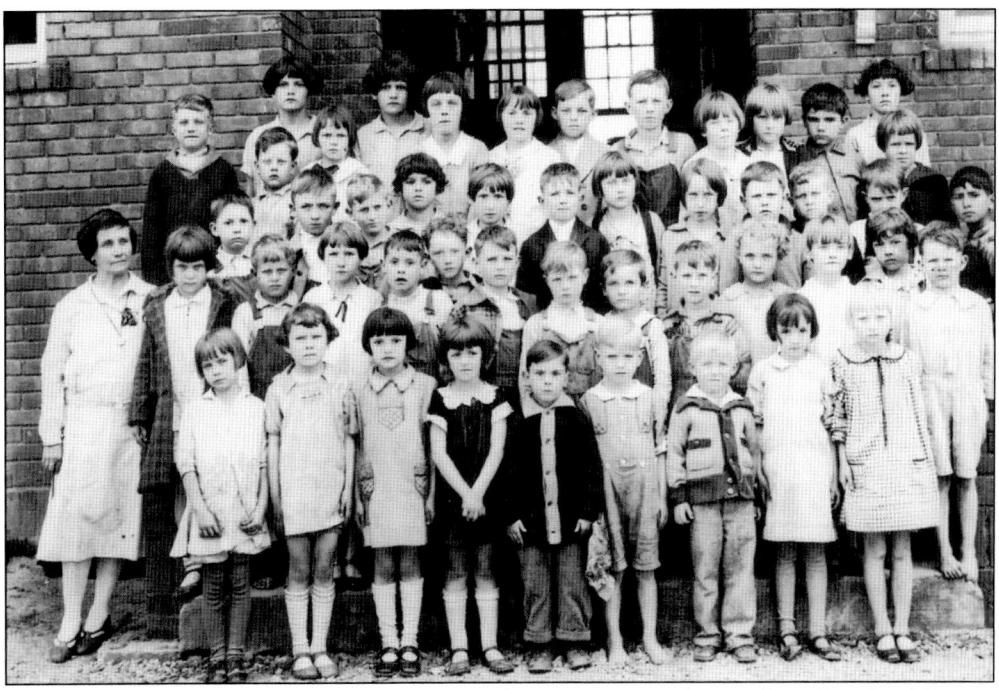

Mrs. L.L. Davis taught this class of students that encompassed several grades. Cecil Lamar Sumners, who became a Mississippi state senator, was in the second grade during this school year. The students have been identified but are too numerous to list in this caption. (Courtesy of Sen. Cecil Sumners.)

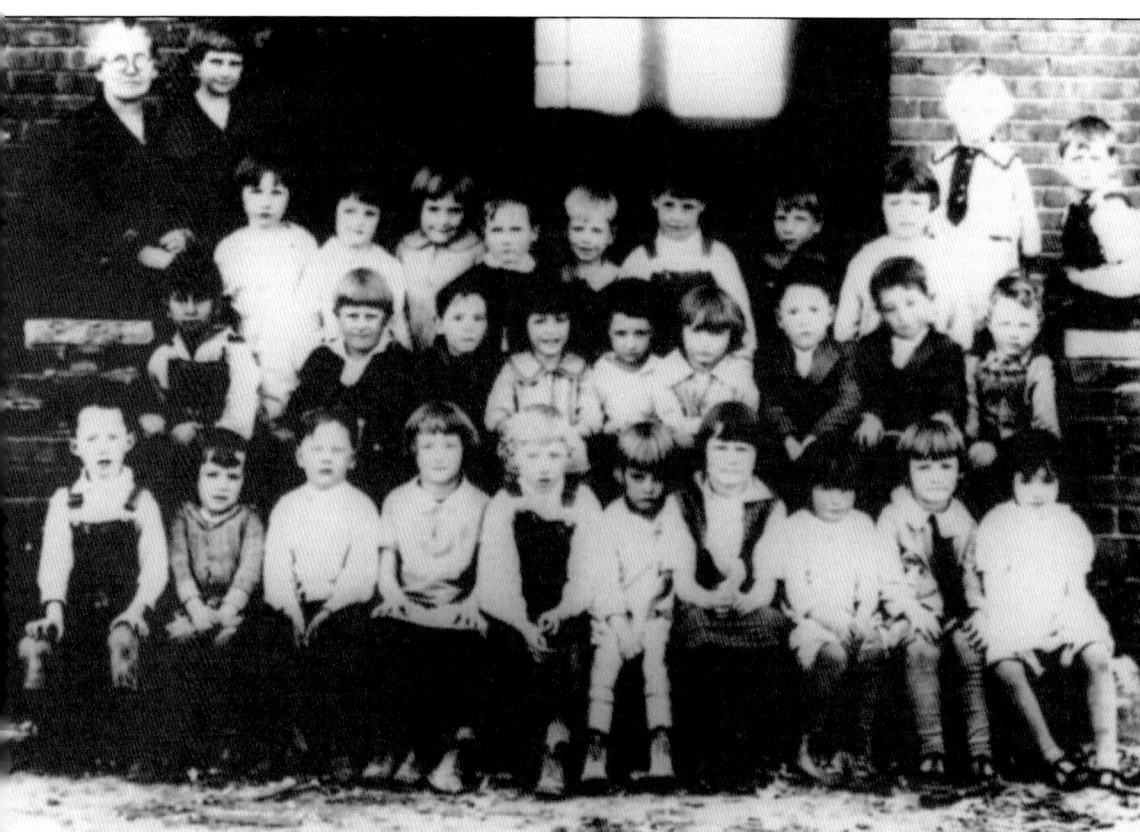

Pictured here is the first-grade class of Belmont in 1925, comprised of, from left to right, (first row) Toy Northington, Maude Cromeans, Braxton Finch, Pauline Credille, "Doc" Gamble, Fleeta Gamble, Doshey Campbell, Helen Moore, Opal Lambert, and Mary Alice Cromeans; (second row) Winford Chambers, unidentified, Cecil Sumners, Frances Shook, unidentified, Edna Shook, ? Nix, John William Cromeans, and J.T. Hallmark; (third row) Mrs. Byram, Helen McFadden, Clytra Sims, Tommie Mae Stanphill, Irene Ozbirn, Philip Davis, Claude Strickland, Edsel Mann, Theron Pounds, Bernell Yarber, Lucille Savage, and Leon Shook.

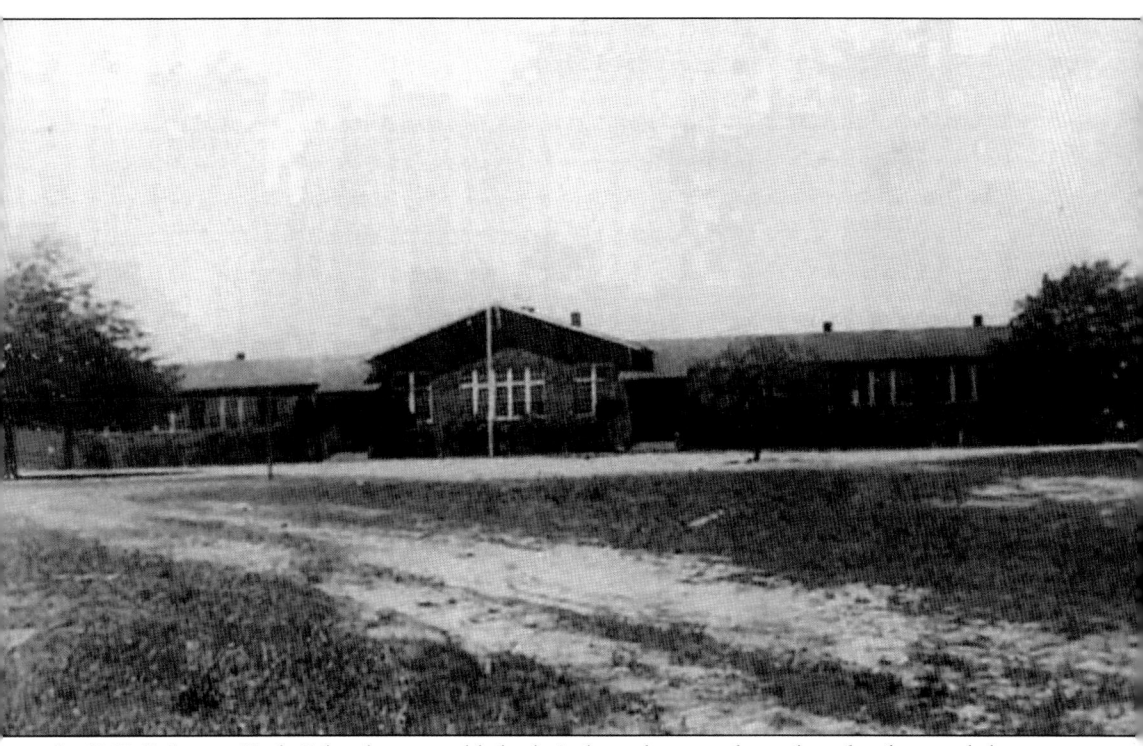
In 1899, Belmont High School was established. A short distance from the school, a much larger building was constructed at the end of the 19th century, which, together with the older one, was supposed to accommodate approximately 200 students. R.L. Shook and his wife, Ann Lindsey Shook, were principal and assistant when the two-teacher expansion was underway. Walter Elledge was one of the first principals at the two-teacher school.

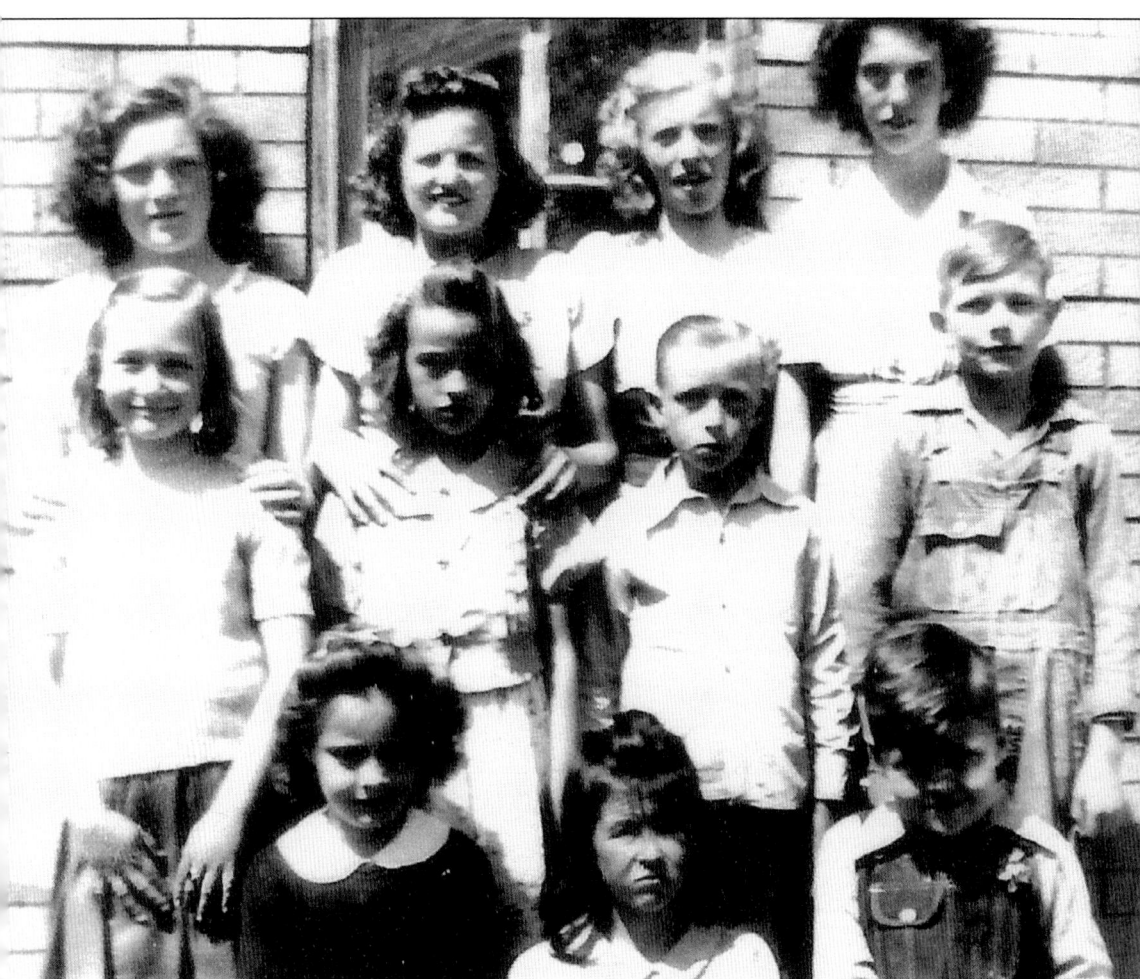

Boggs Chapel School taught grades first through eighth. Students attending the Boggs Chapel School in 1927 were Yvonne Deaton, Ruth Dawson (teacher), Gladys Humber, Eva Mae Strickland, Erline Howe, Verlene Scruggs, Denton Humber, Freeman Floyd, Opaline Thorne, Marcella Pannell, and Bobby Thorne. (Courtesy of Ruth Dawson.)

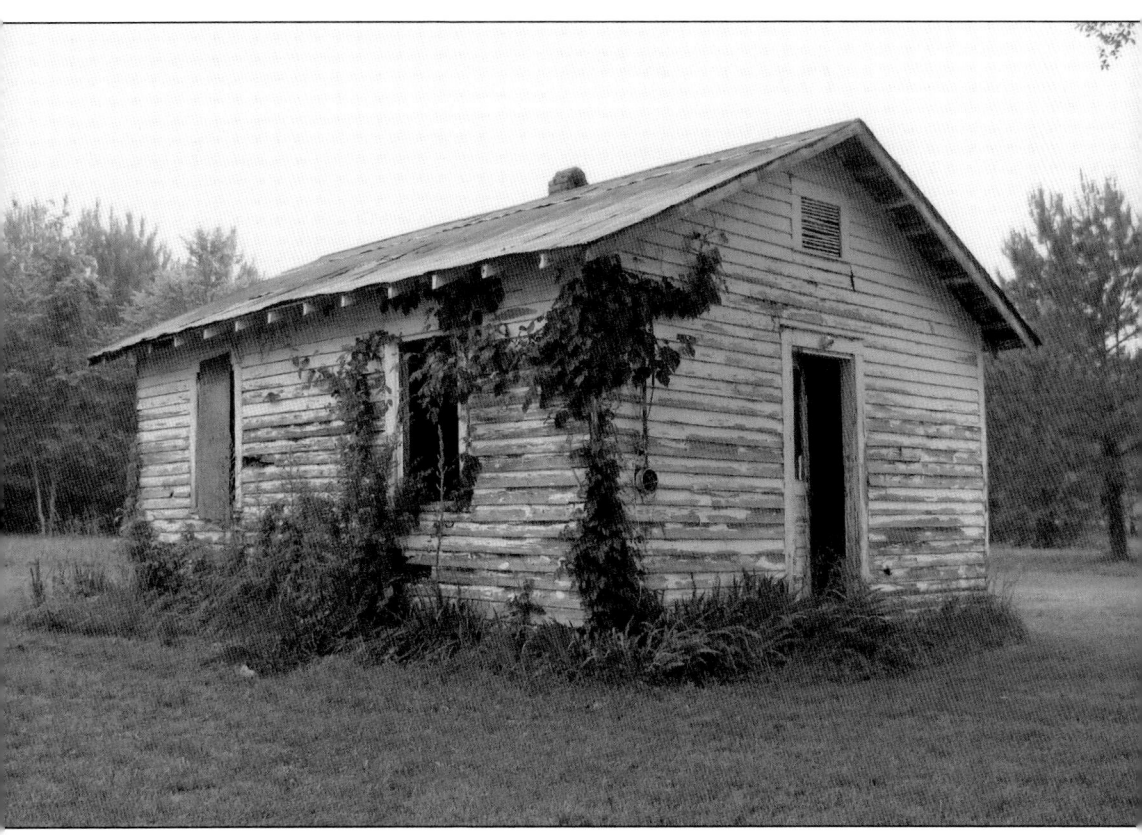

One of the oldest structures in Burnsville is a one-room schoolhouse, known locally as the Burnsville Colored School. The school was constructed in the early 1900s to replace an earlier 1800s schoolhouse that was located approximately one mile away near the railroad. The little schoolhouse still stands today and is a source of pride in Burnsville's heritage. It is pictured here before its restoration in 2011.

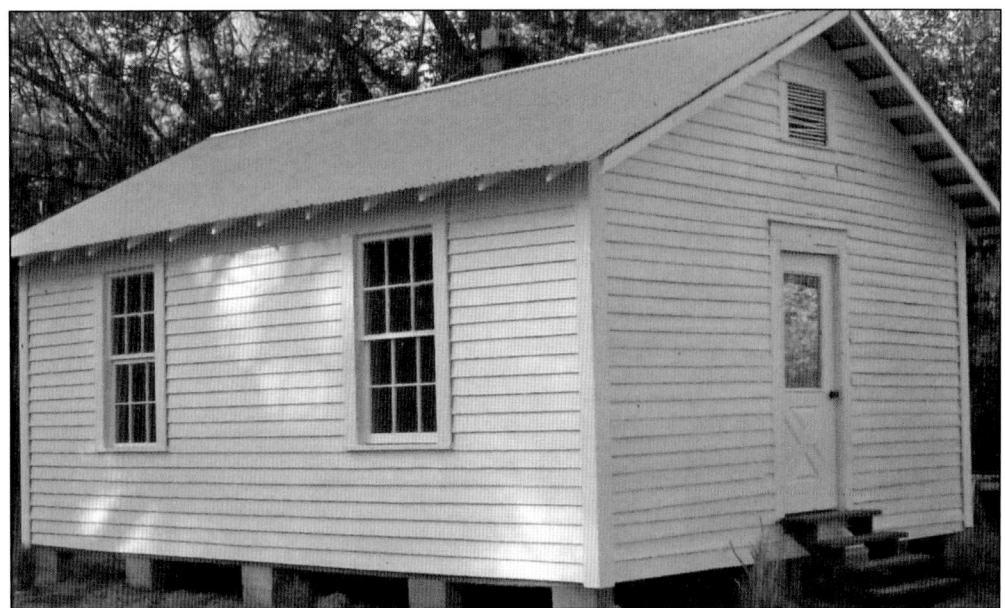

Pictured is the Burnsville one-room schoolhouse after its restoration in 2011. A significant figure in reclaiming the history of the school was the late Clara Hines McClusky, a Burnsville native and schoolteacher, who left to obtain an education and later returned to teach in Burnsville for several years. The schoolhouse was used as a classroom, a sanctuary for African American worship services, and later as a polling place.

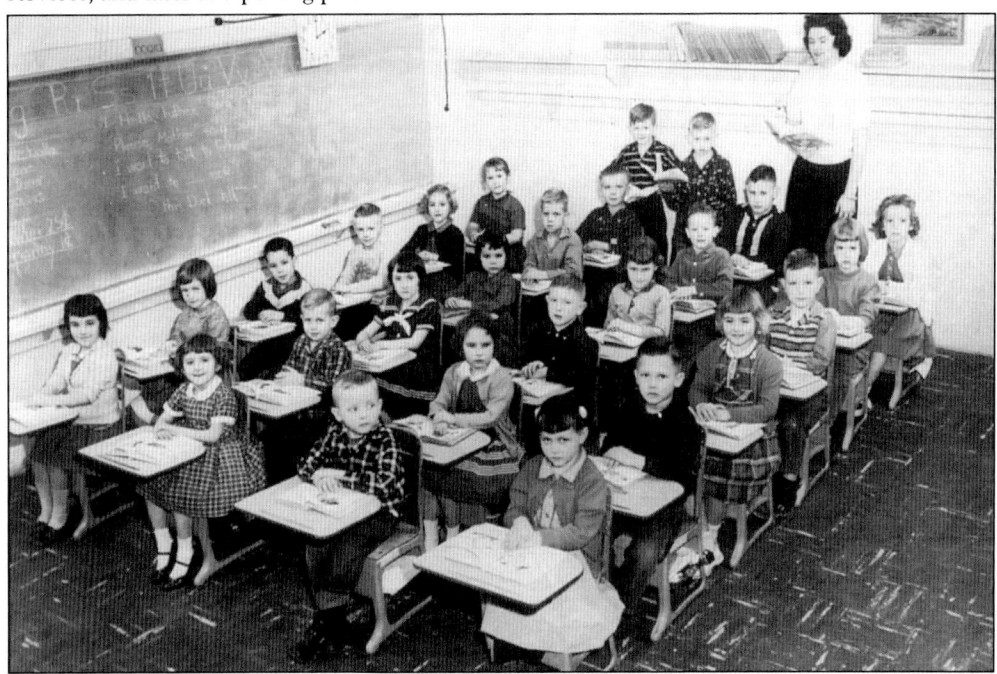

This is a photograph of the first-grade classroom of Erline Belue in the 1959–1960 school year. During the mid-1950s, the town of Burnsville, Mississippi, was "run by women." Women in the town held every office, including mayor, alderwomen, and clerk, from 1953 to 1969—a total of 16 years. Charles Skinner was the principal of Burnsville Elementary School during this time period.

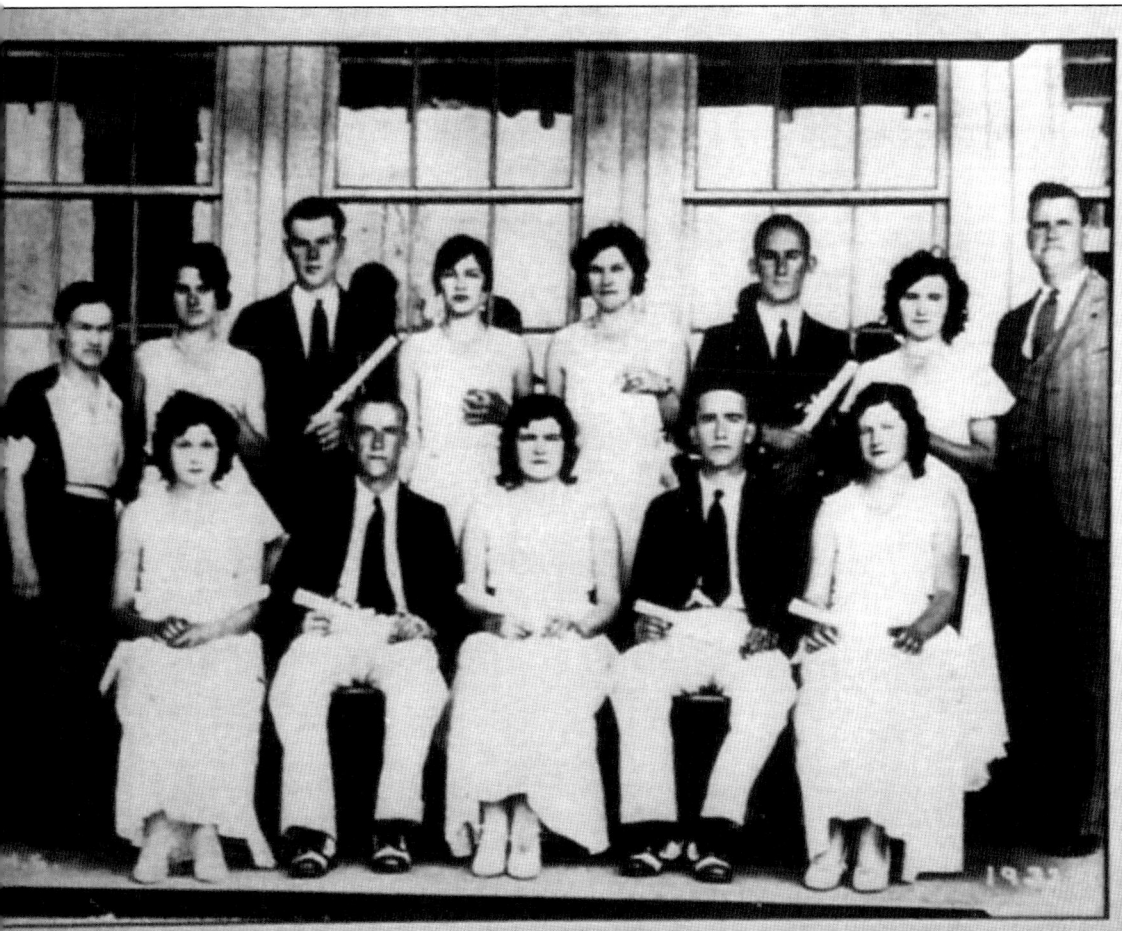

The first graduation for Burnsville High School seniors was held in 1932. Pictured from left to right are (first row) Fleeda Pyron, Floyd Marlar, Jeffie Kennedy, Cleston Scruggs, and Ruby Gober; (second row) sponsor Ruth Harrison, Lessel Pace, Alton Red Coker, Jewel Seago, Mamie Burcham, Minor R. Nixon, Zeddie Compton, and T.L. Cummings.

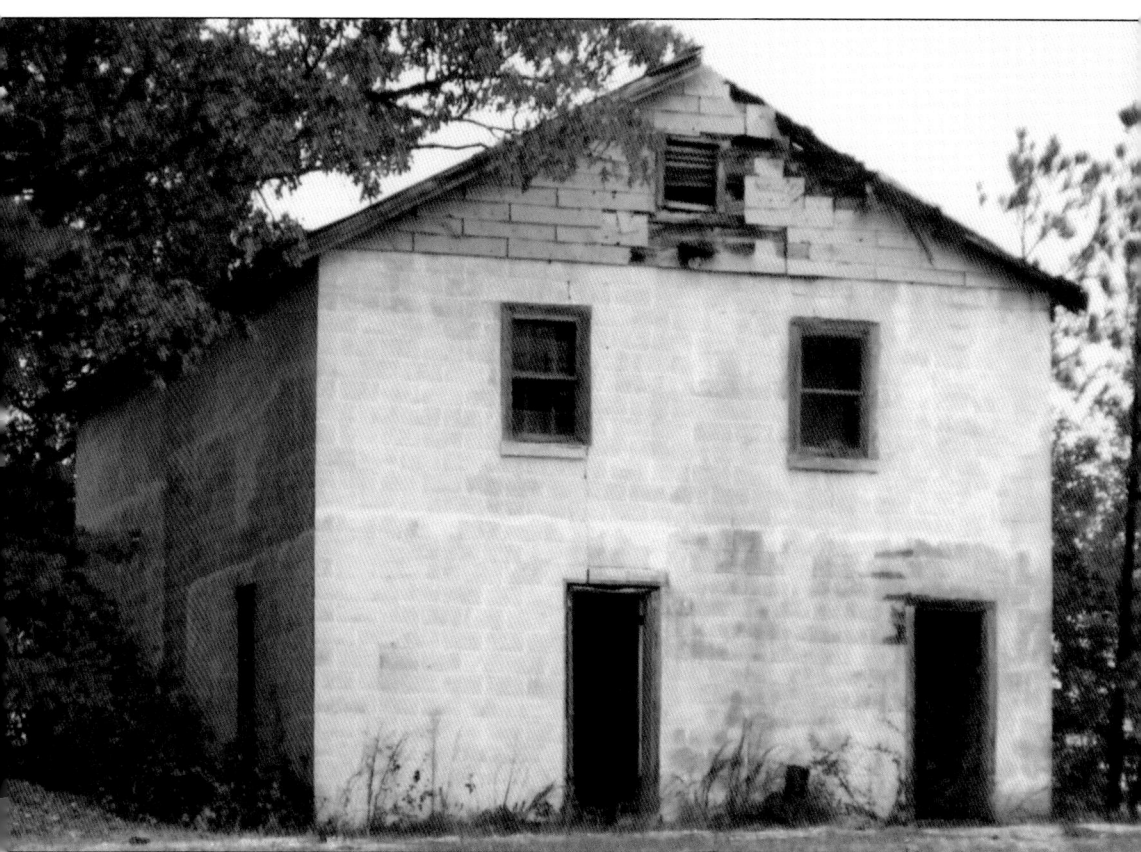

A stream of water called Carter's Branch divides the communities of Carter's Branch and Petertown. Peter Alexander was born into slavery near Nashville, Tennessee, in 1801. Emancipation gave Alexander the freedom to move across the state line into Mississippi, where he purchased land. The Carter's Branch School, constructed for the African-American community, taught grades first through eleventh. Still standing, the school is no longer in use.

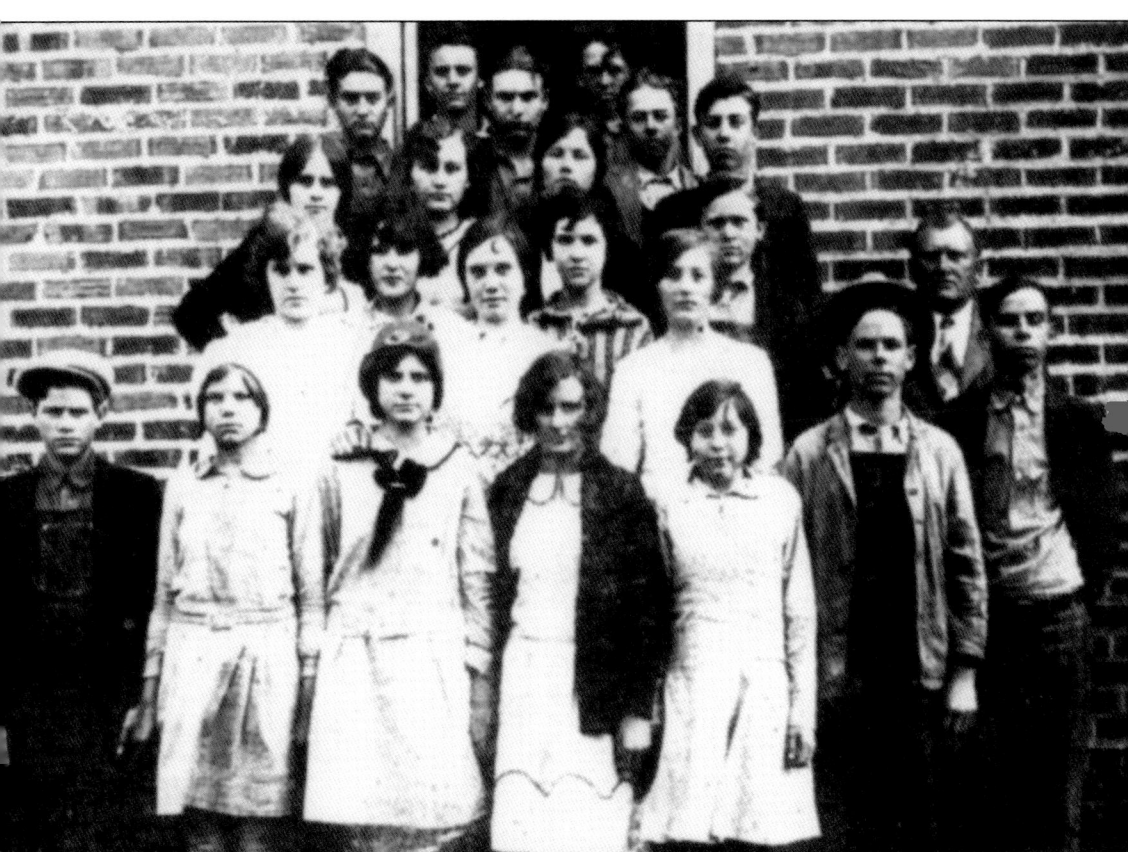

In 1927, the Helton, Patrick, and Harmony Schools consolidated into Central Consolidated School. George Bacon taught grades first through tenth the first two years. Later, Bethel, Hubbard Salem and Walker Cut-Off Schools consolidated with Central. Pictured here are students in A.B. Adams's seventh- and eighth-grade classes in 1930.

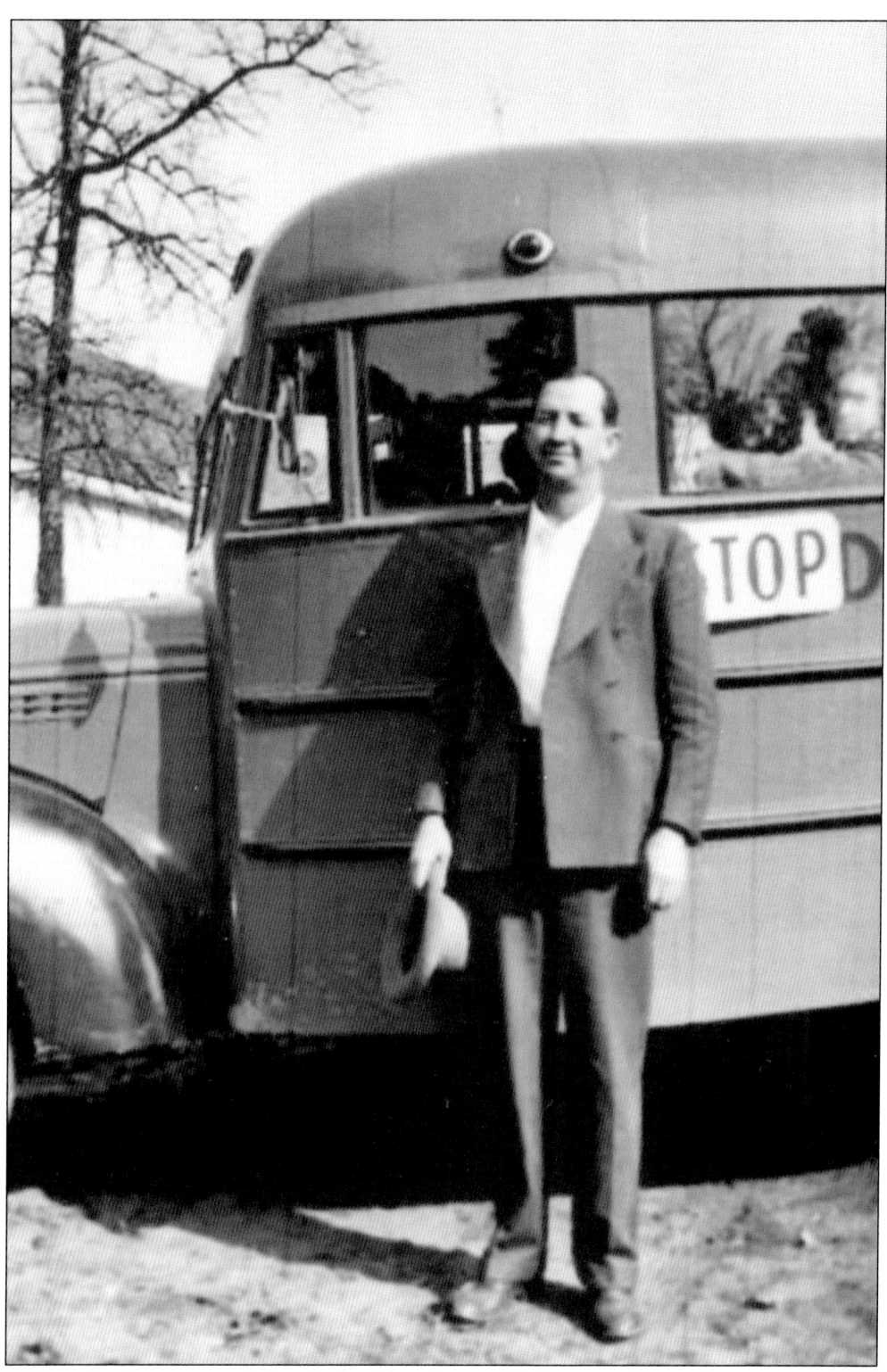
Wallace Anglin was a much-loved school bus driver in Tishomingo County for many years.

This was taken during the 1944–1945 school year of Cripple Deer School. Only some of the children are identified; they are (first row) Clifford Cox, Shirley Ann Page (Wilson), Raymond Cox, and James Ray Page; (second row) Jeanette Trimm (Carr), J. T. Dawson, and Hilda Page (Holman). Irene Bridges taught at this school the year before her marriage. (Courtesy of Irene [Bridges] Nunley.)

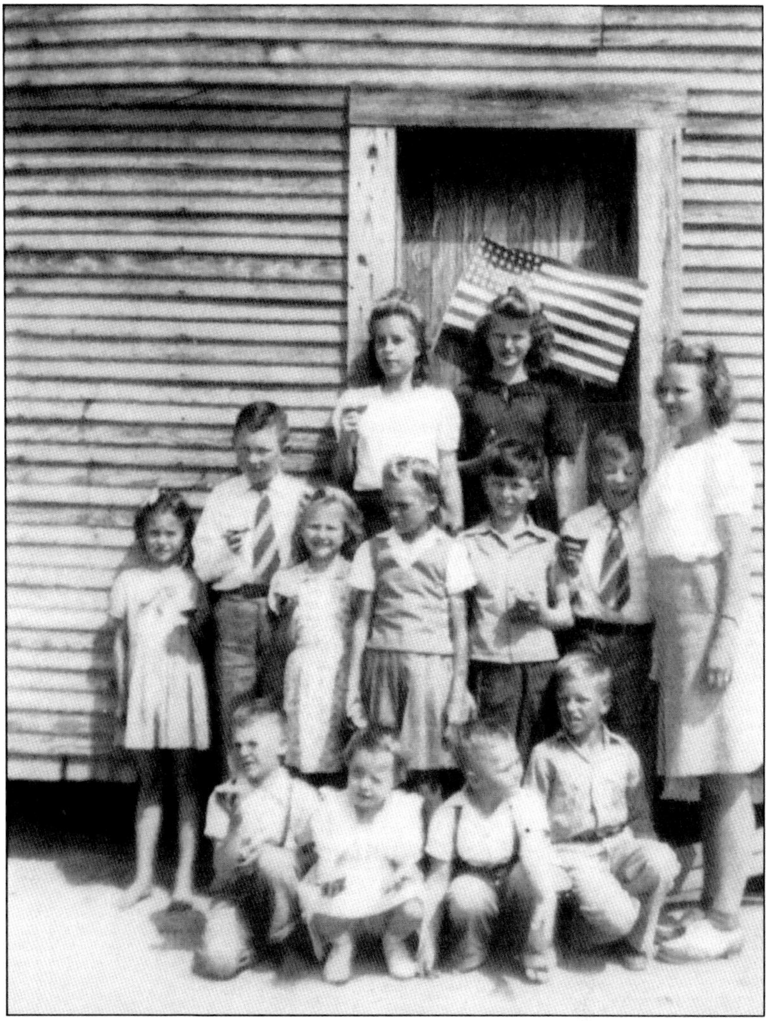

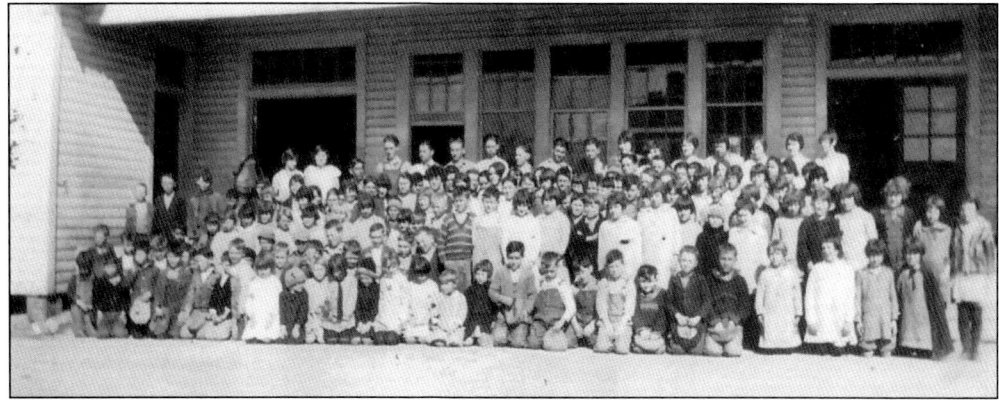

The small community of Dennis was named in honor of the New Providence Church's pastor. In 1908, the village of Dennis, Mississippi, was officially incorporated with 130 residents. The property for a school was deeded to Dennis Methodist trustees by Willis M. and Harriet Davis in 1910. This is a picture of students and faculty taken at the Dennis School in Dennis, Mississippi, in 1921.

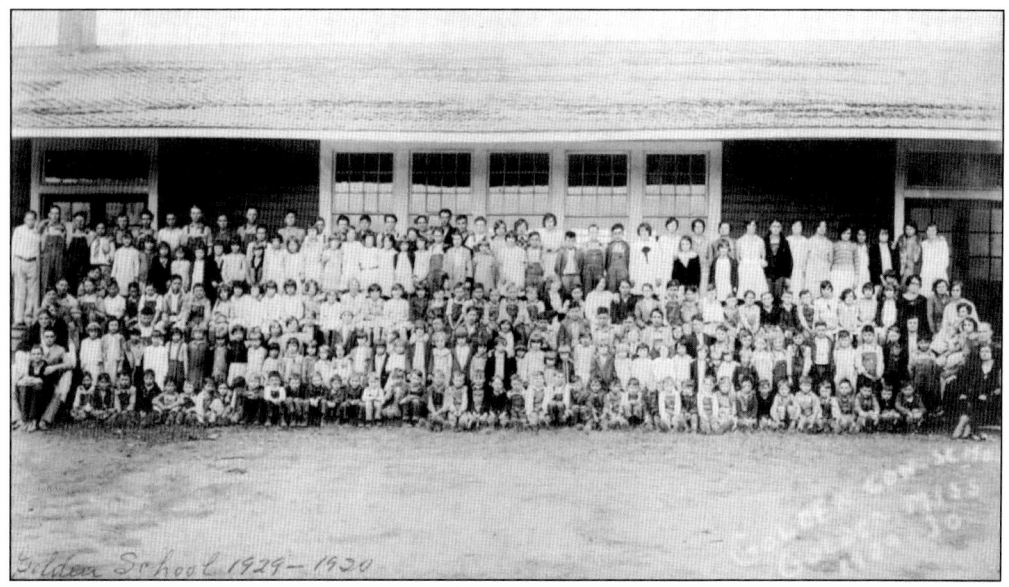

Pictured are the Golden School students for the 1929–1930 school year. Golden, Mississippi, is a small village that came to life with the building of the railroad and the opening of a large lumber mill. With the burgeoning town, a school was necessary to educate their children. Two old churches—Valley and Ebenezer—were established on this site in the early history of the area. School was first held in at least one of these churches before this schoolhouse was erected.

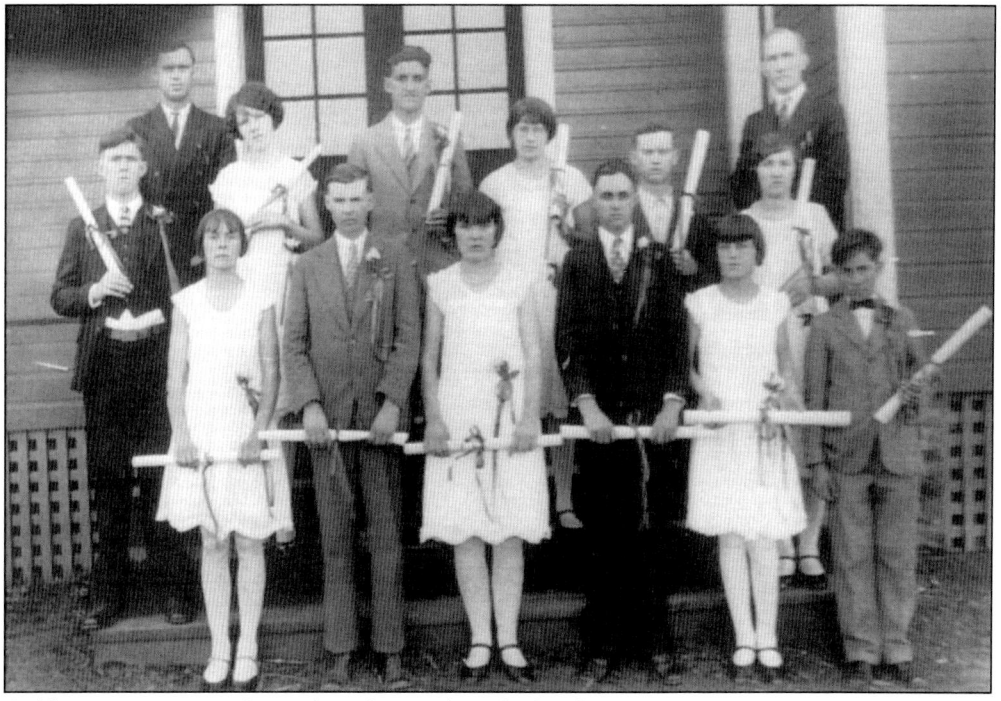

Golden, Mississippi, is located in the south end of Tishomingo County, Mississippi. This is a photograph of students and faculty in the 1927–1928 class of the Golden School. Located third from left is Dr. Raymond Shook, and adjacent to him and wearing glasses is Twilla Smith. The other students are unidentified. (Courtesy of Sharon Embrey.)

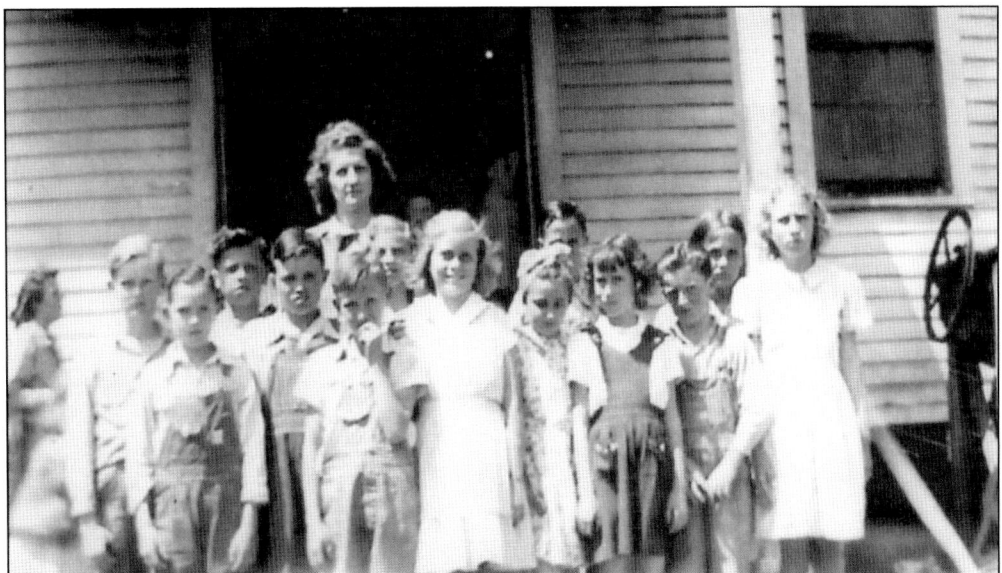

Pictured is the third-, fourth-, and fifth-grade classes of the Gravel Hill School in Tishomingo County, Mississippi. This school taught students in grades first through eighth. If more education was desired, a student needed to transfer to a secondary school. During this 1938–1939 school term, the schoolteacher was Irene (Bridges) Nunley.

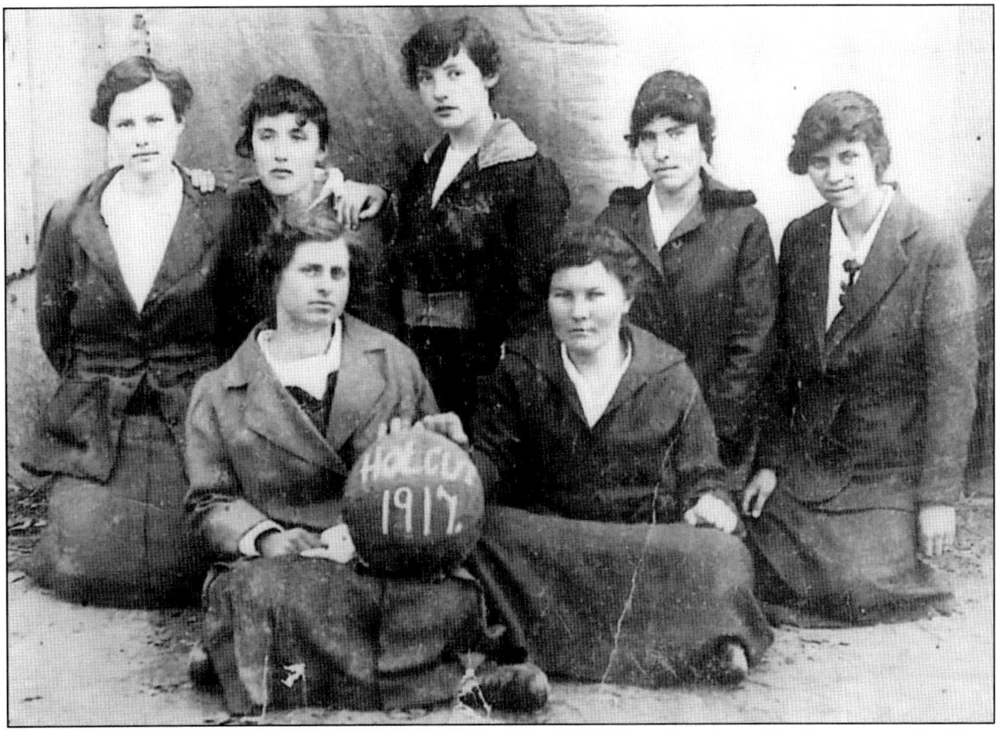

Pictured is the Holcut School girls' basketball team in 1917. The school was first known as the New Lebanon School and later the Nixon School. Then, in the mid-1910s, the school was moved a half mile west of the village of Holcut on Highway 30. It remained there until 1929. V.B. Smith was the first teacher and J.A. Lambert, Tommie Strickland, and Jim Claunch were the first trustees.

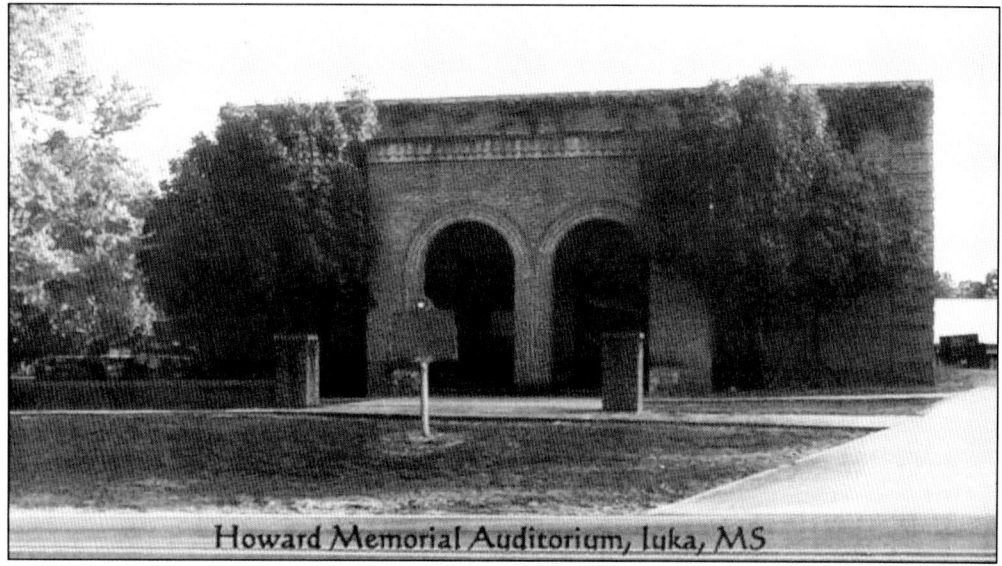

The Howard Memorial Auditorium was built on the campus of the Iuka High School in Iuka, Mississippi, to accommodate various performances and meetings. It was torn down in 2010 to construct a more modern facility. At that time, various items of interest such as photographs and some old desks found in the attic were donated to the Tishomingo County Archives & History Museum.

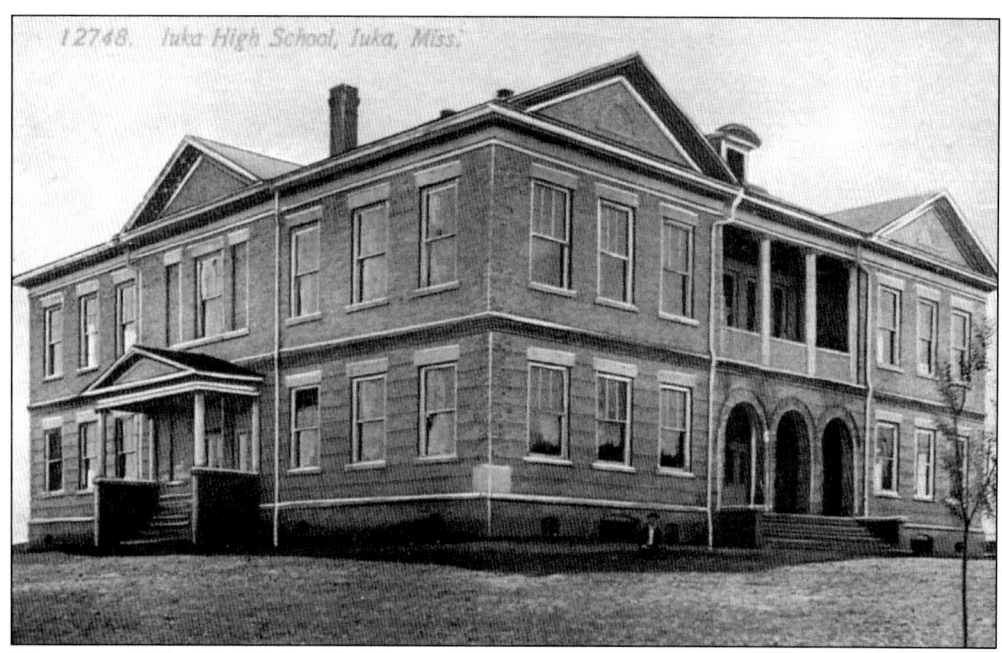

The original Iuka High School building was erected in 1909. Built with buff brick in a Colonial style, it was a steam-heated, modern building with large classrooms, music rooms, an office, library, and spacious auditorium. Later, a fully equipped laboratory for physics and biology was added. By 1923, the school held 12 grades. This building has been torn down.

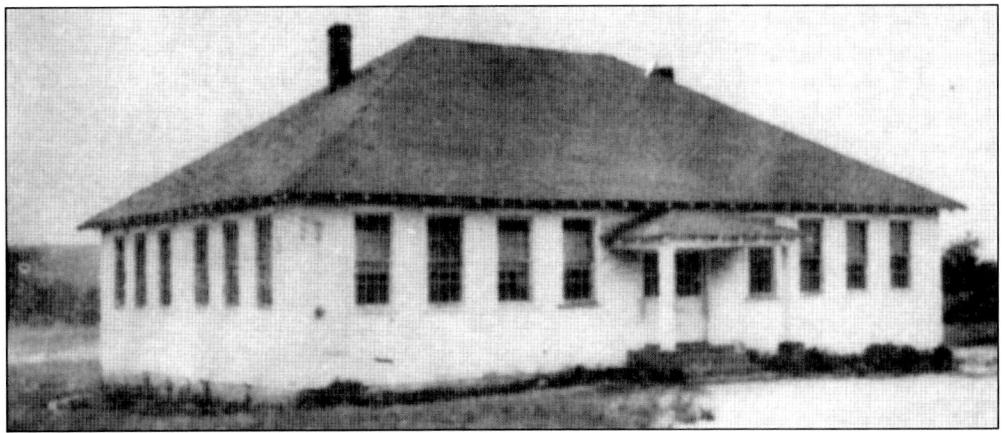

The Holloway School was a three-teacher school near Burnsville, Mississippi, that taught grades first through eighth. The school had a dirt ball court and an occasional box supper. It was part of the consolidation program that included Gravel Hill School, Pleasant Ridge School, Lambert Chapel School, Crossroads School, and the Mulberry School.

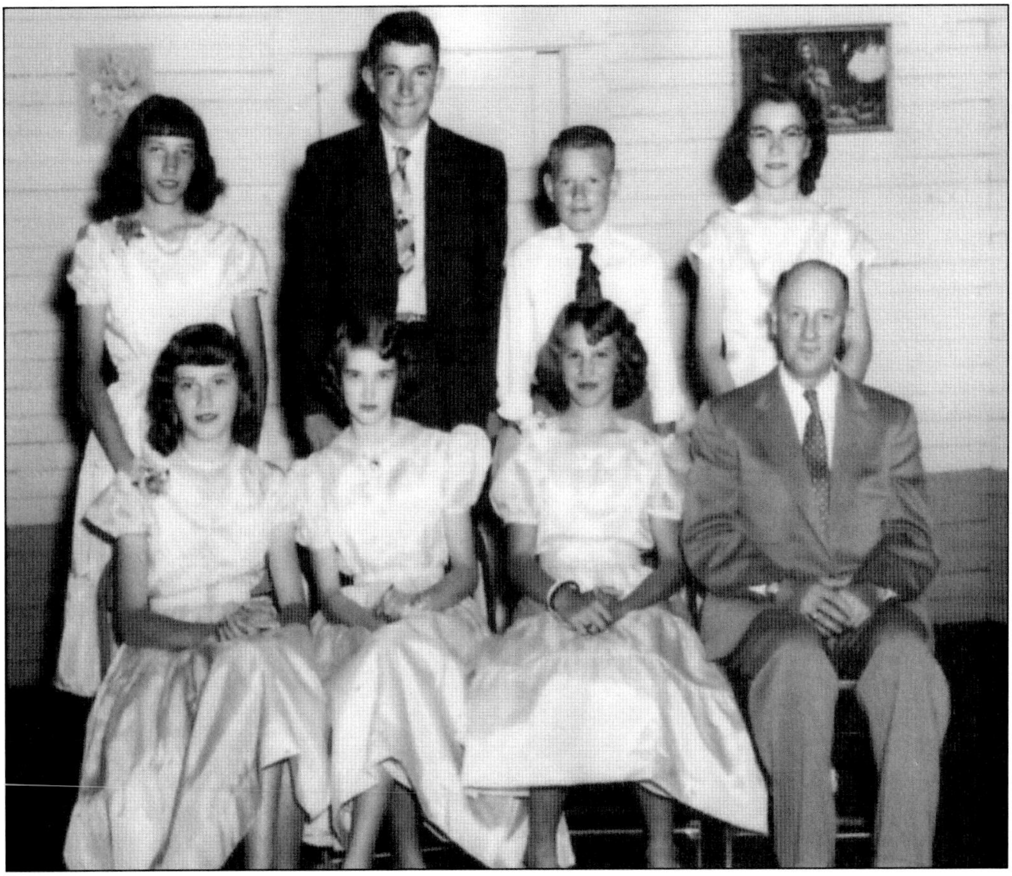

Pictured here are students at the Holloway School graduating from the eighth grade in 1955. They are, from left to right, (first row) Pauline (Johnson) Woods, Shirley (Johnson) Rhodes, Geraldine Whitaker, and principal A.B. Marlar; (second row) Doris Johnson Curtis, Tommy Laird, J.T. Blakney, and Lonie Wilkins. (Courtesy of James Thomas Blakney.)

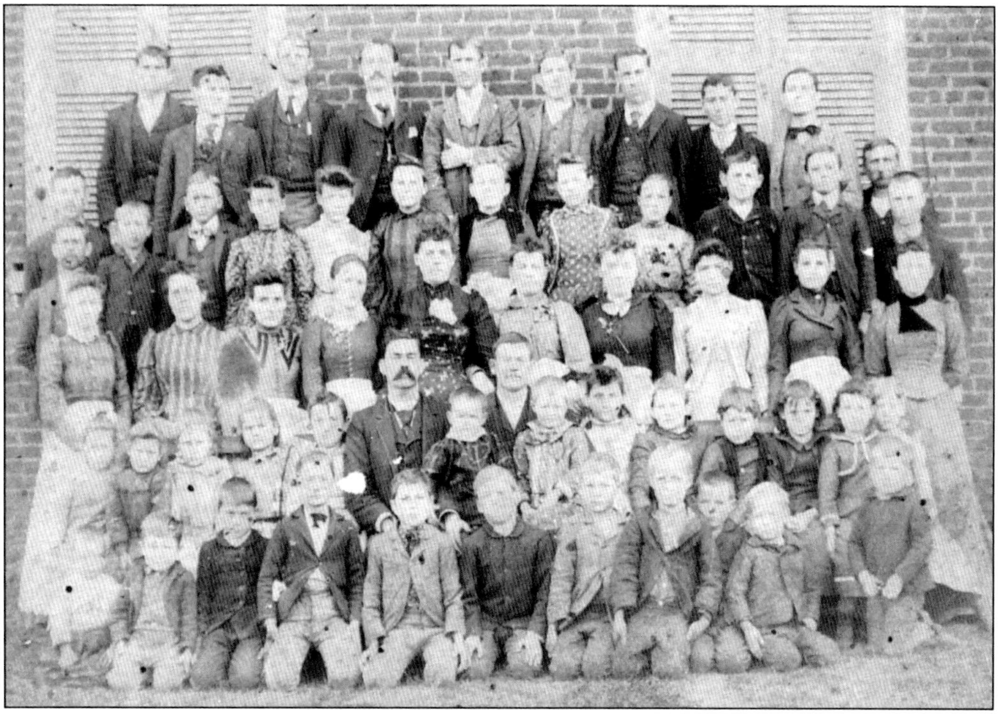

In 1836, Tishomingo County was established with a county seat named Cincinnati. A few weeks later, the town's name was changed to Jacinto in honor of the Battle of San Jacinto, which avenged the Alamo in Texas. Pictured is a group of students at the Jacinto School. Handwritten on the back of this photograph is "March 30, 1895, Jacinto, Miss." (Courtesy of Mary Ellen Ahlstrom.)

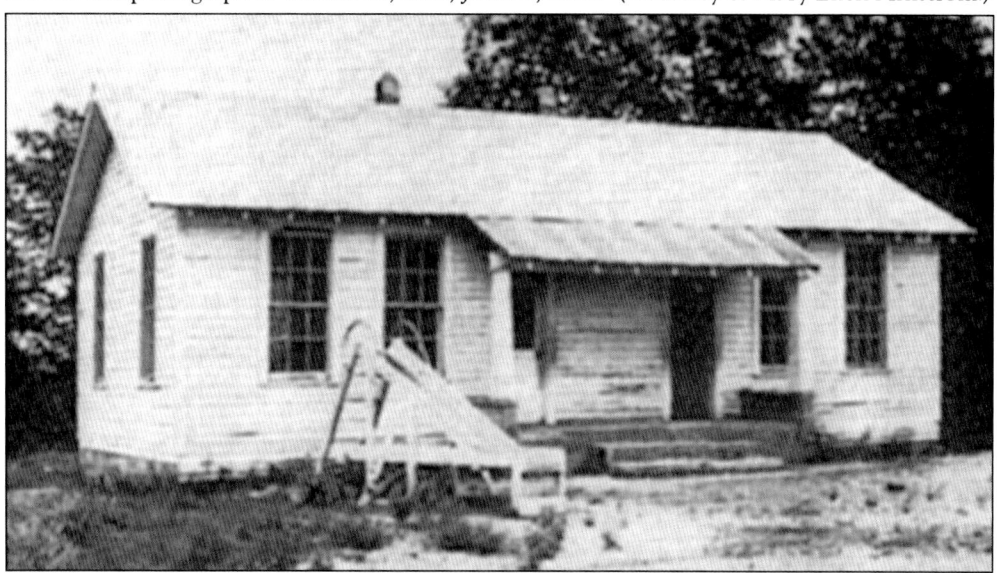

Lambert Chapel School was a small two-room schoolhouse located 1.5 miles from Burnsville, Mississippi, on the Doskie Road. This school existed as far back as the 1850s. Children attended the school from a 6-to-10 mile radius. They traveled by foot, horseback, or any other available means of transportation. James Clyde Lambert helped establish the little school. Grades first through eighth were taught here. The school no longer stands.

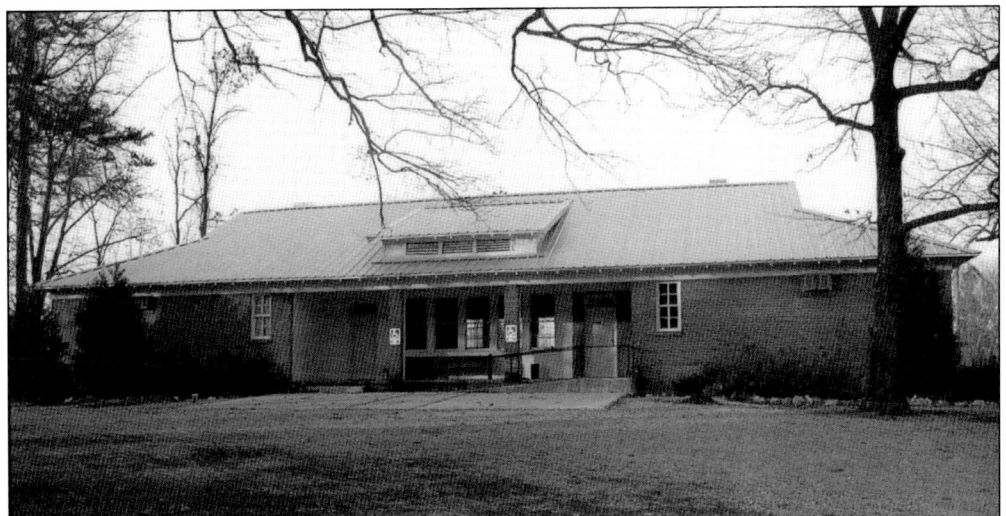

The Midway Consolidated School District was organized on July 15, 1925. It included the Spring Hill and Prospect Schools and a part of Pleasant Hill, New Salem, and Liberty School Districts. Midway School continued as a two-year high school until 1932, when it taught elementary classes only. The faculty members in 1940 were Principal J.V. Hendrix, Cleo Moore, and Ernestine Frederick.

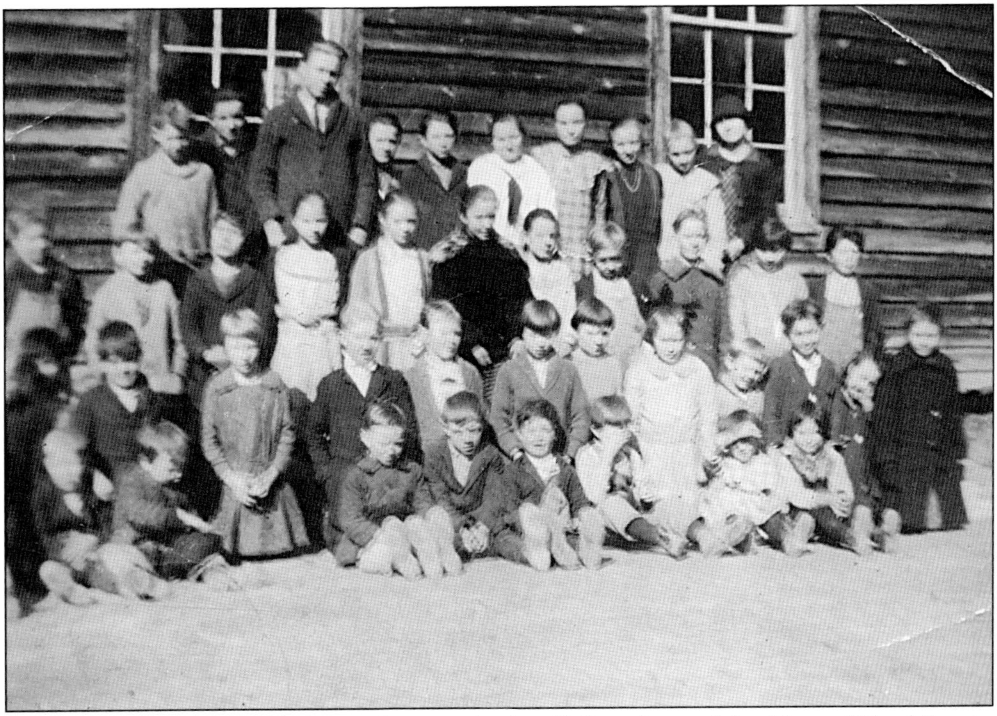

Students and faculty members are photographed in 1920 in front of the Mount Gilead Baptist Church. Classes were held at the church. According to church records, a school existed at the church before Tishomingo County was divided into three distinct counties. The church was organized in 1844. (Courtesy of Truman Barnett.)

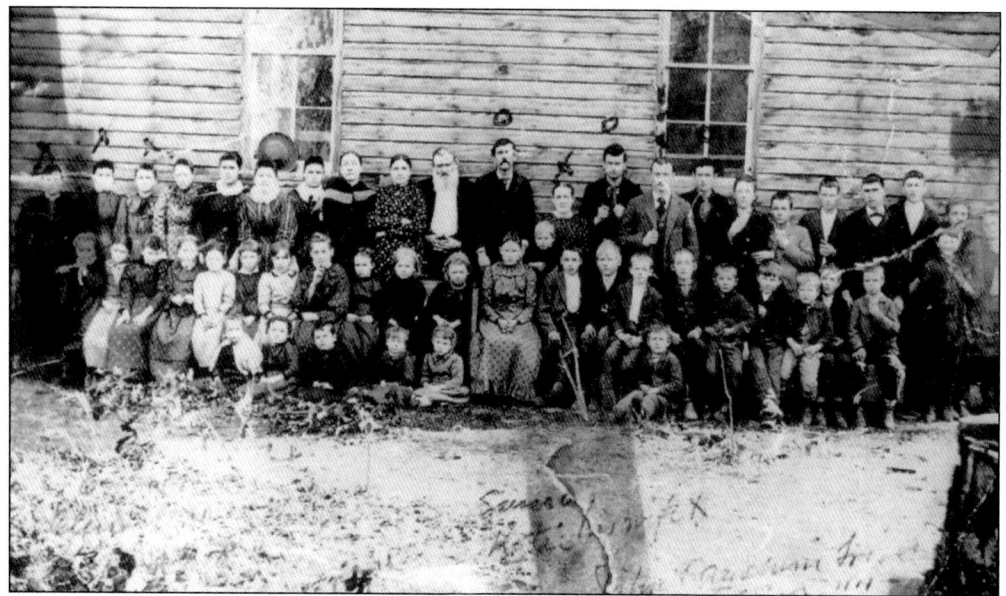

Pictured is school being held in 1896 at the Mount Pleasant Church west of Tishomingo. Students identified in this photograph have the following surnames: Bartnell, Britnell, Butler, Flurry, Hill, McRae, Pitts, Smith, Reno, Reynolds, Trim, Ward, Wigginton, Williams, and Wilson.

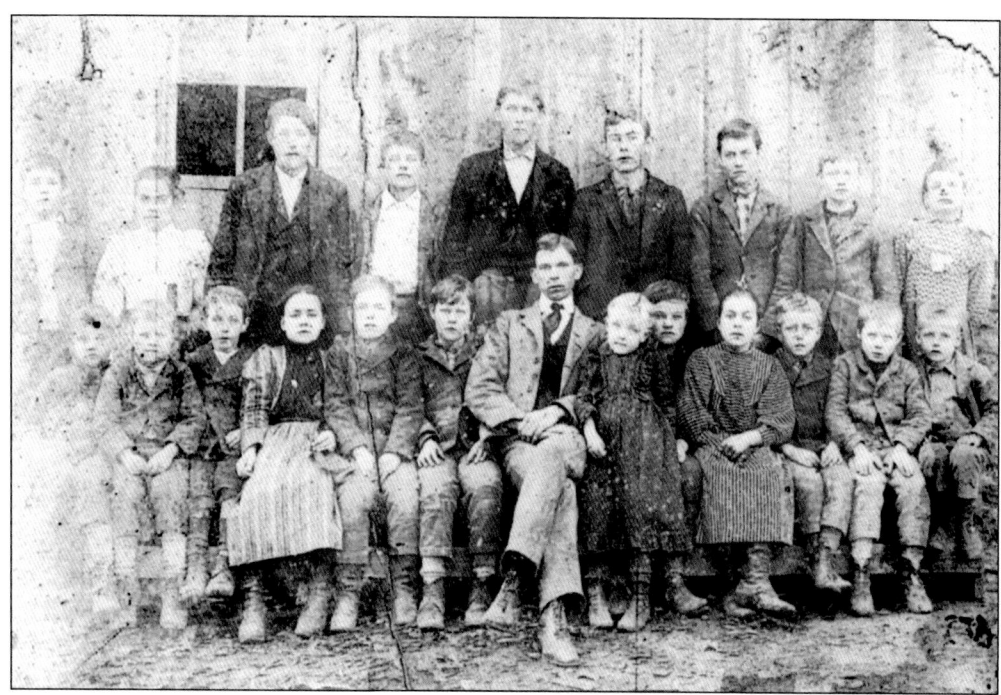

Pictured are students and a faculty member of the Mulberry School in Tishomingo County, Mississippi. The teacher of this class was Arthur Moser, and one of the students was Kendrick Honeycutt. The date of this school year is unknown. The Mulberry School was eventually consolidated with other schools near Burnsville, Mississippi.

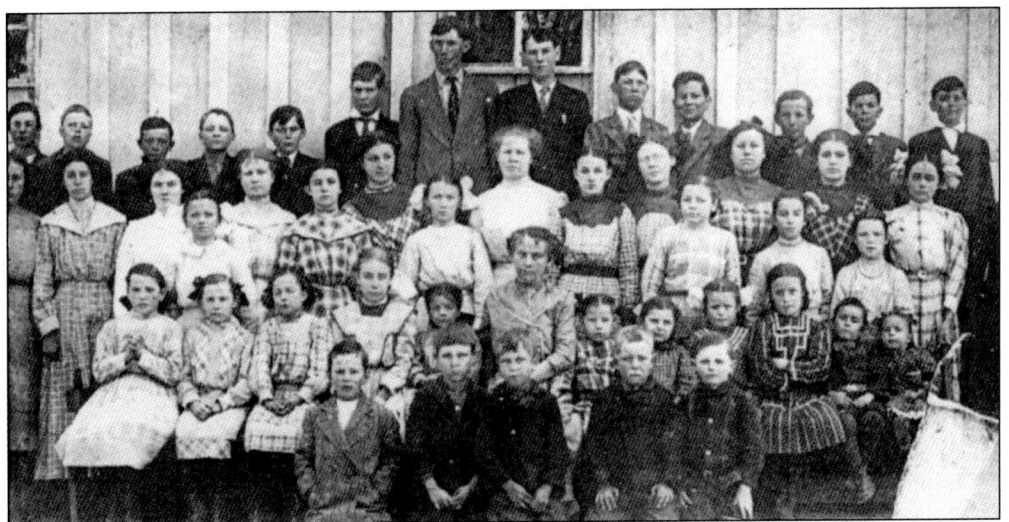

The Oak Ridge School was located in Tishomingo County about three miles west of Iuka near Walker's Switch. This picture of students and faculty was taken about 1913 or 1914. Surnames of students pictured include Adams, Bonds, Davis, Glenn, Hale, Hill, Music, Riley, Seago, Skinner, Taylor, and Woodley.

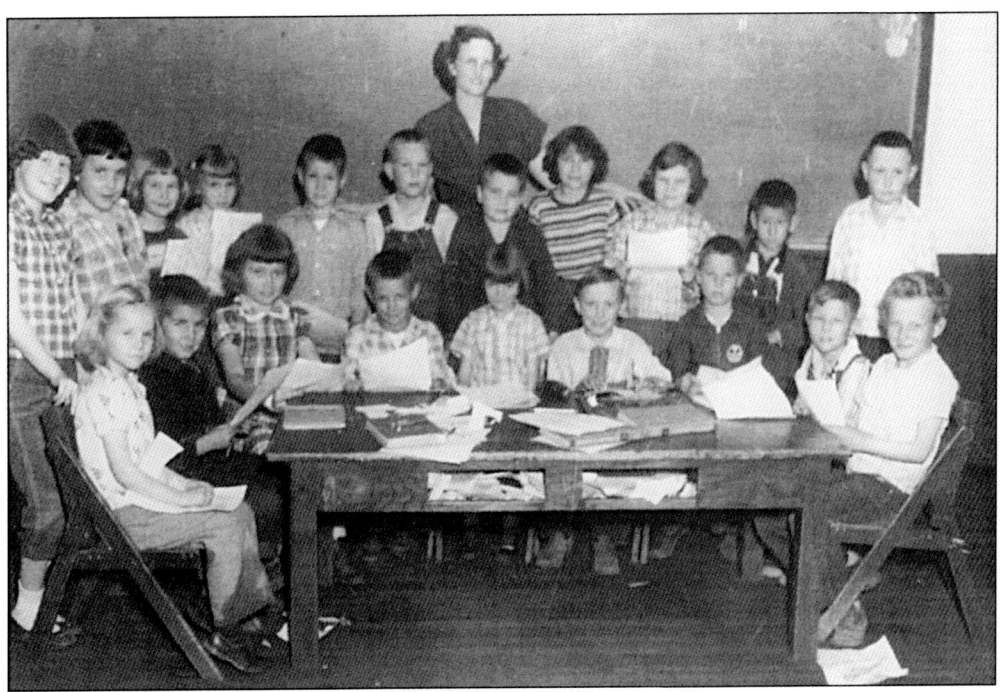

In the late 18th century, the Illinois Central Railroad was built. At that time, the town of Burnt Mills was moved 1.5 miles north, and the name of the small town was changed to Paden in honor of Dr. Tom Paden. Pictured is the first through the third grades at the Paden School. (Courtesy of Ruth Dawson.)

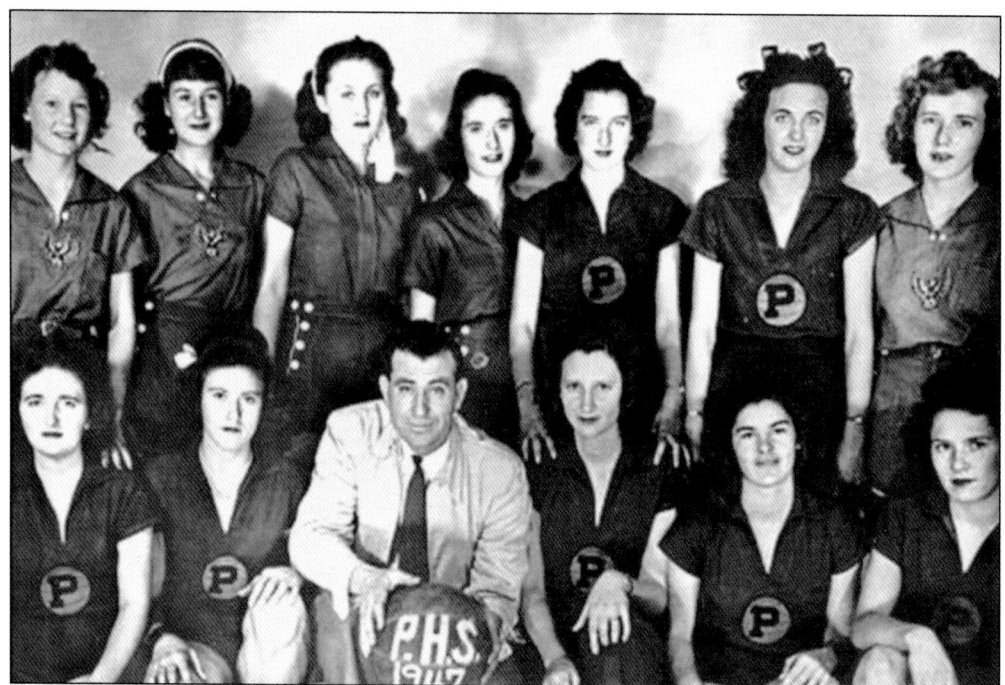

Pictured is the 1947 girls' basketball team of Paden High School. Coach Alver Belue holds the basketball. The girls are, from left to right, (first row) Annie Ruth Florence, Connie Jean McNutt, Coach Alver Belue, Mary Sue McDougal, Geneva Hinton, and Ruth Merrill; (second row) Ouida Weathers, Helen Jane Hill, Sandra Bullock, Helen Ruth Medley, Freida Holley, Louise Green, and Jean Deaton. Shirley Young, also on the basketball team, is not in this photograph.

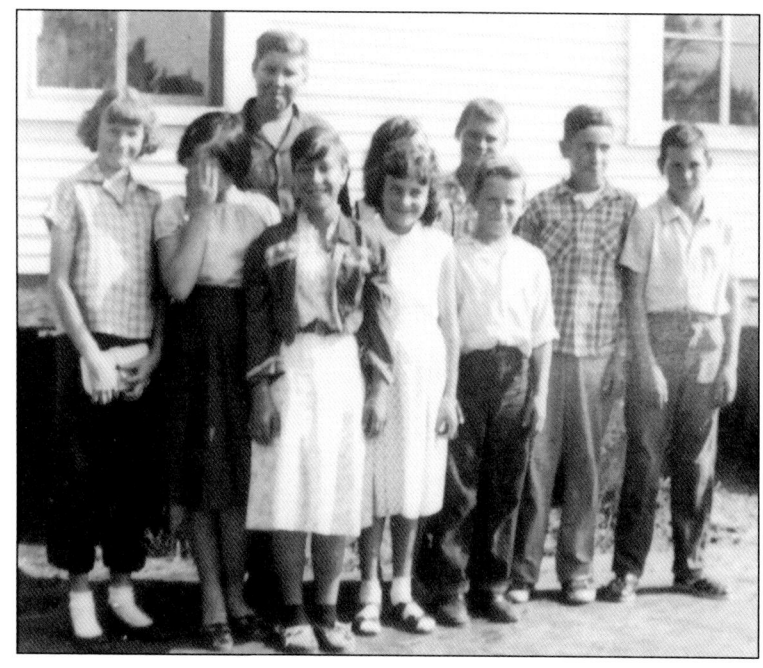

In 1955, students pose outside of the Pleasant Hill School in Tishomingo County, Mississippi. Pictured from left to right are (first row) Peggy Floyd, unidentified, Annette Barrett, Linda Ham, and Austin Moore; (second row) Calvin Hayes, unidentified, Will Hayes, Aaron Bonds, and Leon Barrett.

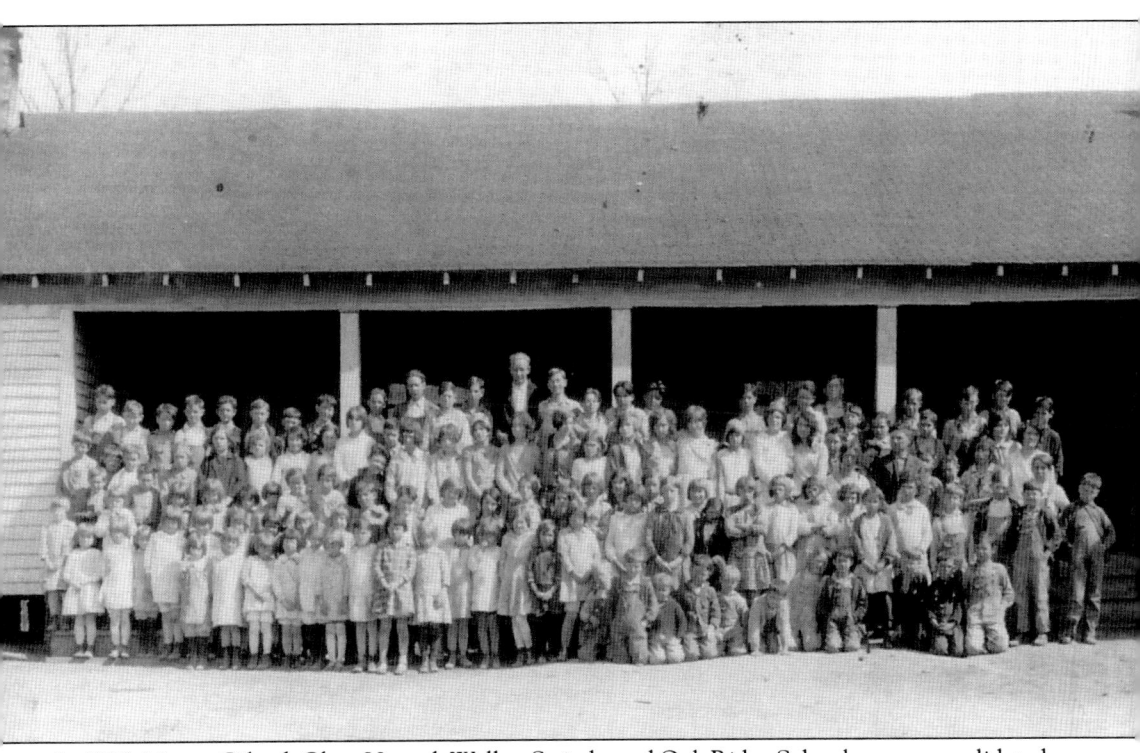

In 1925, Mount Gilead, Glen, Hazard, Walker Switch, and Oak Ridge Schools were consolidated into the Pleasant Ridge School, located near the old Mount Gilead School. Surnames of some students pictured here are Bishop, Bonds, Cummings, Daniels, Davis, Grimes, Haney, Honeycutt, Johnson, Kingham, Lovelace, Loveless, Moore, Rhodes, Scruggs, Thornburg, Tigner, White, and Vandiver. Clara Bingham was the teacher. (Courtesy of Bobby Nelson.)

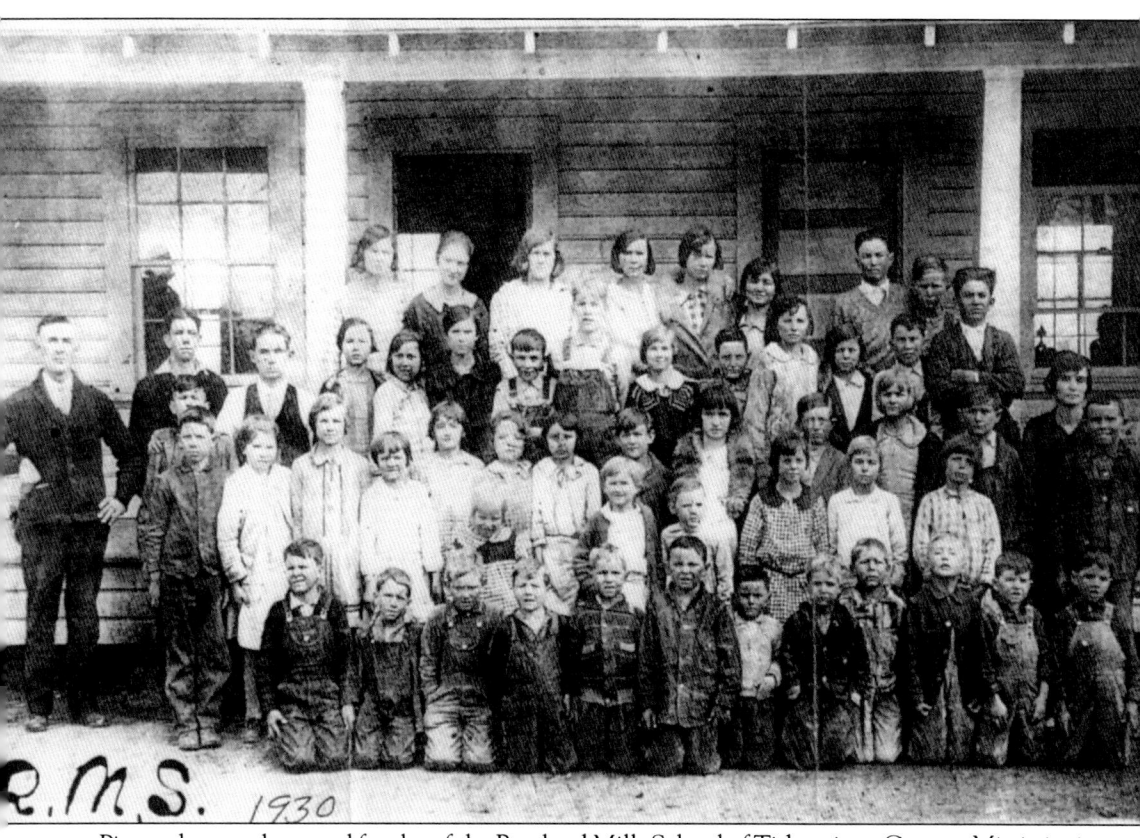

Pictured are students and faculty of the Rowland Mills School of Tishomingo County, Mississippi, in 1930. Surnames of these students are Barnes, Bobo, Bray, Burcham, Castleberry, Clay, Defore, Elliott, Epperson, Hale, Hatcher, Langrum, Ledgewood, McNatt, Newcomb, Ross, Stricklin, White, Whitfield, Woodruff, and Woodrow.

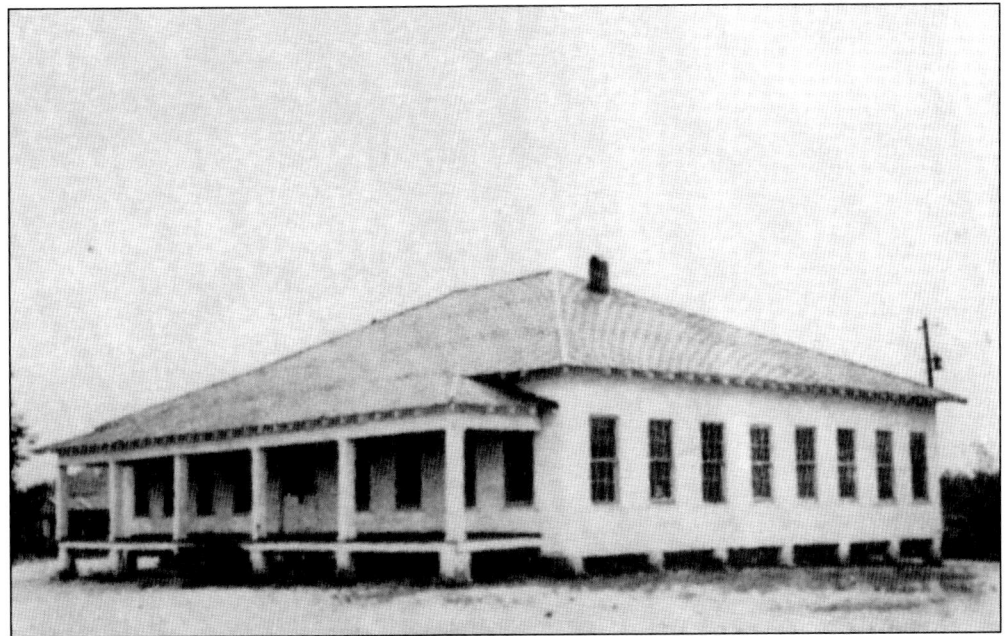

The Snowdown School, located east of Iuka, dates to 1870. Various teachers included Bill Blythe, Bill Ramsey, Wesley Cain, W.M. Hunley, Millie Thacker, Mattie Deardoff, Sallie Castleberry, Horace Long, Fayette Massey, Bob Wood, George Vaughn, Lucian Dean, Leatha Moore, Jess Bennett, Willard Mosley, Blanche Patterson, Dosha Whitehurst, Willard Mosley, Ella Gardner, Christine Haines, Letha Sanders, and Vera Gardner. The Snowdown School and Clear Creek School were consolidated in 1922.

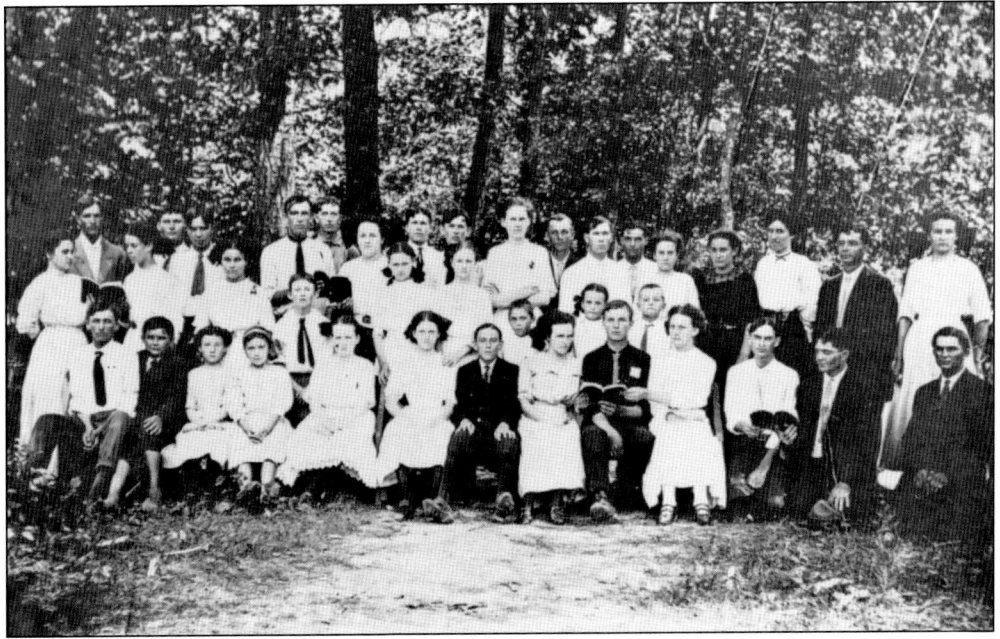

In October 1904, R.L. Wimbish and his wife, Cora, deeded approximately one acre of land, upon which stood a schoolhouse built by G.F. Robinson. From that day forward, it was known as the Spring Hill School.

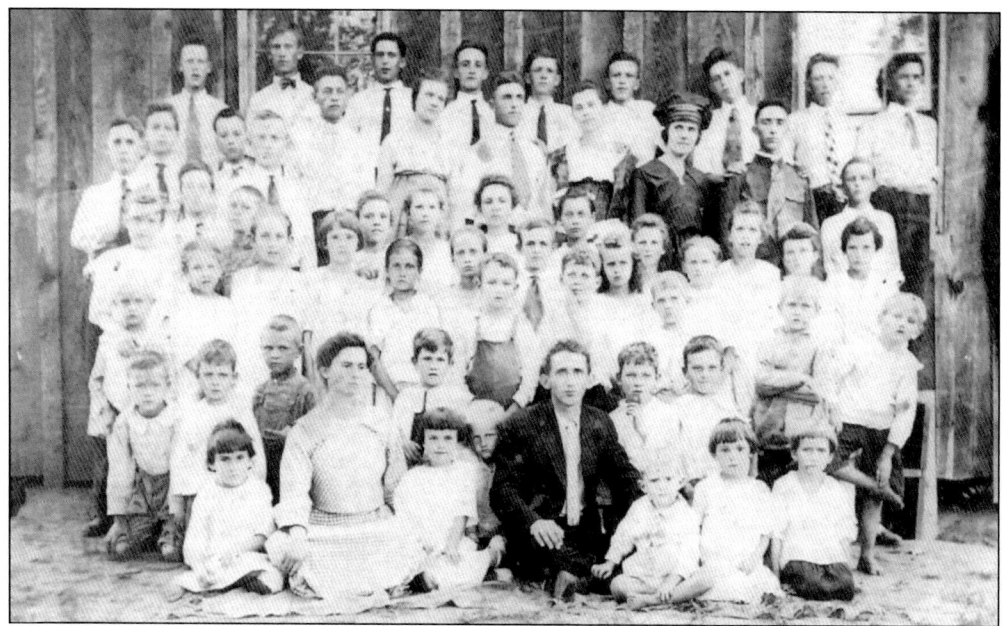

The school built in the community in which Josiah Stephens lived was called Stephens Arbor. It was located several miles below Paden. Josiah died around the time the schoolhouse was established; however, his children were among the students. One teacher who is remembered to this day is Thomas J. Webb. He taught at Stephens Arbor for a number of years. This picture of students was taken in the early 1920s.

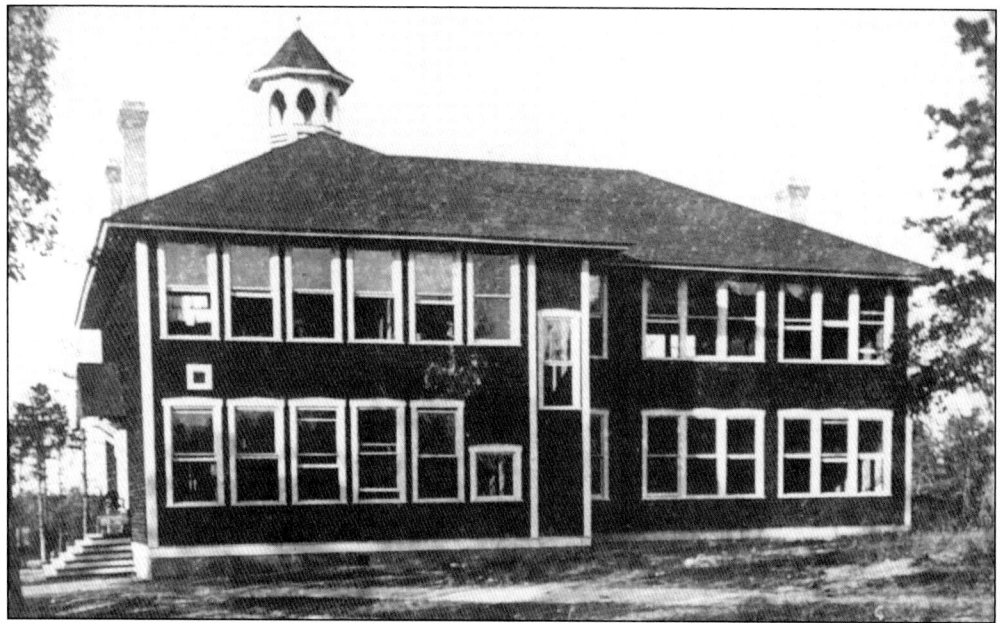

The Tishomingo County Agricultural High School, located at Tishomingo, Mississippi, was 14 miles south of Iuka and 27 miles southeast of Corinth. The beautiful campus had three main buildings. The administration building shown here was built about 1914 in the most up-to-date fashion and was well equipped with modern school furniture. It contained six classrooms and a large auditorium.

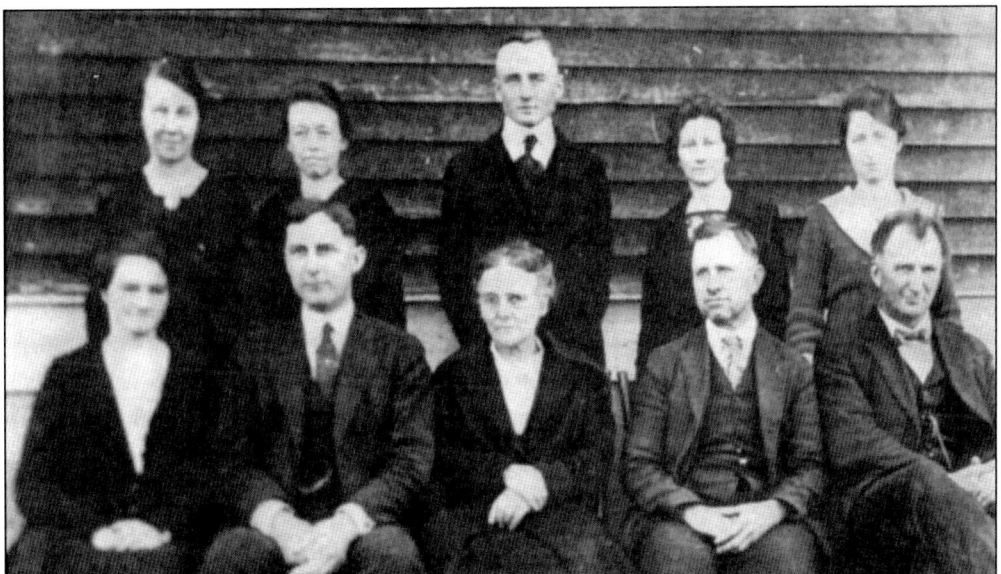

This is a photograph of faculty members at the Tishomingo County Agricultural High School (TCAHS). From left to right are (first row) Mrs. W.R. Nettles, intermediate; William R. Nettles, school superintendent; Anne Holley, assistant matron; Ward Glasgow, principal; and Horace C. Long, math teacher; (second row) Annie Mae Wren, primary teacher; Rosa Lee White, English teacher; L.G. Plyler, agriculture teacher; Mamie Vinzant, home economics teacher; and Allene Gillentine, music teacher.

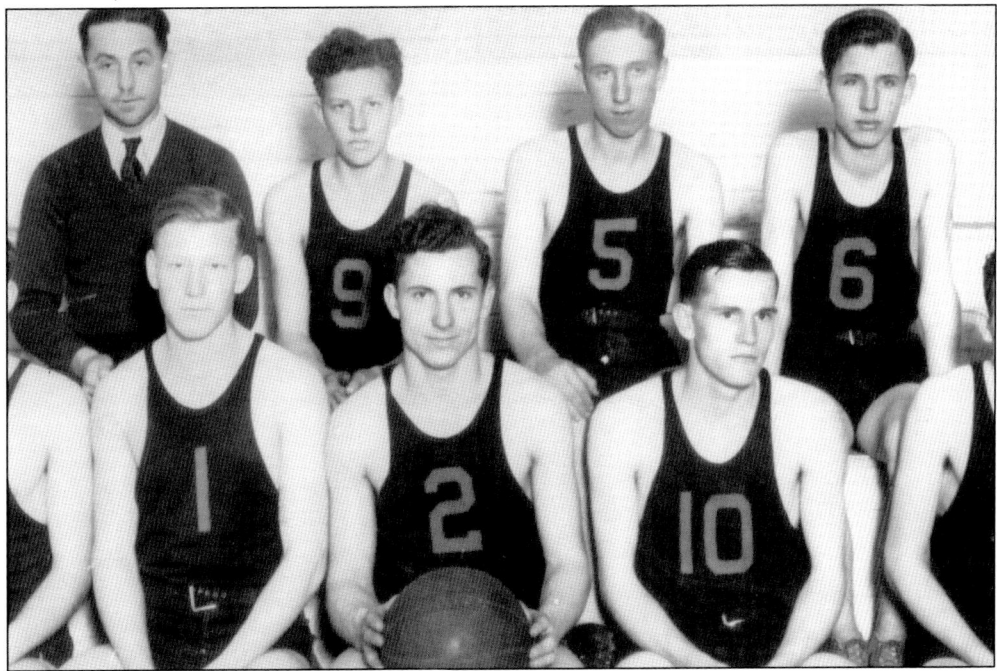

The Tishomingo County Agricultural High School in Tishomingo, Mississippi, prided itself on its boys' basketball team in 1936. Pictured from left to right are (first row) William Nagle, Harold McRae, Carl McClung, Leon Blunt, and Noonan McClung; (second row) L.D. Edwards, Harmon Smith, Bill Southward, and Claude Crow Jr. (Courtesy of W.R. Nettles Jr.)

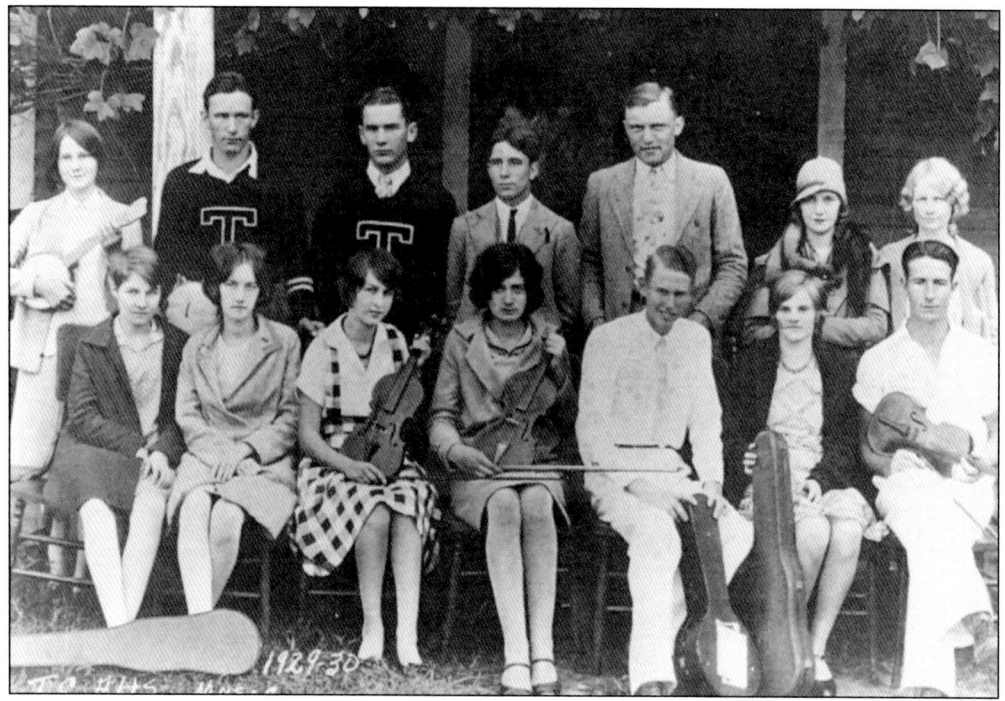

This is a photograph of the members of the music club at the Tishomingo County Agricultural High School of Tishomingo, Mississippi, during the 1929–1930 school year. Pictured from left to right are (first row) Ruth Davis, Mary Blissitt, Lorena Nash, Cletus Loveless, Gadi Timbes, Lucille Pace, and Hubert Wade; (second row) Lorena Oaks, J. Orville "Click" Clark, Earl Holder, Scott Brackeens, Ezra "Bilbo" Bullard, Vivian Davis, and Mary Oaks.

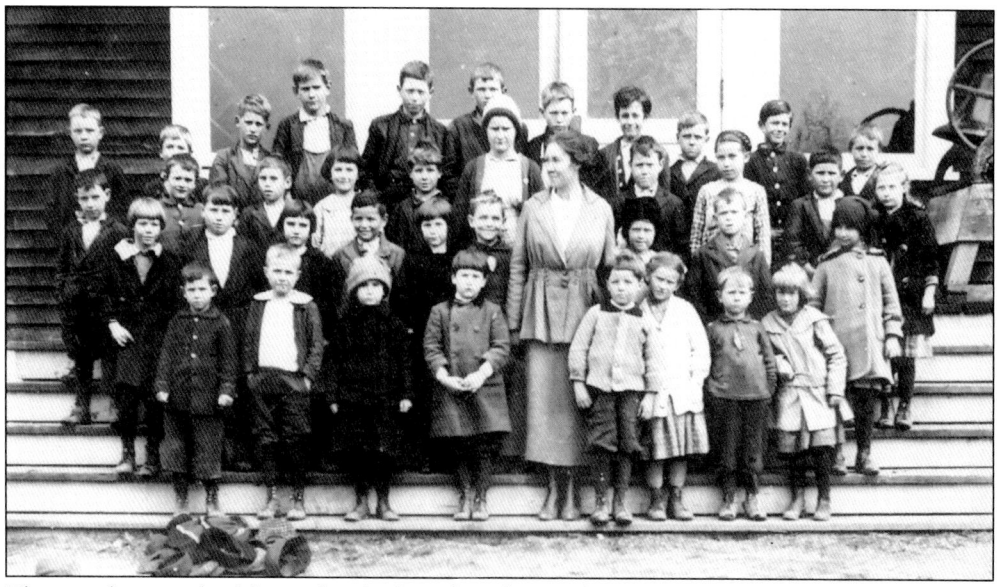

This is a photograph of the student body and teacher in about 1920 for the Tishomingo Grammar School of Tishomingo, Mississippi. The grammar school's classroom was housed in the administration building of the Tishomingo County Agricultural High School for several years after a 1913 tornado leveled the school building in town. The teacher's name is Annie Mae Wren.

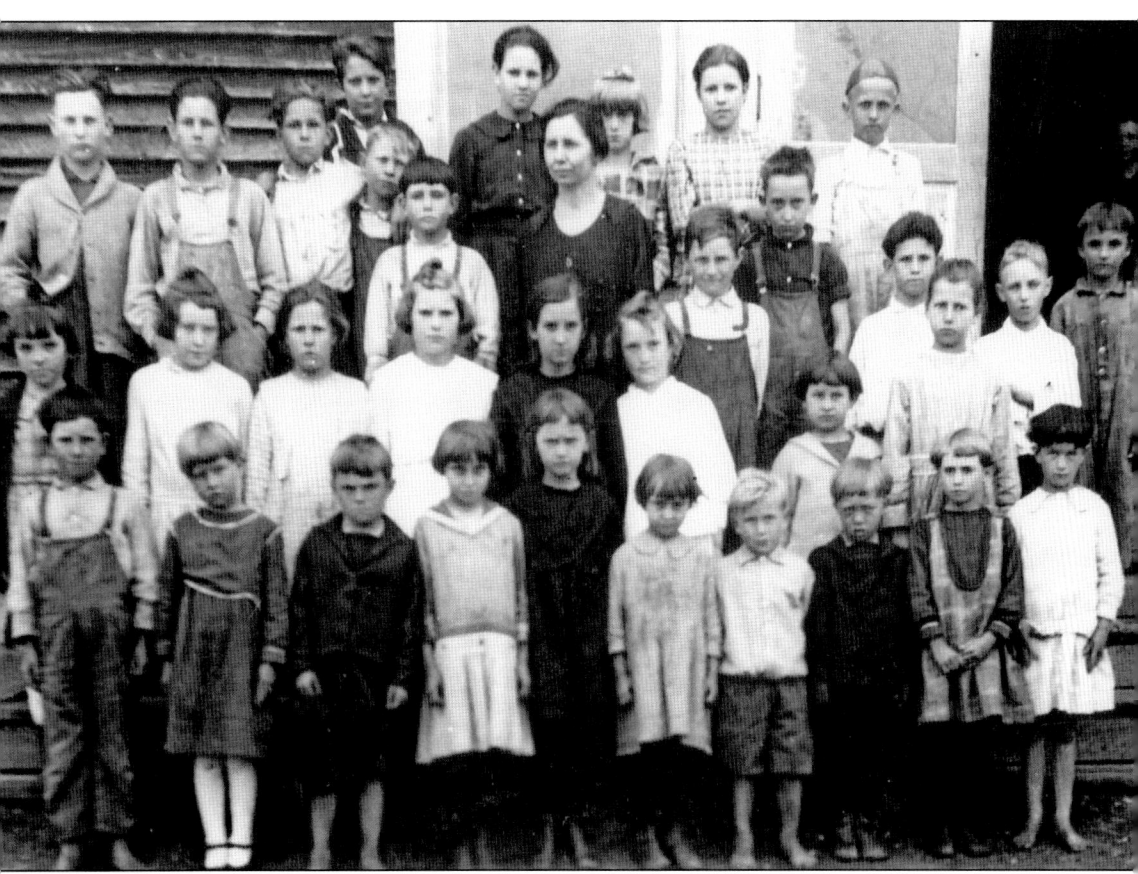

Pictured are students of the Tishomingo Grammar School in about 1921. Surnames of students include Bazzel, Bickerstaff, Blissitt, Blunt, Browning, Carr, Deaton, Finch, Flurry, Gardner, Gray, Hester, King, Long, McAnally, McRae, Nelson, Owens, Pace, Rhodes, Monroe, Ramsey, Storment, Tumlin, and Wren. Mamie Burney was the teacher.

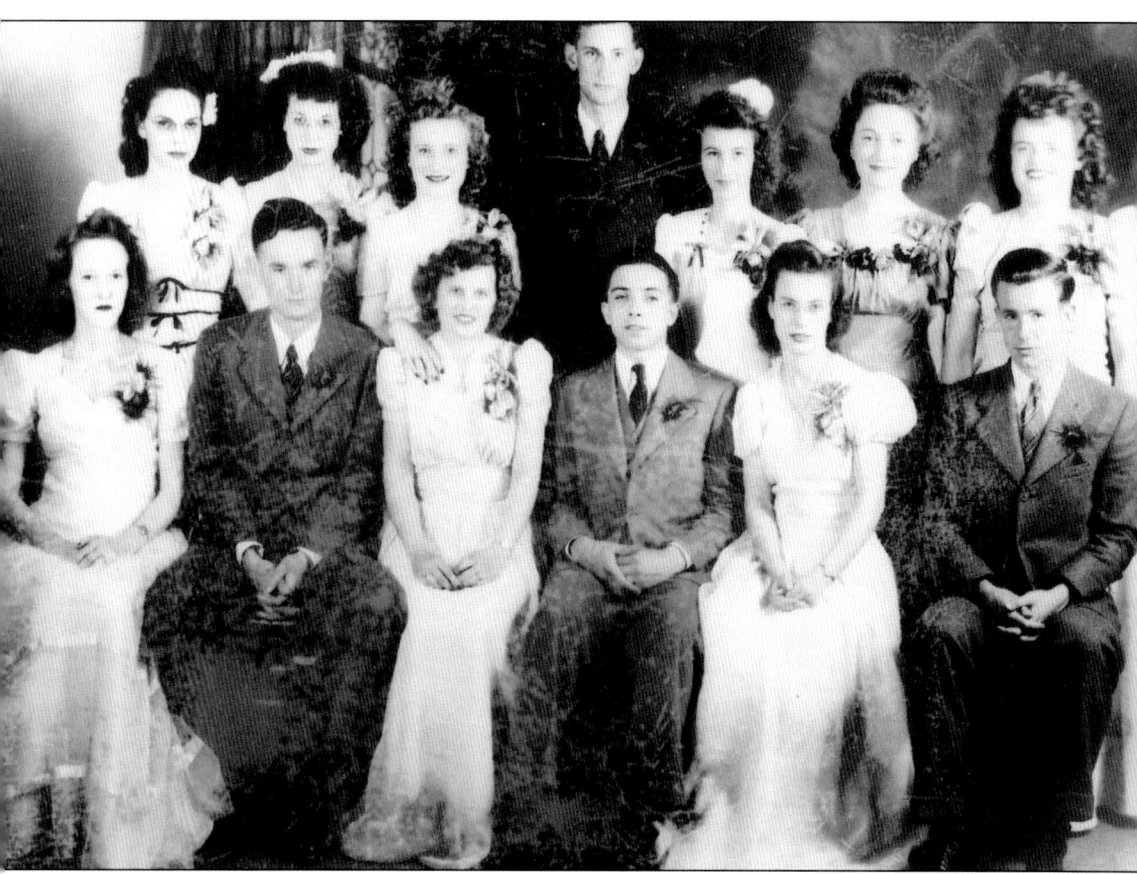

In 1940, the Tishomingo High School class of 1944 had 39 freshmen. World War II took its toll, and only 17 of these freshmen graduated in 1944. Pictured are the 1944 graduates, including (first row) Dorothy Buchanan, Chris Clifton, Ruth (Page) Dawson, Jimmy Vanos, Betsy (Ross) Deaton, and Amos Timbes; (second row) Stella Starkey, Veda Ruth Borden, Christine Deaton, Lyman Hellums, Rachel Pennington, Peggy Deaton, and Vela Mann. Graduates not seen here include Dennis Gray, Evelyn Loveless, Billy Starkey, and Lucille Edmondson. (Courtesy of Ruth Dawson.)

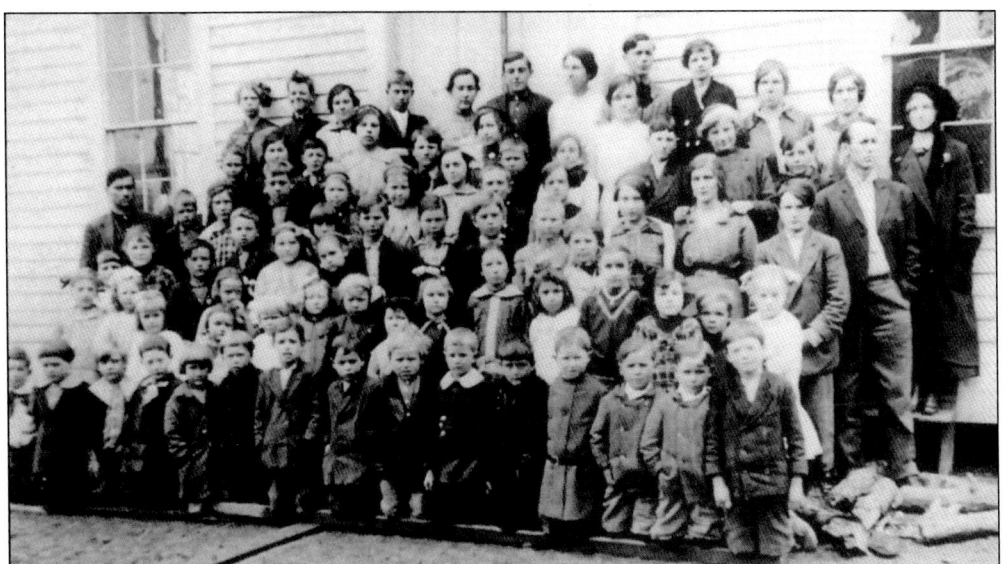

This is the old Wright School, later known as the Paden School, around 1914. The Wright School was the first teaching job for 18-year-old Alta Bell South. She has short hair and appears on the back row in front of the left-side door. On the far right, wearing a hat and standing in front of a window, is Samantha Amanda Cordilla South. She was the teacher's half-sister and cousin.

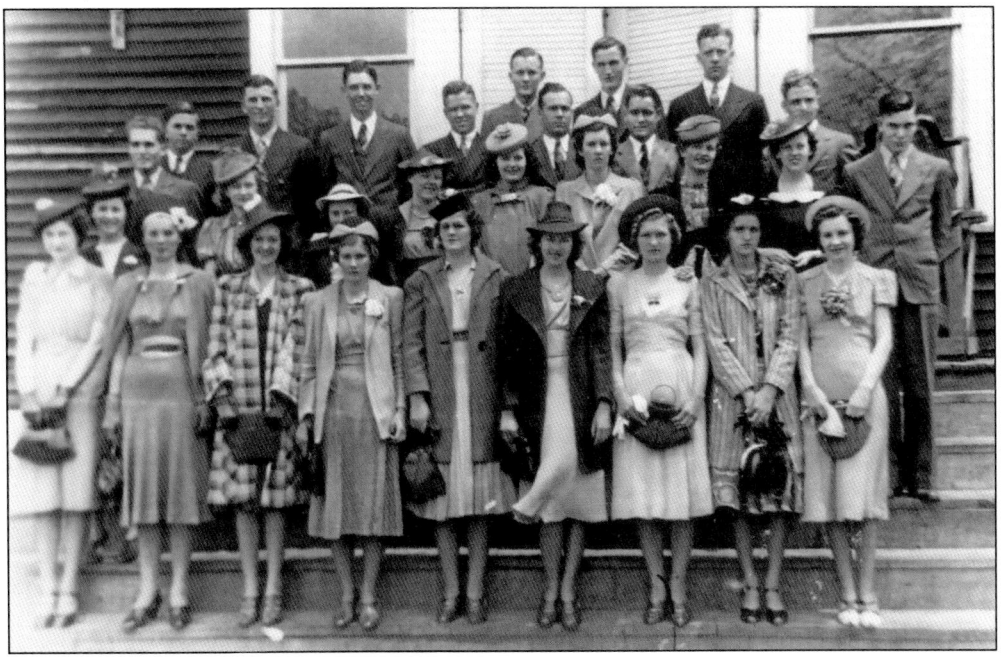

Pictured is the 1939 Senior Class of Tishomingo High School. Identified are, from left to right, (first row) Corine Bell, Elizabeth Philbin, Mary Frances Burns, Minyon Keenam, Shirley Hill, Eleanor Harris, Hazel Ward, Mary Fairless, and Lenora Rhodes; (second row) Maxine Holley, Kathleen Nash, Mary Bea Edmondson, Jennie Maude Gardner, Mary Belle Richard, Yondine Keenam, Hortense Chambers, and Elaine Gardner; (third row) Hurl Puckett, Tulon Tidwell, Cleburn Finch, J. R. Weaver Jr., Frank Campbell, Jack Sheppard, Dempsey Loveless, J.O. Underwood, and Cortez Blunt; (fourth row) Buren Williams, J.A. Blunt, and Harmon Smith.

Discover Thousands of Local History Books Featuring Millions of Vintage Images

Arcadia Publishing, the leading local history publisher in the United States, is committed to making history accessible and meaningful through publishing books that celebrate and preserve the heritage of America's people and places.

Find more books like this at
www.arcadiapublishing.com

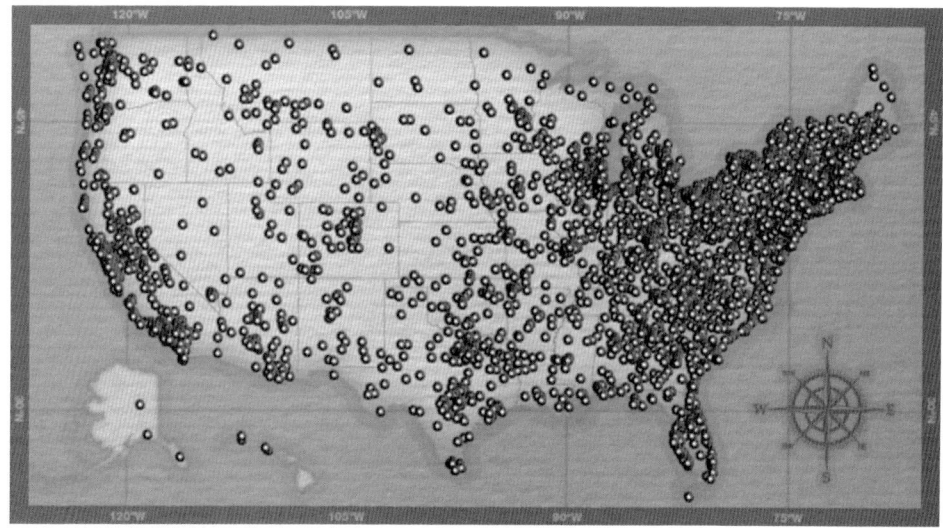

Search for your hometown history, your old stomping grounds, and even your favorite sports team.

Consistent with our mission to preserve history on a local level, this book was printed in South Carolina on American-made paper and manufactured entirely in the United States. Products carrying the accredited Forest Stewardship Council (FSC) label are printed on 100 percent FSC-certified paper.

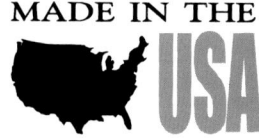